PHYSIOLOGICAL MEASURES OF EMOTION FROM A DEVELOPMENTAL PERSPECTIVE: STATE OF THE SCIENCE

Tracy A. Dennis, Kristin A. Buss, and Paul D. Hastings

W. Andrew Collins
Series Editor

MONOGRAPHS OF THE SOCIETY FOR RESEARCH IN CHILD DEVELOPMENT

Serial No. 303, Vol. 77, No. 2, 2012

WILEY-BLACKWELL

Boston, Massachusetts   *Oxford, United Kingdom*

Kurt Fischer
Harvard University

Doran French
Illinois Wesleyan University

Sarah Friedman
CNA Corporation

Douglas Frye
University of Pennsylvania

Andrew Fuligni
University of California, Los Angeles

Susan Graham
University of Calgary

Elena Grigorenko
Yale University

Megan Gunnar
University of Minnesota

Paul Harris
Harvard University

Susan Hespos
Vanderbilt University

Aletha Huston
University of Texas, Austin

Lene Jensen
Clark University

Ariel Kalil
University of Chicago

Melissa Koenig
University of Minnesota

Brett Laursen
Florida Atlantic University

Eva Lefkowitz
Pennsylvania State University

Katherine Magnuson
University of Wisconsin, Madison

Ann Masten
University of Minnesota

Kevin Miller
University of Michigan

Ginger Moore
Pennsylvania State University

David Moshman
University of Nebraska

Darcia Narvaez
University of Notre Dame

Katherine Nelson
City University of New York

Lisa Oakes
University of California, Davis

Thomas O'Connor
University of Rochester

Yukari Okamoto
University of California, Santa Barbara

Robert Pianta
University of Virginia

Mark Roosa
Arizona State University

Karl Rosengren
University of Illinois, Urbana-Champaign

Judith G. Smetana
University of Rochester

Kathy Stansbury
Morehouse College

Steve Thoma
University of Alabama

Michael Tomasello
Max Planck Institute

Deborah Vandell
University of California, Irvine

Richard Weinberg
University of Minnesota

Hirokazu Yoshikawa
New York University

Qing Zhou
Arizona State University

PHYSIOLOGICAL MEASURES OF EMOTION FROM A DEVELOPMENTAL PERSPECTIVE: STATE OF THE SCIENCE

CONTENTS

ABSTRACT

In the past decade, there has been a dramatic growth in research examining the development of emotion from a physiological perspective. However, this widespread use of physiological measures to study emotional development coexists with relatively few guiding principles, thus reducing opportunities to move the field forward in innovative ways. The goal of this monograph is to present the state of the science on the physiology of emotion from a developmental perspective in order to take stock of the knowledge base at this historical moment in time and to cultivate greater integration and coordination in the field as a whole. The authors of the 13 chapters comprising this monograph provide brief and focused essays that emphasize 5 core themes: the time course of emotion, the context of physiological measurement, the nature of developing physiological and behavioral systems, the specificity of associations between physiological measures and distinct aspects of emotion, and coordination among multiple physiological systems. This monograph has four parts. Part 1 describes integrative measurement approaches to the study of emotion and physiology, including measurement of multiple biological systems and a focus on individual differences in the links between physiology and emotion. Part 2 emphasizes socialization and contextual and environmental factors that influence the physiology of emotion. Part 3 reviews maladaptive physiological processes that underlie or influence affective disruptions and affective psychopathology. Part 4 describes overarching issues in the study of physiology and emotional development, articulating measurement guidelines and cutting-edge methods and statistical techniques. The work presented here represents the current state of the field, as well as exciting new directions that have the potential to revolutionize our understanding of emotional well-being, risk, and psychopathology. Taken together these 13 essays provide an innovative view on the psychophysiology of emotion, emotional well-being, and affective psychopathology from a developmental perspective.

INTRODUCTION TO THE MONOGRAPH: PHYSIOLOGICAL MEASURES OF EMOTION FROM A DEVELOPMENTAL PERSPECTIVE: STATE OF THE SCIENCE

Tracy A. Dennis, Kristin A. Buss, and Paul D. Hastings

The past decade has seen an explosion of developmental research on the physiology of emotion. This emerging field focuses on examining correlates of emotion and also explores complex questions about how biological processes underlie, mediate, and dynamically interact with behavioral phenomena related to the development of emotional well-being and psychopathology. This emphasis on process has moved the field toward examining emotion at multiple levels of analysis, requiring careful and integrated consideration of biology, behavior, and environmental context. Many researchers, however, are unclear about how best to choose among physiological measurement options in order to provide "added value" to their current methodological techniques and to achieve a cross-disciplinary and multimeasurement approach to studying the development of emotion.

The overarching goal of this monograph is to present the state of the science on the physiology of emotion from a developmental perspective. Our aim is to bridge the gap between knowledge of physiological measures and knowledge of their useful application for understanding the development of emotion. Rather than presenting comprehensive summaries of the literature, we invited authors to provide brief, focused descriptions of current, cutting-edge research in order to highlight established and emerging methodological and conceptual approaches. In addition, we asked authors to articulate why specific physiological measures are optimal for capturing unique aspects of emotional processes and affective psychopathology. This goal is critical if, as a field, we are to delineate how physiological measures complement behavioral, questionnaire, and other types of data in order to strengthen the assessment of emotion and its development.

Corresponding author: Tracy A. Dennis, Ph.D., Department of Psychology, Hunter College, The City University of New York, Hunter North Room 636, 695 Park Avenue, New York, NY 10065, email: tracy.dennis@hunter.cuny.edu

No one who conducts physiological research on emotion will deny the inherent challenges we face by pursuing this fascinating topic. One reason for this challenge is the richness and complexity of how emotion and emotion-related processes are defined as they relate to physiology. There continues to be enthusiastic debate about definitions of emotion (Barrett, 2006; Izard, 2007) and other phenomena, such as emotion regulation (Block, Moran, & Kring, 2009; Campos, Frankel, & Camras, 2004; Cole, Martin, & Dennis, 2004). Extended consideration of such definitional issues is beyond the scope of this introduction. In brief, however, we offer definitions that are consistent with the view taken by most of the authors in this monograph and with an article by Cole et al. (2004), who summarize current definitional and methodological challenges faced by emotion and emotion regulation researchers. Essentially, despite differences, a majority of researchers would agree that emotions are evolutionarily adaptive and biologically prepared. Emotions allow the individual to make rapid appraisals of situations that shape equally rapid action readiness tendencies for adaptive behaviors that (a) sustain the conditions that support the well-being of the individual and (b) avoid or contend with conditions that are unfavorable for the well-being of the individual. Most would also agree that emotion regulation refers to " . . . the automatic or controlled, conscious or unconscious process of individuals influencing emotion in self, others, or both" (Gross & Thompson, 2007), although others argue that emotion regulation should also refer to the ways in which emotion regulates other processes, such as cognition and behavior (Cole et al., 2004).

An additional issue to consider is how researchers conceive of the *association* between physiology and emotion. One approach is to equate physiology with emotion, such that emotion is defined as a set of key physiological (and behavioral) phenomena—that is, emotion is constituted by invariant physiological responses, each of which is necessary for a distinct emotion to occur. This perspective, which may have its earliest roots in the classic James–Lange theory of emotion (but see Ellsworth, 1994), would describe emotion as an emergent property of physiology. A different approach would be to identify biomarkers for emotion, or patterns of physiology that correlate with and are observable indicators of key processes and mechanisms underlying the experience and expression of emotion. In this case, a given physiological response is neither necessary nor sufficient for an emotion to occur. Indeed, there are important individual differences in the physiological aspects of how and when emotions are expressed. For example, although in general heart rate increases may be greater when someone is fearful compared to sad, the degree to which this is the case will vary across individuals. Such variability may be a key indicator of risk and resilience factors.

The chapters in this monograph, and arguably most research in the field, take a biomarker approach to examining the physiology of emotion. Biomarkers are biological indicators of a specific process underlying mental

2

and physical disease and well-being. The benefit of a biomarker approach is that when a complex phenotype is being examined, such as an anxiety disorder, a biomarker may help identify key underlying mechanisms that are present in the absence of overt behavioral symptoms, or that are difficult to detect via observable behavior alone. For example, an endophenotype is a specific type of biomarker, one that can delineate behavioral symptoms into more stable phenotypes by articulating specific genetic links (Gottesman & Gould, 2003). Research presented in this monograph highlights some of the most recent and exciting research identifying potential biomarkers and endophenotypes for normative and pathological emotional development. The identification of such biomarkers has the potential to have a powerful impact on the field if they can shed light on normal development, predict psychological risk, and aid in the detection, diagnosis, and treatment of disorder.

There is a four-part structure to the monograph, including sections on integrative approaches to the study of emotion, socialization, psychopathology, and overarching issues and methodological consideration. The first section, "Integrative Approaches to the Study of Physiology and Emotion," focuses on how researchers can use physiology to understand the role of multiple cognitive, affective, and behavioral processes that influence the expression and experience of emotion. Thus, the authors in this section consider a range of phenomena and individual differences, including the interplay between emotion and cognition, temperament, and the stress response. Rather than seeking to minimize variability between individuals in order to reduce "noise," this approach focuses on multiple systems and levels analyses, along with individual differences. Thus, chapters in this section examine meaningful person-level characteristics that can help explain mechanisms of emotional functioning and emotional change across development.

The second section, "Socialization and Environmental Factors in the Physiology of Emotion," considers the environmental and social contexts of physiological measurement, with particular emphasis on the family context. This perspective highlights the fact that the meaning of a physiological measure is intimately connected with the social context within which it is measured. Moreover, both physiology and emotion are developing systems, and the course of their development influences, and is influenced by, important socialization agents and events.

In the third section of the monograph, "Physiology and Affective Psychopathology," the authors discuss maladaptive physiological processes that underlie or influence affective disruptions and affective psychopathology. Chapters in this section report on research using diverse measurement approaches, including neuroendocrine measures of stress reactivity and regulation, cardiac preejection period (PEP) and respiratory sinus arrhythmia (RSA), and pupilometry. Consistent with a developmental psychopathology perspective, the chapters describe how the study of atypical development can enrich our understanding of typical emotional development, and vice versa.

The fourth and final section, "Overarching Issues and Methodological Considerations: What Can Physiological Measures Reveal About Emotion?", provides an overview of core physiological measures used in many studies of emotional development, articulating how emotional processes can or cannot be captured by each measure. This section also describes state-of-the-art methods used with a range of physiological measures and statistical techniques used in EEG and neuroimaging.

These sections, while reflecting a broad range of topics, are united around several core themes. One theme is *time*. It is crucial to document not only "where" emotion happens in the brain and body but also "when," "how quickly," and "how long" emotional processes unfold. Regardless of the nature of the physiological measure being used, timing issues have a critical impact on how each measure can be used to enhance our understanding of emotion. For example, several chapters emphasize a "need for speed"—measures such as EEG and ERP have millisecond precision capable of capturing extremely rapid or covert affective processes. Other chapters focus on measures that can document affective responses over the course of minutes, hours, or days, such as FMRI, RSA, and neuroendocrine measures. Moreover, timing can also refer to developmental processes, discussed in more detail later, such as trajectories of development over time. These questions about the time course of emotion, its physiological underpinnings and development, and fleeting emotional states compared to more enduring emotional traits are at the heart of the many programs of research described in this monograph.

In addition to the issue of time course, chapters in the monograph grapple with the question of how to meaningfully embed physiological measurement in a specific *context*, whether it is the context of parenting, disrupted social experiences, the nature of a specific emotional challenge, or characteristics of the individual, such as temperament. For example, in the section on socialization, Katz and Rigterink examine links between domestic violence and emotion regulation using RSA as a measure of physiological regulation. Their findings suggest that RSA suppression and augmentation could have different implications depending on whether a child is or is not exposed to domestic violence. Moreover, during the preschool versus middle school period, domestic violence affects distinct aspects of children's regulatory abilities measured via RSA. These findings illustrate how environmental and developmental context influences how physiology relates to affective development.

Another important goal of the monograph is to articulate the *specificity* of associations between physiology and emotion. That is, many popular physiological measures are highly sensitive and thus can be used to study diverse aspects of emotional development. Yet this sensitivity, if combined with poor specificity, may reveal little about distinct mechanisms underlying

4

emotional development. For example, a range of affective and behavioral disorders are characterized by decreased activity of the prefrontal cortex during self-regulation or decision making tasks. If this is a common mechanism or cause of disorder, why do some children with this particular biomarker go on to evidence depression, whereas others show conduct problems? Instead, a physiological measure that is more specific and thus predicts some outcomes but not others may reveal more about underlying causes of psychopathology. One approach to obtaining high sensitivity combined with high specificity is to search for multisystem bio-signatures for emotional individual differences, well-being, and disorder.

This notion of multisystem bio-signatures ties into the fourth core theme, the need to *integrate across multiple physiological systems* rather than considering a single system in isolation. As methodological sophistication in the field increases, this goal becomes more tractable. For example, Miscovic and Schmidt explore individual differences in temperamental fear and fearlessness by considering the integration between neural and autonomic measures, such as the role of cerebral asymmetry in cardiac control and neuroendocrine and immune function. Rather than explore a physiological process in isolation, this approach grounds the study of individual differences in the dynamic interplay among biological systems.

Finally, an overarching goal of this monograph is to explore how physiological measures can be used to capture emotional *development.* The importance of considering development in relation to physiology–emotional behavior linkages is well articulated in the chapter by Gunnar and Adam. In particular, they identify points in development in which the association between cortisol and behavior indicators of distress are decoupled. Although there is a critical need to identify biological correlates of emotion at different points in development, this use of physiology to understand dynamic changes in emotion and emotional competence over time is a particularly revealing approach.

In summary, this monograph presents the state of the science in the study of the physiology of emotion from a developmental perspective. By focusing on the themes of time course, context, specificity, integration across systems, and development, we believe this collection of work has the potential to push the field toward a more complete understanding of emotional well-being, risk, and psychopathology.

INTRODUCTION TO SECTION ONE: INTEGRATIVE APPROACHES TO THE STUDY OF PHYSIOLOGY AND EMOTION

Paul D. Hastings, Kristin A. Buss, and Tracy A. Dennis

The first section, "Integrative Approaches to the Study of Physiology and Emotion," presents research that aims to identify sources of individual variation in multiple biological systems that can improve our ability to predict emotional adaptation. While critiques of a multilevel and individual differences approach might label such variation as "noise," this misses an important point. Noise is a variation that is irrelevant or unknown. Individual differences at multiple levels of analysis are variations that are highly meaningful in that they improve prediction of outcomes, outcomes which cannot be adequately explained unless they are evaluated in the context of individual trajectories and variability.

For example, Bell and Diaz write about the interplay between emotion and cognition in the context of developmental EEG/ERP studies. They present a model of emotion–cognition integration in early development that illustrates how the study of neurophysiological correlates of emotion can be greatly enhanced by also considering individual differences in cognition. There are a number of studies focusing on how cognition influences emotion, or how emotion influences cognition. Few studies, however, examine integration such that cognitive and emotional processes are studied as inseparable and as influencing each other in a bidirectional and dynamic manner. For example, specific emotional states may differentially influence cognitive processes like attention, and at the same time these specific emotions are modulated by distinct cognitive control faculties such as working memory. Thus, individual differences in emotion and cognition provide a crucial measurement context for the other. Moreover, Bell and Diaz present suggestive findings that support a central tenet of their model—attentional control influences both emotion and cognition such that they become increasingly correlated over time, with closely linked developmental trajectories. This

Corresponding author: Paul D. Hastings, Ph.D., University of California Davis, Center for Mind & Brain, 267 Cousteau Place, Davis, CA 95618, email: pdhastings@ucdavis.edu

notion of integration rather than interaction is a critical perspective as the field of developmental neuroscience moves farther away from the traditional compartmentalization of the study of emotional and cognitive development, and toward a multisystems approach.

In the next chapter, Adam describes how emotion–cortisol transactions vary within and between individuals as a function of time. This chronometric model describes how HPA-axis changes occur and interact with social and emotional experience over multiple time courses in development—acute, within day, day-to-day, over months and years, and even epigenetic and inter-generational change. Each time scales provide a unique window of insight into stress and emotional development. For instance, Adam reports on a study of state and trait loneliness and cortisol (Doane & Adam, 2009). In this study, the inclusion of temporal covariates such as time of waking and the inclusion of in-dividual differences variables such as interpersonal life stress increased effect sizes and clarified the nature of associations between emotional experience and cortisol. This chronometric model thus provides a powerful framework within which to examine emotion–cortisol links in reference to individual dif-ferences and within specific emotional contexts and developmental periods.

In the final chapter of this section, Miskovic and Schmidt propose a lat-eralized brain–body emotion model for studying individual differences in fearfulness and fearlessness. Given the historical separation between research on central and autonomic correlates of emotion, the authors argue that it is critical to identify how these systems are coordinated to allow for adap-tive emotional responding. They propose that the prefrontal cortex plays a key role in the integration between central and peripheral nervous sys-tem processes that influence the emergence of temperamental vulnerabili-ties and strengths. For example, temperamental shyness may be best under-stood not as a single biological vulnerability but as chronic activation of the brain–body withdrawal system involving sensitization of a right prefrontal cortex–amygdala–sympathoexcitatory network. Importantly, the lateralized brain–body emotion model provides a unifying theoretical framework for integrating disparate findings on the biological correlates of temperamen-tal fear. The research described here is uniquely sophisticated in its attempt to move beyond studying an isolated physiological process, and instead em-bedding the study of temperamental individual differences in the dynamic interplay among biological systems.

In summary, the chapters in this section highlight the complexities and benefits of focusing on individual differences in multiple biological systems. In the same way that geneticists now question the common disease/common variant hypothesis for identifying genetic markers for disease, research in this section suggests that finding a single, common cause of affective behaviors or psychopathology is highly unlikely. We, as a field, must focus on both similarities and differences across individuals and levels of analysis.

EEG/ERP MEASURES OF EMOTION–COGNITION INTEGRATION DURING DEVELOPMENT

Martha Ann Bell and Anjolii Diaz

Examination of the relations between brain electrical activity and emotion can be greatly informed by also considering cognition. Psychologists have long struggled with creating a framework for conceptualizing relations between affect and reason (Izard, 1993; Lazarus, 1982; Zajonc, 1980) and more recently have focused on examining interactions between cognition and emotion from both behavioral and brain-based approaches (Scherer, 2003). Although the field of developmental psychology has traditionally compartmentalized emotion development and cognitive development, there have been recent attempts to integrate these processes conceptually using a neuroscience perspective (e.g., Bell & Deater-Deckard, 2007; Dennis, 2010; Lewis & Todd, 2007; Posner & Rothbart, 2000; Thompson, Lewis, & Calkins, 2008; Zelazo & Cunningham, 2007). Empirical studies with EEG and ERP measures can be used to support these conceptual models (see Fox, Kirwan, & Reeb-Sutherland, this volume, for specifics on measuring EEG/ERP associated with emotion).

In this chapter we propose that the incorporation of cognitive processes in the study of EEG/ERP and emotion relations is state of the science with respect to the examination of individual differences in development (Calkins & Bell, 2010). We begin by examining different models of interrelations between emotion and cognition and selectively review developmental EEG/ERP studies that illustrate each model, including some of our own work. Then we summarize our current conceptualization of emotion–cognition integration in early development (Bell & Deater-Deckard, 2007; Bell & Wolfe, 2004).

Some of the research reported in this chapter was supported by grants HD049878 and HD043057 from the *Eunice Kennedy Shriver* National Institute of Child Health and Human Development (NICHD).

Corresponding author: Martha Ann Bell, Department of Psychology, Virginia Tech, Blacksburg, VA 24061, email: mabell@vt.edu

ASSOCIATIONS BETWEEN EMOTION AND COGNITION

Much like Carlson and Wang (2007), we focus on three basic models for examining the interaction between emotion and cognition. The first two models are unidirectional so as to simplify the study of emotion–cognition relations. It is more likely, however, that emotion and cognition processes continuously influence each other in a dynamic manner (Lewis, 2005), much like the third model.

EMOTION INFLUENCES COGNITIVE OUTCOMES

In the first model, regulation of emotion may have an impact on cognitive outcomes; hence, emotions act to organize thinking, learning, and action (Cole, Martin, & Dennis, 2004). Using this model, researchers may manipulate emotion in the experimental situation and inspect the effect on cognitive performance (Gray, 2001; Richards & Gross, 2000). Similarly, researchers may examine normal variations in emotion reactivity and emotion regulation (i.e., temperament) to study the impact of emotion on cognitive outcomes.

This model has guided several studies in our program of research, including those in which regulatory aspects of temperament were used as a proxy for emotion. With an 8-month-old sample, we sought to predict performance level on an infant executive function task (looking A-not-B, requiring working memory and inhibitory control skills). The percentage of correct classification into high and low cognitive performance groups using measures of task-related frontal/parietal EEG coherence and heart period, as well as maternal-rated infant distress to limitations, was 93% (Bell, 2012). We had, however, predicted that other temperament traits (i.e., duration of orienting, soothability) would be associated with cognitive outcomes because of their links to more regulatory aspects of temperament. This surprising temperament finding led us to examine other aspects of reactivity in relation to cognitive performance.

In a recent study from our lab, we examined fear reactivity in relation to cognitive measures of novelty preference during infancy. In addition to examining mother-rated infant temperament as in our previous infant work, we made behavioral observations of fear reactivity and recorded frontal EEG asymmetries in a group of 10-month-old infants. EEG was recorded at baseline and during fear tasks and our cognitive outcome task, which was novelty preference measured via the visual recognition memory paradigm. Previous research has shown that fear reactivity is associated with right frontal EEG asymmetry in infants (Buss et al., 2003; see Miskovic & Schmidt, this volume, for a brain–body lateralization model of temperamental fear) and infants who present with high fear reactivity also typically exhibit heightened levels of attention to their environments (Calkins, Fox, & Marshall, 1996). Thus, we hypothesized that underlying patterns of general fearfulness may enhance the information processing that is required for the encoding and retrieval associated with recognition memory. Fear reactivity therefore should be associated with novelty preference during recognition memory tasks. We also expected that infants who exhibited higher levels of fear reactivity would have relative right frontal EEG asymmetry during baseline recordings and during the cognitive processing associated with recognition memory.

We found that as a group the infants exhibited left frontal EEG asymmetry at baseline. However, for some of those infants, the left frontal baseline EEG asymmetry changed to right frontal EEG asymmetry in the context of specific fear tasks that were either social (stranger approach) or nonsocial (scary masks and jumping toy spider) in nature. We were able to predict the level of fear behaviors in each context from the magnitude of change from baseline frontal EEG asymmetry to task-related frontal EEG asymmetry (Diaz & Bell, 2011a). What was most salient about our ability to predict the level of fear using frontal EEG asymmetry is that we did not recruit infants based on their temperamental fear reactivity. Furthermore, when we divided the infants into higher and lower fear reactivity groups based on behavioral responses in the three contexts, the more fearful infants also exhibited novelty preference in the recognition memory paradigm. In contrast to our hypothesis, fearful infants demonstrated left frontal EEG asymmetry during the familiarization and paired comparison portions of the recognition memory task. The left frontal areas typically are associated with better feature discrimination during attentional processing (Diaz & Bell, 2010b).

We have also examined the impact of temperament-based emotion on cognitive outcomes during early childhood. With a group of children who were $4^1/_2$ years of age, we were able to correctly classify 90% of the children into high and low cognitive performance groups using task-related frontal EEG power values, maternal-rated child temperament (i.e., approach), and receptive language (Wolfe & Bell, 2004). The cognitive outcomes were measures of early childhood executive function (day/night and yes/no). With a separate group of preschool children between $3^1/_2$ and $4^1/_2$ years of age, we showed that frontal and temporal EEG, as well as maternal-rated temperament (i.e., effortful control), were associated with executive function performance (Wolfe & Bell, 2007). Thus, with infant as well as early childhood samples, we have demonstrated that EEG measures, as well as regulatory and sometimes reactive aspects of temperament (as a proxy for emotion), were predictors of cognitive task performance.

10

COGNITION INFLUENCES EMOTION-RELATED OUTCOMES

In the second model, thinking, learning, and action serve to regulate emotions (Cole et al., 2004). Researchers using this model may examine the effect of cognitive inhibitory responses or other cognitive strategies on emotion regulation (Ochsner & Gross, 2005, 2008). They may also examine how temperament-related influences on cognition may affect the regulation of emotion. Examples of findings from three research teams are highlighted. These teams focus on ERP markers of attentional processing associated with emotion regulation (Dennis, 2010).

Lewis and colleagues have focused on ERP indices of emotion regulation, with particular emphasis on individual differences in attention-related cognitive processes that are recruited for regulating negative emotion (Lamm & Lewis, 2010; Lewis & Stieben, 2004; Woltering & Lewis, 2009). The ERP waveform of interest was the N2, which is associated with effortful attention and response inhibition. One of the anatomical correlates of the N2 is the anterior cingulate cortex, a prominent structure associated with the executive attention system. During a go/no-go task using photos of happy, angry, or neutral facial expressions, preschool children showed greatest frontal N2 amplitudes and fastest N2 latencies to angry faces and smallest amplitudes and longest latencies to happy faces (Lewis, Todd, & Honsberger, 2007). Furthermore, there was a negative correlation between parent-reported fearfulness (measured via temperament questionnaire) and latency of the N2 to angry faces when they appeared in the go condition. Because the N2 effects varied with facial expressions of emotion, Lewis and colleagues interpreted the N2 as an index of emotion regulation.

Dennis, Malone, and Chen (2009) also utilized happy, fearful, and sad faces with children as they performed an attentional task. Differing from the procedures used by Lewis and colleagues, the emotion stimuli used by Dennis were distracters embedded in the attentional task and not the actual stimuli to which the participants were instructed to respond. Larger P1 and frontal Nc amplitudes, associated with early attention processing, to distracting fearful and sad faces were correlated with more effective emotion regulation in 5- to 9-year-old children, with emotion regulation measured as performance on the attention task and as maternal report.

Perez-Edgar and Fox (2007) examined temperament-related attentional differences associated with emotion regulation in 7-year-old children. When the stimuli were affective words, children with higher maternal ratings in attentional control exhibited greater right frontal N2 and lower amplitude P3 to all words regardless of valence. Thus, individual differences in temperament-based attentional control were associated with behavioral and brain-related indices of emotion.

The third model assigns both cognition and emotion as outcomes. Zelazo presents an intriguing hypothesis about emotion–cognition associations in his work on "hot" and "cool" executive functions (e.g., Kerr & Zelazo, 2004). Cool executive functions are those traditionally considered to be focused on cognitive, goal-directed problem solving and they are associated with the functioning of the dorsolateral prefrontal cortex. Hot executive functions are associated with problem solving or with decision making that has significant emotional consequences. Hot functions are associated with functioning of the orbitofrontal cortex. When the problem solving is focused on the regulation of emotion, Zelazo considers executive function to be the same as emotion regulation (Zelazo & Cunningham, 2007).

Zelazo and colleagues use the Children's Gambling Task to study hot executive function. In this task, children play the game in order to receive candies as a reward. They must choose cards from one of two decks in order to receive the candy, with each deck designed to link amount of reward with amount of potential loss. Thus, the children's cognitive decisions are affectively motivated (Kerr & Zelazo, 2004).

Affective responding is also evident in a study by Perez-Edgar and Fox (2005a). Seven-year-old children performed an attentional cuing task under neutral conditions and then performed that same task when told that performance would determine whether or not they would have to give a speech. The task requires orienting to sensory stimuli (bottom-up processing) and the speech condition layers on contextual and individual characteristics (top–down mechanisms). Under the potential speech condition, reaction times were faster and there were more errors. Children with higher levels of maternal-rated shyness had faster reaction times to negative (lose points) versus positive (gain points) attentional cues and also had greater N1 and N2 amplitudes relative to the low shy children (Perez-Edgar & Fox, 2005a). These temperament group differences were not evident during the neutral task condition, indicating that the interactions between emotion and cognition only occurred during the motivationally significant potential speech condition. This finding highlights the value of assessing EEG/ERP components of emotion regulation during emotionally salient task conditions.

Dennis and Chen (2007) report a similar finding with adults. As previously noted, this research team has developed a protocol where happy, fearful, and sad faces are used as distracters embedded in an attentional task. When instructed to respond to nonemotion stimuli during the task, adults who self-rated as high in threat sensitivity exhibited enhanced N2 to fearful faces and this was linked to sustained executive attention performance. For adults who self-rated as low in threat sensitivity, greater N2 was associated with decrements in executive attention. In this study, the fearful faces provided the context for the coupling of emotion and cognition.

Brain electrophysiology measures have proven important for the examination of emotion–cognitive associations. Thus far we have described various EEG and ERP correlates of emotion, with an emphasis on related cognitive processes. Next we turn to a brief discussion of the use of electrophysiology in studying the integration of emotion and cognition during development. We begin with a definition of *integration* and then highlight that the brain systems that we (Bell & Deater-Deckard, 2007; Bell & Wolfe, 2004) and others (e.g., Dennis, 2010; Lewis, 2005; Rothbart, Sheese, & Posner, 2007) propose are the foundations for emotion–cognition integration.

CONCEPTUAL FRAMEWORK FOR EMOTION–COGNITION INTEGRATION

Gray (2004) defines *integration* with respect to emotion and cognition. When conceptually linked, cognitive and emotion processes are not completely separable and their subprocesses influence each other selectively. Specific emotional states can differentially influence information processing, and cognitive control can modulate various emotion experiences (Gray, 2001). This is illustrated by the studies of Perez-Edgar and Fox (2005a) and Dennis and Chen (2007) discussed above. In each study, individual differences in emotion regulation and performance on attentional tasks were associated with context-related patterns of brain electrical activity.

Our conceptualization of emotion–cognition integration incorporates the bidirectional influences between emotion and cognition that are the focus of the third model we described above (see Figure 1). Our model is focused on the brain mechanisms of the executive attention system, encompassing the anterior cingulate cortex and other areas of the prefrontal cortex (see Bell & Deater-Deckard, 2007, for details of this model). The anterior cingulate has sections that process cognitive and emotional information separately. The cognitive section is connected with the prefrontal cortex, parietal cortex, and premotor and supplementary motor areas and is activated by tasks that involve choice selection from conflicting information (Engle, 2002). The emotion section is connected with the orbitofrontal cortex, amygdala, and hippocampus, among other brain areas, and is activated by tasks with emotion content (Fichtenholtz et al., 2004). It was previously thought that there was always activation of the cognitive section and suppression of the affective section during cognitive processing and activation of the affective section along with suppression of the cognitive subdivision during emotion processing, thus rendering emotion and cognition as separate processes neurologically (Bush, Luu, & Posner, 2000). Recent brain imaging studies with adults, however, show that the activation–suppression relations between cognitive and affective sections

13

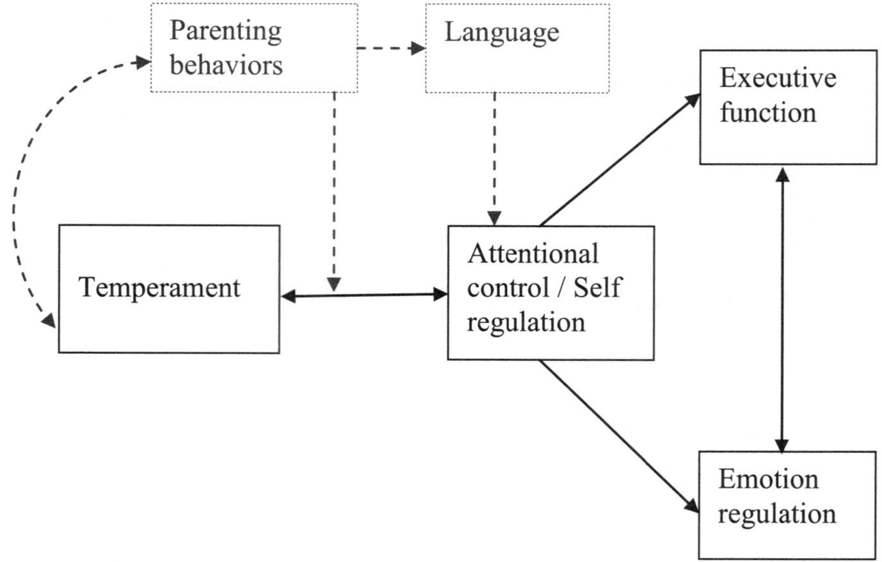

FIGURE 1.— Model of hypothesized emotion–cognition relations. Attentional control directly influences both emotion and cognition. We hypothesize that with development, emotion and cognition become increasingly correlated, with constitutional differences in child temperament contributing to the developmental outcomes of attentional control, executive function, and emotion regulation (adapted from Bell & Wolfe, 2007).

of the anterior cingulate cortex can be complex. For example, emotionally incongruent trails on the word–face Stroop (e.g., a positive word overlaid upon a face with a negative valence) are associated with increased activation of the cognitive subdivision of the anterior cingulate cortex (Haas, Omura, Constable, & Canli, 2006). Similarly, during the emotional counting Stroop there is decreased activity in the affective subdivision of the anterior cingulate, but increased activity in that same subdivision during the display of emotionally valenced words (Bush et al., 2000). This research finding, along with Posner and Rothbart's strong developmental framework of the attentional control associated with certain self-regulatory aspects of temperament, is one of the reasons for the current focus on the anterior cingulate cortex and the executive attention system in the study of the *development* of emotion–cognition integration (Rothbart, 2004; Rothbart et al., 2007). Nondevelopmental conceptualizations of emotion–cognition integration/interactions have focused on other brain structures, such as the amygdala (Phelps, 2006).

We consider temperament-based attentional control as critical for the self-regulation associated with emotion–cognition integration, as do other developmental scientists (Henderson & Wachs, 2007; Rothbart et al., 2007). Early regulation of temperament-based emotional distress is enhanced by the

14

development of attentional control associated with the executive attention system (Ruff & Rothbart, 1996). Attentional control is required for resolving conflict among thoughts, feelings, and responses (Rueda, Posner, & Rothbart, 2005) and, thus, important for the developing self-regulation of both emotion and cognitive processes (Kopp, 2002).

We hypothesize that attentional control processes exert influence on both cognition and emotion so that they may become increasingly correlated over time, with interlocking developmental trajectories demonstrating the significance of both cognition and emotion as outcome measures. Currently, we are examining the development of attentional control, cognition (i.e., executive functions), and emotion regulation across infancy and early childhood using both behavioral and EEG measures. In this longitudinal study we are using separate measures of cognition and emotion so that we can track the developing trajectories for each. We are also collecting measures of temperament and language, given the influence of each on cognitive and emotion development (Henderson & Wachs, 2007; Wolfe & Bell, 2004, 2007).

Some of our initial findings show associations between attentional processing measures of looking time, emotion regulation skills during distress, and frontal EEG activity (Diaz & Bell, 2011b). Specifically, 5-month-old infants who process information quickly (i.e., are short lookers during familiarization of a stimulus, as opposed to long lookers; Colombo, Mitchell, Coldren, & Freeseman, 1991), appear less distressed during the arm restraint task, as indicated by behaviors and frontal EEG activity during the task. Specifically, the short lookers are more likely than the long lookers to employ a regulatory strategy where they focus on something other than the source of their distress (i.e., mother) during the arm restraint task. Furthermore, the short lookers exhibit greater task-related increases in frontal EEG power during arm restraint than the long lookers. We and others have interpreted these increases in frontal EEG power as the electrophysiology associated with effortful cognitive processing (Bell, 2001, 2002; Morasch & Bell, 2009; Orekhova, Stroganova, & Posikera, 2001). We use the same interpretation during the arm restraint task. When the short looking infants were faced with duress, they used their efficient information processing skills and their effortful control of attention to regulate.

When these same children are 24 months of age, performance on cognition and emotion tasks, as well as task-related changes in frontal EEG, are related to measures of inhibitory control (Morasch & Bell, 2011). Specifically, we were able to predict 29% of the variance on a maternal-report measure of temperament-related inhibitory control using performance on a cognitive conflict task (A-not-B with invisible displacement), a delay task (crayon delay), a compliance task (acceptance of EEG electrodes), and verbal ability, although performance on the delay task did not contribute unique variance to the model. In addition, we could also predict 29% of the variance on the maternal report of temperament-related inhibitory control using conflict task EEG, after controlling for performance on the conflict task. Specifically, lateral frontal power values in each hemisphere, as well as task performance, provided unique variance to the model. As we continue to see these children throughout early childhood, we will gather the data to be able to test our hypothesis that our cognitive and emotion-related measures will become more correlated over time.

We include language and parenting behaviors in our model as well (Bell & Wolfe, 2007). The development of language, in conjunction with continuing development of the frontal cortex, may encourage early advances in the voluntary control of emotion and cognition (Ruff & Rothbart, 1996). Maternal interactive style is related to emotion regulation behaviors in infants and young children (e.g., Calkins & Bell, 2010); however, not much attention has been given to the role of parenting to the development of executive functions. It is likely that infant cognitive status (i.e., length of attention, memory) interacts with some aspects of caregiving to influence cognitive development (Colombo & Saxon, 2002). In our model, parenting behaviors are moderators of the associations between temperament and attentional control. For example, caregivers may support infants' attentional development in efforts to relieve early infant distress (Ruff & Rothbart, 1996). We are examining if there are specific parental behaviors that are associated either concurrently or longitudinally with the development of attentional control and, thus, with associations between executive functions and emotion regulation.

CONCLUDING REMARKS

There are different ways of conceptualizing emotion–cognition integration (Calkins & Bell, 2010) and we have emphasized the regulatory aspects of emotion and cognition associated with attentional control in this brief chapter. This particular framework allows for the identification of common psychobiological processes and we have presented three basic models for examining these relations using EEG/ERP measures. We have shown that there are complex processes by which emotions relate to cognition and ultimately to developmental outcome. Thus, we propose that the examination of emotion must include concurrent examination of cognitive processes in order to understand these dynamic and neurologically related processes.

EMOTION–CORTISOL TRANSACTIONS OCCUR OVER MULTIPLE TIME SCALES IN DEVELOPMENT: IMPLICATIONS FOR RESEARCH ON EMOTION AND THE DEVELOPMENT OF EMOTIONAL DISORDERS

Emma K. Adam

In understanding the associations between emotional experience and physiological processes, time is a central variable. Most physiological processes are moving targets—they change from moment to moment and over the course of days, months, and years. Stress-sensitive physiological systems, such as the hypothalamic-pituitary-adrenal (HPA) axis and the sympathetic nervous system, are in fact *designed to change over time* in relation to changing internal and external conditions. This notion of adaptive flexibility in physiological functioning has been termed "allostasis," in contrast to models emphasizing the importance of physiological stability or "homeostasis" (McEwen, 1998; Sterling, 2003). Adaptive changes in physiology occur both in response to, and in anticipation of, experience, with the goal of helping the body prepare for, cope with, and recover from social, emotional, and physical challenges (McEwen, 1998; Sterling, 2003).

In this chapter, I focus on the HPA axis as an allostatic system and introduce a chronometric model (see Figure 2) suggesting that HPA-axis changes (as indexed by changing salivary cortisol levels) occur in response to social and emotional experience over *multiple time courses* in development. I provide examples of research on children and adolescents showing the relevance of various time courses of cortisol change (ranging from moment-to-moment changes to changes occurring over the course of days, months, and years) for understanding individual differences in state and trait emotion and the development of emotional disorders. Using illustrations from my own research on adolescents at risk for the development of major depressive disorder (MDD), I show how a consideration of multiple time scales of cortisol change, combined with careful design, measurement, and use of multilevel analyses, can

Corresponding author: Emma K. Adam, Program on Human Development and Social Policy, School of Education and Social Policy and the Institute for Policy Research, Northwestern University, 2120 Campus Drive, Evanston, IL 60208-0001, email: ek-adam@northwestern.edu

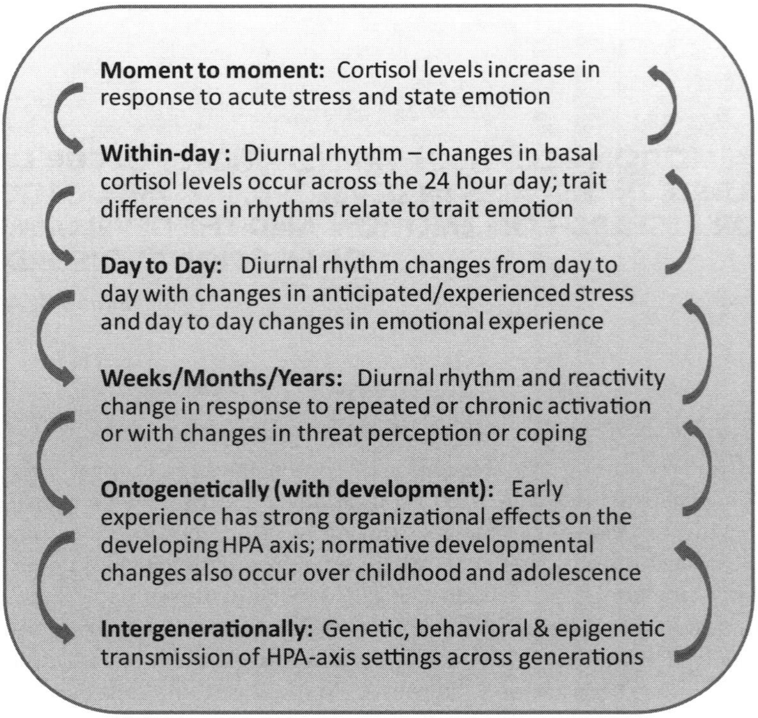

FIGURE 2.—Multiple time frames of change in the hypothalamic-pituitary-adrenal axis in relation to social and emotional experience.

reveal the subtle and dynamic interplay that occurs between emotional experience and cortisol in the course of everyday life and with development. This chapter particularly highlights the monograph themes of "time" or "time course" and "development," illustrates other monograph themes of "context" and "specificity," and notes how other research in this monograph fits within the chronometric model introduced herein.

MOMENT-TO-MOMENT CHANGES IN CORTISOL (ACUTE REACTIVITY)

The most commonly studied time scale of cortisol change is acute reactivity, in which within-person changes in cortisol in response to an acute stressor or momentary (state) emotion are measured in either laboratory (Dickerson & Kemeny, 2004; Gunnar, Talge, & Herrera, 2009) or naturalistic settings (Adam, 2006; Smyth et al., 1998; van Eck, Berkhof, Nicolson, & Sulon, 1996). As noted in Gunnar and Adam (this volume), cortisol levels

18

peak in saliva approximately 20–25 min poststressor, but take up to an hour to recover to prestress baseline levels. Speaking to the theme of specificity, although some studies have linked momentary negative mood states, such as worry, sadness, and anger, to acute increases in cortisol (e.g., Adam, 2006), reviews of the experimental acute reactivity literature in children, adolescents, and adults suggest that situations that pose threats to the social self are the most consistent and powerful acute activators of the HPA axis and that positive social relationships may serve as effective buffers of cortisol reactivity (Dickerson & Kemeny, 2004; Gunnar et al., 2009; Gunnar & Quevedo, 2007). Thus, social context plays a powerful role in contributing to and buffering acute cortisol reactivity, with social threat being an important ingredient for acute cortisol increase. As discussed later in this chapter, and in Gunnar and Adam (this volume), there is also some evidence that associations between state emotion and momentary cortisol change with development, with acute cortisol reactivity declining after infancy and increasing again over the transition to adolescence. Cortisol increases cannot therefore be considered a simple proxy or indicator for the presence of negative emotional states. Acute cortisol reactions are likely to occur under negative emotional conditions in which threats to the self are high, and support is low, and may change with age/developmental stage.

CIRCADIAN CHANGES (WITHIN-DAY CHANGES OR CORTISOL DIURNAL RHYTHMS)

Cortisol levels follow a strong circadian pattern across the day. In studies that examine cortisol levels across the full waking day, approximately 70% of the variation in cortisol is due to time of day (Adam & Gunnar, 2001). The basal or diurnal cortisol rhythm is typically characterized by high levels upon waking, a substantial (50–60%) increase in cortisol concentration in the 30–40 min after waking (the cortisol awakening response or CAR), and a subsequent decline over the remainder of the day, reaching a low point or nadir around midnight (Kirschbaum & Hellhammer, 1989; Pruessner et al., 1997; Weitzman et al., 1971).

The circadian or basal patterning in cortisol occurs as part of the basic circadian machinery for regulating alertness, appetite, and metabolic function (Dallman et al., 1994). Nonetheless, stress and emotional experience may cause cortisol levels to increase above typical basal levels at any point in the day (thus, reflecting acute reactivity, above) (Adam, 2006). Also, both individual differences in emotion (trait emotion) and changes in emotion within persons over time (daily emotional state) have been found to modify the shape of the diurnal cortisol rhythm (Doane & Adam, 2010; Hauner et al., 2008; Polk, Cohen, Doyle, Skoner, & Kirschbaum, 2004).

Two key elements of the basal rhythm that have been shown to be responsive to emotional experience are the CAR and the diurnal cortisol slope (decline in cortisol levels across the waking day) (Adam & Kumari, 2009; Saxbe, 2008). When the diurnal cortisol slope is modeled as rate of change in cortisol from wake time to bedtime (i.e., doesn't include the CAR), the size of the CAR and the steepness of the diurnal cortisol slope are not strongly correlated and relate in different ways to psychosocial and emotional variables. They thus represent relatively independent indicators of basal cortisol function (Adam & Kumari, 2009; Saxbe, 2008). Another basal cortisol indicator, the average cortisol level across the waking day, as measured by the area under the diurnal cortisol curve, does not relate as consistently with emotional experience.

How state emotional experience modifies diurnal cortisol rhythms is described later; here, I briefly describe research on trait emotional functioning and basal/diurnal cortisol. Diurnal cortisol patterns start to emerge in infants by 3 months of age (Price, 1983), and individual differences in these rhythms are evident throughout childhood and adolescence. In examining trait emotional correlates of the CAR, one study found that adolescents with high levels of introversion had a lower CAR (Hauner et al., 2008), and another found that adolescents with high levels of trait anger had a larger CAR (Adam, 2006). More research has been conducted on trait emotion and cortisol slopes. For example, among preschool-age children, flatter slopes from morning to afternoon in day care settings have been associated with greater sadness and shyness, high social fear, and poor inhibitory control (Dettling, Gunnar, & Donzella, 1999; Vermeer & van Ijzendoorn, 2006; Watamura, Donzella, Alwin, & Gunnar, 2003). However, similar associations are not obtained in the home setting (Dettling et al., 1999), suggesting that these results may reflect reactivity to the child care setting, rather than trait differences in rhythms, and highlighting the importance of social context in understanding emotion-cortisol associations. In adolescents, there is evidence of flatter slopes from wake time to bedtime among male adolescents with high levels of neuroticism (Hauner et al., 2008) and among youth with high trait loneliness (Doane & Adam, 2010); these trait associations were not explained by emotional state on the days of cortisol measurement. In interpreting associations between trait emotion and cortisol, it is helpful to examine the extent to which associations are accounted for by the measurement context and by differences in state emotion. In interpreting diurnal cortisol rhythms, it is important to note that flatter rhythms can result both from higher afternoon or evening levels and from lower morning levels (DeSantis et al., 2007; Dettling et al., 1999). Cortisol levels that follow the typical diurnal pattern—high wakeup levels, a strong decline from waking to bedtime, and a moderate CAR—tend to be associated with more desirable trait and state emotional functioning.

20

DAY-TO-DAY CHANGES IN CORTISOL ACTIVITY

Studies often average cortisol rhythms across multiple days of measurement in order to improve the measurement of "trait" diurnal cortisol rhythms, as day-to-day variation is often considered "noise." More recently, research (mostly in adults) found that cortisol rhythms change in meaningful ways from day to day in relation to changing social and emotional experience. For example, the CAR is accentuated the day after adolescents and adults experience high levels of sadness and loneliness (Adam, Hawkley, Kudielka, & Cacioppo, 2006; Doane & Adam, 2010), and diurnal cortisol levels are flatter on days with higher levels of anger/frustration (Adam, 2006). Day-to-day changes in cortisol rhythms can also be anticipatory. For example, professional ballroom dancers have a higher CAR on days they have an upcoming competition (Rohleder, Beulen, Chen, Wolf, & Kirschbaum, 2007). In preschoolers, cortisol levels at the beginning of the child care day are *lower* than corresponding levels at that time of day at home, perhaps protecting against elevations that tend to occur across the child care day (Dettling et al., 1999). Indeed, recent interpretations suggest that ability of diurnal cortisol patterns (and in particular the CAR) to flexibly adapt to changing daily demands is important hallmark of healthy HPA-axis functioning (Adam, 2006; Mikolajczak et al., 2010). Most research on day-to-day changes in cortisol rhythms has been conducted on late adolescents and adults—more developmental research on day-to-day variation in basal cortisol rhythms is needed. Examining how cortisol rhythms change in response to and in anticipation of daily experience provides insights into the potentially functional role of cortisol in mediating responses to daily challenges.

CHANGE OVER MONTHS AND YEARS

HPA-axis changes also occur over the course of months and years. These include normative developmental changes and responses to both early and cumulative developmental experience.

Normative developmental changes are described in more detail in Gunnar and Adam (this volume). Briefly, cortisol reactivity is robust beginning in infancy, and diurnal cortisol rhythms are evident in infants as young as 3 months of age but continue to mature over the first few years of life (Gunnar & Quevedo, 2007; Price, Close, Fielding, 1983). A relative stress hyporesponsive period, in which reactivity is harder to achieve, occurs from approximately 2 years of age through early adolescence; as a result, it may be more difficult to identify social and emotional correlates of HPA-axis activity during this time (Gunnar & Quevedo, 2007). In early adolescence, basal cortisol and cortisol reactivity to stressors appear to increase, particularly in girls, and increases correlate with stage of pubertal development (Adam, 2006; Gunnar, Wewerka, Frenn, Long, & Griggs, 2009; Stroud et al., 2009; Stroud, Papandonatos, Williamson, & Dahl, 2004). These latter changes are hypothesized to underly increased rates of depression, especially in girls, that also emerge over this time period (Stroud et al., 2004), but more research is needed on this point.

Chronic/Cumulative Stress Exposure

Beyond the impact of momentary and daily emotional experience on concurrently measured cortisol levels, exposure to chronic stress (and presumably, accompanying chronic negative affective arousal) can cause persistent alterations in basal cortisol activity and reactivity. The timing of cortisol measurement poststressor matters—reviews of both child (Gunnar & Vazquez, 2001) and adult research (Miller, Chen, & Zhou, 2007) suggest that following a stressful life event, basal cortisol levels may initially be elevated but, over time, may drop to below normal, resulting in a profile that is as likely hypocortisolemic (chronically low basal cortisol and flatter diurnal rhythms). Thus, the HPA axis may adapt to chronic stress over the course of weeks, months, and even years, and the direction of the association found may depend on the amount of time that has passed poststressor.

Chronic social-relational, and especially family stressors, are particularly likely to be linked with chronic alterations in cortisol activity (Adam, Klimes-Dougan, & Gunnar, 2007; Repetti, Taylor, & Seeman, 2002). For example, children living in a home with low levels of marital satisfaction and low maternal warmth have higher average cortisol and flatter diurnal rhythms (Pendry & Adam, 2007). Exposure to transitions in household composition (Flinn & England, 1995) and child maltreatment (Cicchetti & Rogosch, 2001; Shea, Walsh, McMillan, & Steiner, 2004) have also been associated with alterations in cortisol activity (for a review of their research on child maltreatment and cortisol, see Cichetti and Rogosch, this volume). On a positive note, interventions designed to improve social circumstances appear to have a positive impact on HPA-axis functioning; children in foster care homes participating in caregiving interventions have diurnal cortisol profiles that are more similar to profiles of children in a normal care environment (Dozier, Peloso, Gordon, Manni, & Gunnar, 2006; Fisher, Gunnar, Dozier, Bruce, & Pears, 2006). In these studies, data on children's emotional responses to stressors are rarely available. More research is needed on whether the impacts of chronic social stress (and reductions thereof) on the HPA are mediated by immediate emotional reactions to or ongoing changes in emotional experience.

Early Developmental Experience

Positive early social experiences, in particular sensitive and contingent caregiving during the first few years of life, are fundamentally important in that they contribute to lifelong patterns of both emotional and biological (including HPA axis) functioning in later interpersonal contexts, with the absence of adequate early contingent caregiving having important negative consequences for later biological regulation, including HPA-axis activity (see the chapters by Feldman and Strang, Hanson, and Pollack, this volume). Evidence from both animal models and humans suggests that stress experiences occurring in the first few years of life may have more dramatic effects on long-term emotional and HPA-axis functioning than similar stressors encountered later in childhood (Halligan, Herbert, Goodyer, & Murray, 2004; Shea et al., 2004). In addition, exposure to early life stress may modify the impact of later stress experiences on the HPA axis. Essex and colleagues (2002), for example, found that afternoon cortisol levels were elevated among 4.5-year-olds with currently depressed mothers, but only if those mothers had also been depressed during their infancy. They hypothesized that early experience had sensitized the infant HPA to be more responsive to later stressful life experiences. Heim and colleagues suggested that neurobiologically and developmentally distinct subtypes of depression exist, with altered cortisol activity (including elevated basal cortisol and increased reactivity) only likely to be present among depressed individuals who encountered early life stress (Heim, Newport, Mietzko, Miller, & Nemeroff, 2008). Thus, early social-developmental experiences may (1) alter the current functioning of the HPA axis and (2) may alter/moderate associations between later emotional experience and cortisol. Knowing about an individual's developmental past is therefore essential to understanding the present functioning of their HPA axis.

Genetics, Epigenetics, and Intergenerational Changes

Some portion of trait individual differences in HPA-axis activity originates in genetic differences. Twin studies identify a heritable component to HPA-axis reactivity and various aspects of basal patterning, and numerous genetic polymorphisms relevant to the functioning of the HPA axis have been identified (Wüst et al., 2004). A purely genetic model of individual differences in HPA-axis functioning allows change only in the next generation with changes in the genome—a very slow time scale of change in HPA-axis functioning. More recent epigenetic models (Weaver et al., 2004) suggest that the effects of HPA-relevant genetic polymorphisms on later functioning are not set in stone. In rodent models, alterations in adult behavioral and HPA-axis functioning occur as a result of early maternal care, and such changes are mediated by epigenetic modifications of glucocorticoid receptor regions of DNA (Weaver et al., 2004); it seems likely that similar epigenetic mechanisms may underlie the effects of early experience on later HPA-axis functioning in humans, described earlier. Some forms of epigenetic modification have been shown to be heritable across generations in plant and animal models (Whitelaw & Whitelaw, 2006). Should this prove to be true in humans for epigenetic modifications of HPA-axis relevant genes, epigenetics would also provide a biological mechanism (to complement known behavioral mechanisms) by which emotional experiences within a life span would be passed to the next generation.

Loneliness Example—Considering Three Time Courses in a Single Study

The fact that associations between emotional experience and cortisol can occur over multiple time scales is perhaps best illustrated by research in which several time scales of emotion–cortisol associations are simultaneously examined. In a recent study of loneliness and cortisol, we predicted that trait loneliness, a form of chronic psychosocial strain, would be associated with a flattening of the diurnal cortisol rhythm, but we were also interested in whether state loneliness, including experiencing lonely moments or lonely days, would also predict more acute alterations in cortisol levels. In order to maximize the generalizability of our results, and to ensure that we were studying associations between loneliness and cortisol as they actually unfold in the context of adolescents' daily lives, we used a modified experience sampling protocol, in which momentary diary reports, time linked with salivary cortisol samples, were gathered six times per day for 3 days in naturalistic settings (see also Dahl, Silk, and Siegle, this volume, regarding the advantages of ecologically valid measurement approach). In our study, a three-level multilevel growth curve model was employed, with momentary loneliness modeled at Level 1, day-to-day changes in loneliness modeled at Level 2, and trait loneliness (and other trait characteristics) modeled at Level 3. As expected, trait loneliness significantly predicted a flatter average diurnal cortisol rhythm across the days of testing (Doane & Adam, 2010). In addition, day-to-day changes in loneliness predicted daily changes in the CAR, with higher prior day loneliness predicting a larger CAR the next morning. We hypothesized that this increased CAR following a "lonely day" may serve to provide an energetic "boost" to assist the individual in engaging more effectively with the social world the next day ("boost hypothesis"; Adam et al., 2006). Finally, momentary increases in loneliness predicted momentary elevations in cortisol, but only for those adolescents who also had high levels of chronic interpersonal stress over the past year (Doane & Adam, 2010).

Following these adolescents forward longitudinally, we found that adolescents with a higher baseline CAR are significantly more likely to develop an episode of MDD over the following year (Adam et al., 2010). This suggests that short-term CAR "boosts" may come at a cost of long-term emotional health, a cost that may not have been apparent without following youth over a time frame of months to years. It is important to note that current MDD is *not* associated with an elevated CAR in these youth; rather, youth with current (and past) MDD have flatter diurnal cortisol slopes. This highlights the importance of *using prospective longitudinal data* to examine the role of the HPA axis in the etiology of emotional disorder. Given the allostatic nature of the HPA, *risk factors* for the development of emotional disorder may not still be identifiable among individuals already showing signs of disorder, since *changes* in the HPA axis are thought to be involved in etiology of depression, and the experience of the disorder itself may further alter the HPA (Adam, Sutton, Doane, & Mineka, 2008). Dynamic associations between emotional experience and cortisol occur over multiple time frames. Failure to identify and carefully plan data collection efforts to capture the appropriate time frame(s) of change in cortisol and emotion could result in underestimations of the associations between HPA-axis activity and emotional experience.

Psychological and Neurobiological Mechanisms of HPA-Axis Change

A full chronometric model of the HPA axis should consider (1) the extent to which acute HPA-axis activations add up to contribute to associations with occurring over longer time scales and (2) the psychological and neurobiological mechanisms mediating HPA axis change at each time scale. For this brief chapter, it must suffice to note (as depicted in Figure 2) that bidirectional cross-talk and interactions across time scales are expected and that changes across differing time scales are likely mediated by differing aspects of the underlying neurobiology of the HPA axis, ranging from genetic and epigenetic mechanisms to changes in receptor populations and responses in the pituitary and adrenal to changes in emotional and cognitive inputs to the HPA axis, such as threat appraisals and coping resources.

Importance of Considering Multiple Influences on Cortisol

It is important to note that cortisol does not respond uniquely, or specifically, to emotional experience. As summarized in Figure 3, many other aspects of current and past experience have been linked to individual differences in basal cortisol activity and reactivity. To more effectively reveal associations between emotion and cortisol, it is important measure and model various confounding and moderating influences, including factors measured on the

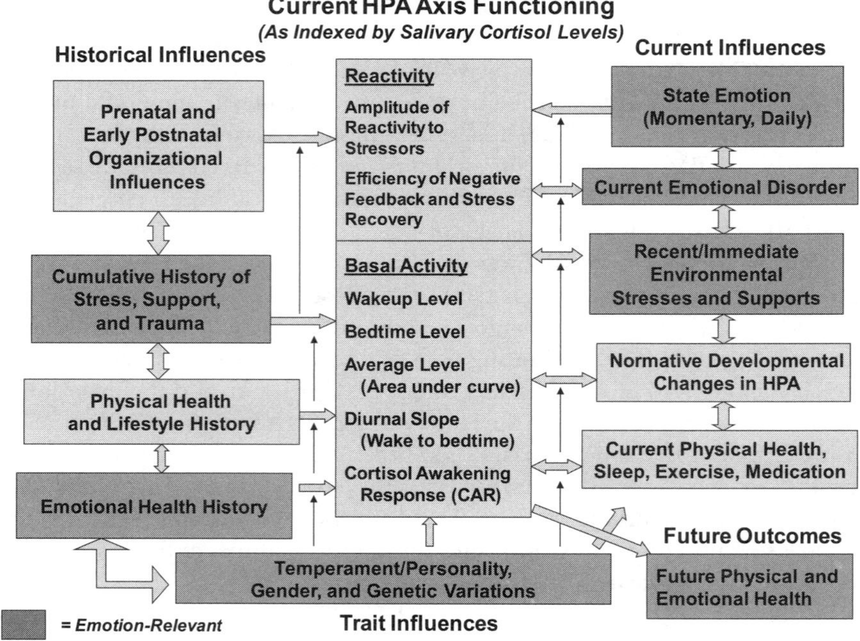

FIGURE 3.—Historical and current influences on HPA-axis functioning as indexed by salivary cortisol levels, highlighting the role of emotion and emotional disorder.

days of testing, in the recent past, and earlier in individuals' developmental histories. For example, in examining associations between state and trait loneliness and cortisol, we included day-varying covariates, such as time of waking each day, and person-level covariates, such as the presence of current MDD, caffeine, and nicotine use and recent interpersonal life stress (see Doane & Adam, 2010). Typically, we found that addition of multiple covariates for known confounding and moderating influences, rather than reducing effect sizes, tend to improve the strength and clarity of associations between emotional experience and cortisol.

Summary and Conclusion

To understand individual differences in cortisol, and its relations with state and trait emotional experience, one must understand the dynamic quality of this hormone—that cortisol levels and patterns change over multiple time scales in response to changes in emotional experience. It is also important to understand that within-person changes and individual differences in

26

cortisol are not specific to emotional experience—there are many other confounding and moderating influences on HPA-axis activity. Future research should consider (and measure and model) how multiple influences on cortisol interact, over multiple time scales ranging from moments to years, to contribute to individual differences in the associations between emotional experience and cortisol. Future research should also take a multisystem, integrative approach, examining the meaning and impact of cortisol change in light of co-occuring changes in other stress-sensitive biological systems, and should attempt to identify the neurobiological mechanisms underlying the various patterns and time courses of HPA-axis change.

NEW DIRECTIONS IN THE STUDY OF INDIVIDUAL DIFFERENCES IN TEMPERAMENT: A BRAIN–BODY APPROACH TO UNDERSTANDING FEARFUL AND FEARLESS CHILDREN

Vladimir Miskovic and Louis A. Schmidt

The study of the biological bases of temperament has shifted, historically, from a focus on peripheral interactions (e.g., Eppinger & Hess, 1910) to central nervous system circuits (e.g., Davidson, 2000; Fox, 1991; Rothbart, Sheese, & Posner, 2007). This shift has been driven largely by increased opportunities for the noninvasive *in vivo* study of the human brain, such as electroencephalography (EEG) and functional neuroimaging (fMRI) measures. Relatively few attempts, however, have been made toward integrating central and autonomic measures in the study of individual differences in temperament and emotion. There are, at least, two reasons for this lack of integration: (1) the culture within contemporary psychophysiology has traditionally considered central and autonomic contributions to emotion in parallel (Larsen, Berntson, Poehlmann, Ito, & Cacioppo, 2008), and (2) the field has been limited by a lack of theoretical frameworks from which to derive testable hypotheses. This state of affairs is lamentable since the study of central–autonomic coupling in emotion promises to generate more sophisticated insights into the biological foundations of temperament than those offered by traditional approaches (see Bauer, Quas, & Boyce, 2002; Beauchaine, this volume). Fortunately, recent advances in the field of affective neuroscience, both theoretical and methodological, have made a synthesis increasingly tenable.

For one, there is a growing appreciation that the ways in which the brain regulates the internal viscera impose specific neurobehavioral constraints (e.g., Porges, 2001), and that somato-visceral afferent activity also has a

This research was supported by grants from the Natural Sciences and Engineering Research Council of Canada (NSERC) and the Social Science and Humanities Research Council of Canada awarded to Louis A. Schmidt, and a Vanier doctoral scholarship from NSERC awarded to Vladimir Miskovic under the direction of Louis A. Schmidt.

Corresponding author: Vladimir Miskovic, email: vlad.miskovic@gmail.com or Louis A. Schmidt, email: schmidtl@mcmaster.ca

considerable influence on higher, central function (Berntson, Sarter, & Cacioppo, 2003; Craig, 2002; Damasio, 1994). Affective information processing is no longer considered the sole purview of central circuits but is viewed as extending down to the viscera (Cameron, 2009; Schulkin, Thompson, & Rosen, 2003). In keeping with these advances, several contemporary investigators have integrated notions of brain–body coupling in theories of affective development and function (Benarroch, 1993; Craig, 2005; Porges, 2001; Thayer & Lane, 2000).

Technological developments have been equally important in attempting to integrate central and peripheral approaches to temperament and emotion. With the advent of faster and more powerful computers over the past several decades, researchers have moved beyond analog signals written on chart drives to acquiring and processing biological signals at computational speeds approximating real time. Improvements in bioamplifier design, including greater input impedances, have allowed researchers to record from more electrodes with less preparation time, an important concern when dealing with pediatric populations for whom it is difficult to remain still in constrained laboratory conditions (Schmidt & Segalowitz, 2008). Developmental researchers are becoming increasingly able to noninvasively index relatively specific aspects of biology simultaneously (e.g., source dipoles of brain electric currents, as well as sympathetic and parasympathetic control of heart rate). These advancements have the promise to provide unprecedented insights into the dynamics of emotional expression, experience, and regulation, if they are integrated into larger theoretical models.

This chapter has four goals: (1) to review the lateralization of two basic motivational networks, both in the body and the brain; (2) to provide an elaboration of a brain–body model and emphasize its importance in the study of individual differences in human temperament and emotion; (3) to illustrate how this model can be used to organize an accumulated body of data regarding temperamental shyness; and (4) to suggest future avenues of research using the model to understand other temperamental styles such as fearless children.

Our model, illustrated in Figure 4, aims to remedy the brain–body split in the psychophysiology of emotion. An important caveat concerns the model's reliance on evidence drawn from adult studies. We will return to these issues in our concluding remarks.

LATERALIZED FUNCTION IN THE STUDY OF TEMPERAMENT AND EMOTION

One salient dimension of lateralization that is important for understanding individual differences in temperament and emotion involves neurobehavioral systems for appetitive approach and defensive withdrawal.[1]

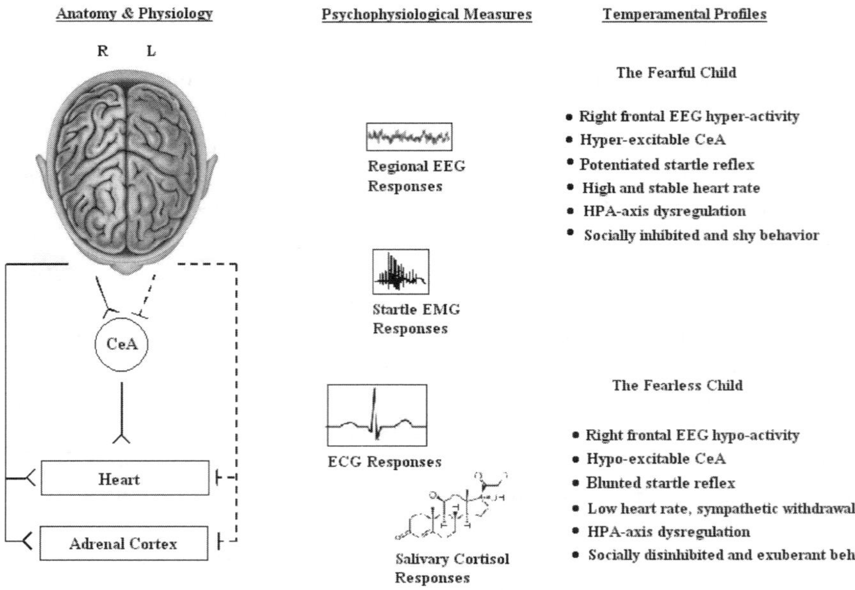

FIGURE 4.—Schematic illustration of an extended lateralized brain–body model that can be applied to studying individual differences in temperament. Also included are the relatively noninvasive psychophysiological measures that are available to index different levels of this hierarchical model in developmental populations. The model can be used to organize a disparate set of findings on two contrasting temperamental styles: temperamental fearfulness and temperamental fearlessness.
Note: Schematic diagram is not drawn as anatomically realistic. CeA = central nucleus of the amygdala; the solid lines represent excitatory pathways; the dashed lines represent inhibitory pathways. CeA excites both the heart and the adrenal cortex.

Below we review evidence for extensive brain–body lateralization of these highly conserved systems.

Lateralization of Efferent and Afferent Autonomic Function

There is considerable evidence for asymmetrical effects in neural cardiac regulation (Hugdahl, 1995; Wittling, 1995, 1997). At low levels of the neuraxis, the primary division of labor is between chronotropic and inotropic/dromotropic control, governed by right- and left-sided autonomic efferents, respectively. However, findings from several distinct lines of research suggest that a different principle governs cortical lateralization of autonomic regulation.

The notion of cerebral asymmetry in cardiac control is derived from multiple paradigms. For example, clinical studies involving patients with unilateral cerebral infarct (Andersson & Finset, 1998; Oppenheimer, Kedem,

& Martin, 1996; but see Korpelainen, Sotaniemi, Huikuri, & Myllyla, 1996), hemispheric barbiturate inactivation studies (Hilz et al., 2001; Lane, Novelly, Cornell, Zeitlin, & Schwartz, 1988; Rosen, Gur, Sussman, Gur, & Hurtig, 1982; Yoon, Morillo, Cechetto, & Hachinski, 1997; Zamrini et al., 1990; but see Ahern et al., 2001), and unilateral electric stimulation protocols (Oppenheimer, Gelb, Girvin, & Hachinski, 1992) suggest that the right hemisphere controls sympathetically mediated cardiac acceleration, while the left hemisphere controls parasympathetically mediated cardiac deceleration.[2]

Similarly, noninvasive studies with healthy controls have contributed evidence for the differential involvement of the cerebral hemispheres in autonomic control. Walker and Sandman (1979) found that spontaneous increases in heart rate were associated with enhanced amplitudes of right-hemispheric evoked potentials. Likewise, visual hemifield studies have shown that emotional stimuli delivered to the right hemisphere lead to increases in blood pressure and sympathetically mediated cardiac changes (Hugdahl et al., 1983; Wittling, 1990; Wittling, Block, Schweiger, & Genzel, 1998). By contrast, left hemisphere stimulation is associated with parasympathetically mediated cardiac depression (Wittling, Block, Genzel, & Schweiger, 1997). Most recently, Foster and Harrison (2006) demonstrated a relation between the magnitude of cerebral asymmetry at rest and heart rate—individuals having more activity in the right forebrain exhibited faster resting heart rates.

In addition to asymmetries in autonomic efferent control, there is also evidence of identical asymmetries in cortical representation of homeostatic afferents. Sympathetic and parasympathetic sensory inputs are represented predominantly in the right and left hemispheres, respectively (see Craig, 2005). This visceral feedback likely influences aspects of subjective state (Craig, 2002; Damasio, 1994) and cortical affective information processing (Berntson, Sarter, & Cacioppo, 2003).

Peripheral Lateralization of Endocrine and Immune Function

Peripheral lateralization also extends to neuroendocrine and immune function. Specifically, the left hemisphere is associated with reduced cortisol concentrations/immunopotentiation, and the right hemisphere with cortisol secretion/immunosuppression (Davidson, Coe, Dolski, & Donzella, 1999; Henry, 1993; Kalin, Larson, Shelton, & Davidson, 1998; Neveu, 1993; Vlajkovic, Nikolic, Nikolic, Milanovic, & Jankovic, 1994; Wittling & Genzel, 1995; Wittling & Pfluger, 1990).

Based on the evidence reviewed above, Wittling (1995, 1997) and Craig (2005) hypothesized that the cerebral hemispheres are characterized by two different response modes. The left hemisphere supports an energy-enriching, inhibitory response mode, while the right hemisphere supports an energy-consuming, excitatory mode (but also see Thayer & Lane, 2009). Activation of either response system entails bodywide changes that support distinct neurobehavioral states (either of appetitive approach or defensive withdrawal).

A CENTRAL-SOMATIC INTEGRATION HYPOTHESIS

The above evidence of cerebral asymmetries in the relative control of peripheral function is remarkably consistent with the cerebral asymmetry of approach–withdrawal tendencies (see Craig, 2005). Davidson (2000) and Fox (1991) were the first to observe and describe how frontal asymmetries in EEG alpha power desynchronization (a marker of cortical activation) were related to individual differences in temperament and emotion in adults and children. Specifically, activity in the left prefrontal cortex (PFC) indexes a circuit that sustains feelings of positive affect and appetitive approach. Activity in the right PFC, on the other hand, indexes a neural withdrawal/defense system and is associated with a negative affect bias. The left and right PFC regions likely represent the most rostral extensions of approach–withdrawal systems. The lateralization observed at the level of the cerebral cortex may have been a natural concomitant of increasing encephalization, culminating in higher primates including humans.

Research on the central and autonomic bases of emotion, however, has proceeded largely in parallel (Larsen, Berntson, Poehlmann, Ito, & Cacioppo, 2008), with little attention given to integrating the two in theories of affective function (see Benarroch, 1993; Craig, 2005; Porges, 2001; Thayer & Lane, 2000, for notable exceptions). More recently, different central and autonomic components have been conceptualized as coupled "bio-oscillators" (Benarroch, 1993) that must be effectively coordinated to allow for adaptive emotional responding (Thayer & Lane, 2000). The PFC is likely to play a special role in the integration of diverse response systems (autonomic, endocrine) in line with the executive function of the frontal lobes. The influence of the left and right PFC on autonomic and endocrine function can be exercised either indirectly via modulation of limbic activity or directly by projections to the autonomic motor neuron pools (Berntson, Cacioppo, & Quigley, 2007).

Figure 4 presents a schematic diagram of the lateralized brain–body emotion model reviewed in this chapter. This model is based chiefly on functional and anatomic data outlined more extensively elsewhere (Craig, 2005; Wittling, 1995, 1997) as well as on recent evidence from the human and nonhuman animal affective neuroscience literature (see Berridge, 2003; Davidson, 2003, for reviews). According to this model, the central nucleus of the amygdala (CeA) functions as the "hub" of a general defense system (Amaral, 2002; Kalin, Shelton, & Davidson, 2004). The CeA exerts a sympathetic-excitatory drive and results in a cardioacceleratory response (through sympathetic activation and vagal withdrawal) that sustains energy-consuming defensive behavioral strategies (Saha, 2005; Yang et al., 2007). Activation of this defense circuit also leads to engagement of the hypothalamic–pituitary–adrenal (HPA) axis, with glucocorticoid release providing the metabolic basis for peripheral bursts of activity and central processing of threat (Schulkin, Morgan, & Rosen, 2005). Neural regulation by the PFC provides a negative feedback signal that effectively dampens this energetically costly defensive drive. Animal models suggest that PFC inhibition is accomplished either through GABAergic inhibition of the lateral and basal amygdaloid nuclei (Grace & Rosenkranz, 2002) or through projections to the inhibitory intercalated cells of the amygdala (Quirk & Mueller, 2007).

A popular hypothesis (Davidson, 2002; Schmidt & Fox, 1999) is that PFC-based regulation of the amygdala is lateralized. In humans, higher glucose metabolism in the left PFC is strongly related to reduced bilateral amygdalar glucose metabolism (Abercrombie et al., 1996), while a pattern of greater brain electrical activity in the left PFC predicts faster extinction of fear learning (Davidson, 1994) and increased ability to down-regulate negative emotions (Jackson et al., 2003; Johnstone, van Reekum, Urry, Kalin, & Davidson, 2007). Most recently, we (Miskovic & Schmidt, 2010) provided preliminary evidence that greater left PFC activity in the resting EEG predicts attentional avoidance of rapidly presented pictures conveying social threat. The left PFC may, therefore, constitute the principal "brake," while asymmetric activity favoring the right PFC is associated with a sticky "accelerator" mode that involves systemic, bodywide changes. In support of this suggestion, a recent study using functional brain and cardiac imaging showed that participants with a greater signal change in the amygdala and the right frontal and insular cortices in response to threat of shock exhibited the greatest potentiation of myocardial contractility (an index of sympathetic activation) (Dalton, Kalin, Grist, & Davidson, 2005).

A study from our group likewise found that participants who exhibited right-lateralized frontal EEG activity during an anger-induction task showed greater increases in systolic and diastolic blood pressure than nonright lateralized participants (Waldstein et al., 2000). Similarly, right PFC activity during the performance of cognitive tasks shows a strong positive relation with heart rate, either as a result of parasympathetic withdrawal or sympathetic activation (Tanida, Sakatani, Takano, & Tagai, 2004).

The lateralized brain–body emotion model integrates findings showing asymmetries in peripheral function with asymmetries in the central circuits of emotion. We suggest that the two brain–body networks are differentially responsive to positive and negative incentive stimuli, with these phasic perturbations likely superimposed on tonic differences in activity. The idling state of the two extended central-somatic networks during resting conditions may serve as a diathesis that interacts with different challenges to shape an individual's emotional range. Importantly, while some investigators have emphasized opponent processing between approach and withdrawal (Dickinson & Dearing, 1979; Konorski, 1967), others have conceptualized them as largely orthogonal systems, with distinct operating characteristics (Cacioppo & Berntson, 1999) and the possibility of coactivation (Miller, 1959; Schmidt, 1999).

Finally, it should be noted that contrary to the argument advanced here, others (Thayer & Lane, 2009) have hypothesized that the right PFC, rather than the left, exerts the primary inhibitory influence over threat-elicited sympathoexcitatory responses. However, this neuroanatomical pathway is largely based on neuroimaging and pharmacological work examining chronotropic control of heart rate, without being directly related to the cerebral asymmetry models of motivation and emotion (Craig, 2005). As noted by Thayer and Lane (2009), it is important to caution against overly simplistic hypotheses concerning hemispheric activation and recognize that the ensemble of neural structures involved in mediating adaptive responses are best understood as forming flexible and context-specific functional coalitions. It is our opinion that the schematic illustrated in Figure 4 provides a reasonable hypothesis for integrating the wide range of disparate findings that have emerged from the human and nonhuman animal affective neurosciences.

THE FEARFUL CHILD: CLUES FROM TEMPERAMENTAL SHYNESS

The lateralized brain–body emotion model can be used to understand and explain some individual differences in temperament. One of these temperamental styles is shyness. Temperamental shyness refers to an early appearing and stable form of shyness that is observed in approximately 10–15% of typically developing children (García Coll, Kagan, & Reznick, 1984; Kagan, Reznick, & Snidman, 1987). Temperamental shyness is associated with fearfulness and restraint in the face of social and nonsocial forms of novelty and has been a key focus of our research group. A large body of evidence has accumulated suggesting that temperamental shyness is linked to a unique pattern of central and peripheral physiology, both at rest and in response to various stressors (Kagan, 1994; Schmidt & Fox, 1999). Importantly, the lateralized brain–body emotion model provides a unifying theoretical framework for integrating the disparate set of findings on the biological correlates of this temperamental profile.

According to the model described earlier and illustrated in Figure 4, deficient negative feedback input from the left PFC leads to disinhibition of the CeA hub and a tonic activation of the right hemisphere defense system. Temperamental shyness can be understood as a "run-away" positive feedforward effect, involving sensitization of a right PFC-amygdala-sympathoexcitatory network, due to a genetic predisposition, adverse early experience, or (most likely) some combination of the two (see Fox et al., 2005; Fox, Hane, & Pine, 2007; Schmidt, Fox, & Hamer, 2007). From a dynamic systems perspective (Thayer & Lane, 2000), an irregular feedforward circuit accounts for many features of pathological anxiety. This profile is reflected in the psychophysiological correlates of temperamental shyness, involving greater relative right frontal EEG activity (Fox et al., 1995, Fox, Schmidt, Calkins, Rubin, & Coplan, 1996; Schmidt & Fox, 1994; Schmidt, Fox, Schulkin, & Gold, 1999; Theall-Honey & Schmidt, 2006), high and stable heart rates (i.e., low vagal tone) (Kagan, Reznick, & Snidman, 1987, 1988; Schmidt & Fox, 1994), increased sympathetic myocardial contractility (Buss, Davidson, Kalin, & Goldsmith, 2004), enhanced amygdala activation and potentiation of amygdala-based reflex circuits (Beaton et al., 2008; Schmidt & Fox, 1998; Schwartz, Wright, Shin, Kagan, & Rauch, 2003; Snidman & Kagan, 1994), and HPA-axis aberrations (Buss, Davidson, Kalin, & Goldsmith, 2003; Kagan, Reznick, & Snidman, 1987, 1988; Schmidt et al., 1997; Schmidt, Santesso, Schulkin, & Segalowitz, 2007). Importantly, the disinhibition of the CeA and a right cerebral bias in autonomic regulation have systemic effects that affect the entire body. Centrally, a perceptual framework for fear is activated, which makes detection of threat more likely (Pérez-Edgar et al., 2010; Rosen & Schulkin, 1998; Schmidt & Schulkin, 2000), and, peripherally, cardiac and endocrine resources are utilized to provide the metabolic substrates for energy-consuming defensive behaviors.[3]

Chronic activation of the brain–body withdrawal system is metabolically costly (Schulkin, 2003). Consistent activation of the energy-consuming right hemisphere response mode and, consequently, the continued experience of stress likely leads to an accrual of allostatic load. Allostatic load occurs when short-term emergency responses are sustained over long periods of time, subsequently leading to a breakdown of regulatory physiological mechanisms (Schulkin, McEwen, & Gold, 1994).

How does central and peripheral integration unfold developmentally? The work to date on this issue has largely been derived from cross-sectional studies of fear and shyness in infants and children and has not been examined developmentally. Buss and colleagues (2003) noted that infants with extreme levels of right frontal EEG asymmetry also exhibited high cortisol and more sadness-related behavioral expressions during a withdrawal task. Schmidt and his colleagues reported increases in right frontal EEG activity and heart rate in preschoolers (Theall-Honey & Schmidt, 2006) and early-school-age children (Schmidt et al., 1999) who were classified as temperamentally shy during the processing of negative emotions induced by video clips and anticipation of a self-presentation task, respectively. Although the central and autonomic measures each independently explained emotional processing in shyness, Schmidt and colleagues did not report the correlated activity between the

TABLE 1

FUTURE DIRECTIONS FOR BRAIN–BODY RESEARCH ON TEMPERAMENTALLY FEARFUL
AND FEARLESS PROFILES

Future research directions for the fearful child
- Immune function, both baseline levels and response to pathogenic provocation
- Cardiac health outcomes across the life span
- Possible homeostatic adjustments of the HPA axis into adolescence and adulthood (Schmidt, Santesso, Schulkin, & Segalowitz, 2007)
- Readiness to rapidly acquire or inability to extinguish conditioned aversive associations, reflecting hyperexcitable amygdala function or impaired top-down inhibition
- Metabolic function outcomes across the life span (e.g., glucose intolerance, diabetes prevalence)
- Further characterization of potential subtypes, = (e.g., conflicted *versus* avoidant withdrawal)

Future research directions for the fearless child
- Deficits in amygdala activation or impaired potentiation of amygdala-based circuits (e.g., the startle reflex)
- Impaired ability in the acquisition/or rapid habituation of conditioned aversive associations, reflecting hypoexcitable amygdala function or impaired top-down inhibition
- Dopamine neurotransmission deficits, reflected in event-related potential components like the P300
- Neuroendocrine function, involving hypo- or hyperarousal of the HPA axis
- Characterizing the differences between exuberant children with and without inhibitory control

central and autonomic measures. Table 1 summarizes some of the questions suggested by the integrated brain–body model that remain to be empirically tested in the future using longitudinal research designs with children.

THE FEARLESS CHILD: FUTURE DIRECTIONS FOR TESTING THE MODEL

The lateralized brain–body emotion approach can be used to make testable experimental predictions concerning other temperamental styles. For example, a temperamentally fearless child may be at risk for later externalizing behaviors (Fowles, Kochanska, & Murray, 2000), as these children display a reduced ability to regulate the emotions of anger and aggressive approach. A plausible hypothesis is that this fearless profile is maintained by deficient withdrawal mechanisms *coupled* with dysregulated approach systems, possibly due to impairments in central dopaminergic function (Beauchaine, Gatzke-Kopp, & Mead, 2007). These predictions can be tested in the future using noninvasive psychophysiological measures that index central, autonomic, and endocrine response systems in conjunction (see Figure 4). A body of evidence suggests that, at the peripheral level, fearlessness is reflected in low heart rate and blunted electrodermal responses, indicative of reduced sympathetic tone

(Raine, 1996). Deficits in sympathetic responding, however, represent only a part of the equation. Beauchaine's (2001; see also Beauchaine, this volume) model of externalizing behavior problems demonstrates the benefits of an integrated physiological approach by emphasizing the need for indexing simultaneous activation in both autonomic branches. We would suggest that still more stands to be gained by the inclusion of central measures, such as spontaneous (Santesso, Reker, Schmidt, & Segalowitz, 2006) and evoked (Polich, 2007) EEG. For instance, event-related components such as the P300 wave, known to be sensitive to dopaminergic neurotransmission (Polich, 2007; Polich & Criado, 2006), can be used to further explore the hypothesis of compromised dopamine function in this temperamental style. In Table 1, we have suggested some tentative future directions for using biological measures to examine temperamental fearlessness.

DEVELOPMENTAL AND TEMPORAL CONSIDERATIONS

A key challenge for future research will consist of charting the developmental processes that guide patterns of central–somatic integration and their relation to emotional expression and regulation. For example, although previous studies have provided strong evidence for the relations between individual biological response systems and particular temperamental profiles (see the preceding sections on temperamentally fearful and fearless children), there has been scarce work examining the joint contribution of multiple physiological systems.[4] More recently, several studies have examined multivariate relations between different response components of the autonomic nervous system in children and adolescents (e.g., Boyce et al., 2001; Buss, Goldsmith, & Davidson, 2005; Salomon, Matthews, & Allen, 2000), leading to more refined theories of physiology–behavior relations. Future longitudinal studies will be necessary to more fully elucidate the changing patterns of integration between biology and behavior across the life span.

CONCLUSION AND IMPLICATIONS

We have emphasized the importance of considering brain–body interactions in the study of individual differences in temperament. We have used examples of temperamentally fearful and fearless children to illustrate how an integrated psychophysiological model can be used to contextualize findings from different levels of analysis. An important caveat concerns the model's reliance on evidence from adult studies. It is possible that distinct organizing principles operate across different stages of development and that the nature of brain–body lateralization is time dependent. Additionally, it will be interesting to examine the influence of early experience on lateralization, given the evidence for such effects in animal studies (Denenberg, 1981). An interesting suggestion is that atypical or reversed lateralization could lead to the most problematic outcomes (Wittling & Genzel, 1995). For example, we recently found evidence that adolescent females exposed to child maltreatment exhibit lateralized abnormalities in EEG coherence and that this predicts the degree of psychiatric impairment (Miskovic, Schmidt, Georgiades, Boyle, & MacMillan, 2010).

Improvements in the speed and relative information yield of psychophysiological measures will continue to accrue in the future and investigators interested in temperamental differences will need to take note (see Molenaar & Gates, this volume). However, technological advances become meaningful only in the presence of *conceptual* advances (Kagan, 2006) and these tools will only lead to a more sophisticated understanding of the biological bases of human temperament and affect if they are integrated into unifying theoretical frameworks. Our hope is that this chapter has provided a brief example of one such framework.

NOTES

1. In principle, these motivational tendencies have been postulated by researchers working with organisms ranging from invertebrates to mammals (Dickinson & Dearing, 1979; Konorski, 1967; Lang, Bradley, & Cuthbert, 1990; Miller, 1959; Schneirla, 1959) and closely mirror the BIS/BAS distinction made in Gray's (Gray & McNaughton, 2000) conceptual nervous system.

2. There are numerous exceptions to a straightforward left-parasympathetic/right-sympathetic dichotomy—some of the discrepancies may derive from methodological inconsistencies, but others likely reflect the dynamic and rapidly shifting nature of cortical control over autonomic function. Perhaps the safest interpretation of the findings is to stress that, as with other dimensions of lateralization, hemispheric differences in autonomic control are not "all-or-none" but rather "more-or-less."

3. It is important to note, however, that distinct subtypes of temperamental shyness exist that vary in the degree to which the left hemisphere approach system is activated (Schmidt & Fox, 1999). These subtypes differ in the amount of anxiety experienced (Cheek & Buss, 1981), risk for substance use and abuse (Page, 1990; Santesso, Schmidt, & Fox, 2004), as well as central (Schmidt, 1999) and autonomic (Schmidt & Fox, 1994) physiology.

4. In addition to examining between-system coherence, it is vitally important to establish the relative temporal stability *within* neural systems required for affective expression and regulation. Developmental studies meeting this challenge are ongoing (Hannesdóttir et al., 2010; Schmidt, 2008; Smith & Bell, 2010).

INTRODUCTION TO SECTION TWO: SOCIALIZATION AND ENVIRONMENTAL FACTORS IN THE PHYSIOLOGY OF EMOTION

Paul D. Hastings, Kristin A. Buss, and Tracy A. Dennis

The second section of the monograph, "Socialization and Environmental Factors in the Physiology of Emotion," places the themes of context and development front and center. Children's emotional and physiological development, and the development of the relations between their physiological and emotional functioning, occurs within the contexts of their relationships. For most children, the first and most important relationships are with the family, and these chapters document how parents make fundamental, pervasive, and lasting contributions to their children's emotional physiology. Further, they show that when a healthy family context is missing, the physiological underpinnings of healthy emotional development are disrupted.

Feldman reviews her program of research on parent–infant synchrony, the process of multisystem entrainment between parents and infants in the first year of life that underlies the formation of primary attachment relationships. On an acute time scale, synchrony reflects the moment-to-moment temporal concordance between social partners, but it is the affective context of relationships—including parent-infant, child-peer, and romantic partners—that defines the meanings of physiological and behavioral change in both social partners. Integrating evidence for synchrony across neural, hormonal, autonomic and behavioral systems, Feldman charts the intricate growth and blossoming of synchrony over the first 12 months of life. She documents the benefits of synchrony for the development of emotion regulation, adaptive functioning and well-being. Importantly, Feldman's work reveals the bidirectional and transactional relations between biological and behavioral development; physiological systems and processes are both shaped by, and contribute to, children's and parents' behavior in affectively close relationships. Further, threats to early parental availability, including prematurity and postpartum

Corresponding author: Paul D. Hastings, Ph.D., University of California Davis, Center for Mind & Brain, 267 Cousteau Place, Davis, CA 95618, email: pdhastings@ucdavis.edu

depression, are shown to compromise the normative developmental process of synchrony at both biological and behavioral levels.

The following chapters in this section also show that studying deviations from well-functioning family contexts can be effective for highlighting the contributions made by socialization to the development of affective physiology. Katz and Rigterink consider the development of respiratory sinus arrhythmia (RSA), an index of parasympathetic contribution to emotion regulation capabilities, in children exposed to domestic violence. Spouses who engage in domestic violence also introduce perturbations to a child's emotion socialization, and Katz and Rigterink focus on emotion coaching as a key aspect of effective parenting that is diminished in the context of domestic violence. Considering the specificity of biological measures and emotional processes, higher baseline RSA is thought to reflect traitlike capacity for emotion regulation. RSA suppression to social threats or stressors is considered an adaptive statelike application of emotion regulation, whereas RSA augmentation under such conditions is interpreted as heightened vigilance to cues of danger or challenge. Katz and Rigterink show that the experience of domestic violence in early childhood is concurrently associated with failures to suppress RSA in children who manifest behavioral maladjustment, and is predictive of smaller gains in baseline RSA by middle childhood. Thus, there is a progression from state (and possibly transitory) to trait (more enduring) in how one physiological basis for effective emotion regulation might be eroded by early or chronic exposure to an adverse family context.

Support for this conclusion is strongly enhanced in the chapter by Strang, Hanson, and Pollak, by their examinations of emotion physiology in maltreated and institutionalized children. Echoing the idea of hypervigilance to danger suggested by Katz and Rigterink, Strang and colleagues use the temporal resolution and specificity of ERP to show that maltreated children devote greater neurocognitive resources to detecting and monitoring anger in adults' facial expressions. More enduring physiological impacts of maltreatment appear to be evident from structural MRI examinations of brain regions linked to socioemotional functioning. In children adopted from understaffed international orphanages, the severity of neglect is reflected in hormonal disruptions during interactions with their adoptive mothers, perhaps revealing physiological mechanisms for the attachment-related difficulties often shown by postinstitutionalized children. Thus, the themes of context, development and specificity are front and center in this program of research. Strang and colleagues conclude with a set of important methodological considerations that researchers would do well to keep in mind when establishing their protocols for studying the physiology of emotions in children.

As a set, these three chapters extend our understanding of how physiological functioning is involved in parents' socialization and children's adaptive and maladaptive emotional development. Decades of research have documented how variations in family context and socialization experiences are associated with children's emotions and adjustment. The chapters in this section help to lay the essential groundwork for a vital new direction: Understanding the physiological mechanisms and processes by which children internalize their socialization experiences and come to experience, understand, express and regulate their emotional lives.

PARENT–INFANT SYNCHRONY: A BIOBEHAVIORAL MODEL OF MUTUAL INFLUENCES IN THE FORMATION OF AFFILIATIVE BONDS

Ruth Feldman

Synchrony, a concept coined by the first researchers on parenting in social animals (Rosenblatt, 1965; Schneirla, 1946; Wheeler, 1928), describes the dynamic process by which hormonal, physiological, and behavioral cues are exchanged between parent and young during social contact. Over time and daily experience, parent and child adjust to the specific cues of the attachment partner and this biobehavioral synchrony provides the foundation for the parent–infant bond (Fleming, O'Day, & Kraemer, 1999). Affiliative bonds—defined as *selective* and *enduring* attachments—are formed on the basis of repeated exposure to the coordination between physiological states and interactive behavior within each partner, between partners, and between the physiology of one and the behavior of the other. Such social bonds, in turn, set the framework for the infant's emotional development and shape the lifelong capacity to regulate stress, modulate arousal, and engage in coregulatory interactions, achievements that are central components of the child's social–emotional growth (Feldman, 2007a). Moreover, the experience of biobehavioral synchrony in the first months of life sets the biological and behavioral systems that enable the child to provide optimal parenting to the next generation, thereby forming the cross-generation transmission of attachment patterns (Feldman, Gordon, & Zagoory-Sharon, 2010a).

During the sensitive period of bond formation, infants' brains are sensitized to the mutual influences between physiological systems, behavioral indicators, and their interactions. Studies in mammals propose that this process of synchrony—the system's sensitivity to the coordination of physiology

Research reported in this chapter was supported by the Israel Science Foundation (#01/941, #1318/08), the US-Israel Bi-National Science Foundation (2001-241, 2005-273), the March of Dimes Foundation (12-FY04-50), the NARSAD foundation (Independent Investigator Award), and the Irving B. Harris Foundation.

Corresponding author: Ruth Feldman, Department of Psychology and the Gonda Brain Sciences Center, Bar-Ilan University, Ramat-Gan, 52900, Israel, email: feldman@mail.biu.ac.il

and behavior in the two partners—spans the period of early gestation to weaning, which in humans is considered the period between early pregnancy and the end of the first year of life (Feldman, 2007b). During this time, infants must experience the synchrony between their own physiology and behavior and the mother's body, physical presence, and sensory cues (e.g., maternal touch, smell, heart rhythms) and the species-specific maternal repertoire for optimal social and emotional growth (Hrdy, 1999). Over the past decade, research in my lab attempted to define this process of biobehavioral synchrony; address its genetic, hormonal, autonomic, brain, behavior, and mental components; and study its implications for emotional development across childhood and up to adolescence. We examined similarities and differences between the parent–infant bond and two other processes of bond formation observed across mammalian species—pair and filial—which in humans are expressed during periods of "falling in love" with a romantic partner and in children's emerging friendships with a "best friend." The data presented here across several biobehavioral systems provide initial evidence that during periods of bond formation, parent and infant's brains transform to accommodate the inclusion of the other as an attachment partner by means of biobehavioral synchrony. Such processes enable the formation of human attachment, and attachment relationships, in turn—at least according to some perspectives—serve as the central motivating force that guide individuals throughout life and define the apex of the human condition.

From a theoretical standpoint, the focus on observed parent–infant behaviors and their physiological underpinnings as a prerequisite for theory building has been the cornerstone of Bowlby's (1969) ethological-based attachment theory. According to the early ethologists (Lorenz, 1950; Timbergen, 1963), theoretical perspectives on the nature of social adaptation in mammals must begin with a meticulous documentation of behaviors that emerge or intensify during bond formation. Indeed, Bowlby's far-reaching formulations on the attachment system across the life span were based on careful observations of infants' reactions to maternal presence and absence, daily routines, and changes in internal arousal. By focusing on concrete bonding-related behaviors, Bowlby advocated a bottom-up theory of human development that is evolutionary based. This perspective has been further elaborated by the empirical programs of Hofer and colleagues (Hofer, 1995), which spelled out the provisions embedded in the maternal physical presence and their impact on the pup's physiological systems, and Meaney and colleagues (Meaney, 2001; Szyf, McGowan, & Meaney, 2008), who detailed the effects of the mother's postpartum behavior on the offspring's brain plasticity, stress reactivity, and social behavior. Such biobehavioral coupling was thought to provide the basis for the infant's lifelong physiological regulation and social adaptation and the cross-generation transmission of attachment. In this context, it is important to note that the concept of *synchrony* describes only the *temporal concordance* between processes that occur simultaneously or sequentially and does not imply any heuristic system of symbols (e.g., "cognition" or "affect"). As such, *synchrony* as an overall framework is especially suited for a bottom-up model that centers on discrete building blocks as they cohere into a theoretical model. Conceptual perspectives in neuroscience recently addressed the process of synchrony as the mechanism that underlies consciousness and supports the brain's capacity to form a unitary event out of the simultaneous activity in discrete brain regions (Damasio, 1999; Edelman, 2004), as stated by Llineas (2001, p. 120): "timeness is consciousness." This transition from mechanisms of a "central organizer" to those of temporal synchrony marks the shift from a top-down to a bottom-up viewpoint. Such a paradigm shift has not yet been incorporated into developmental research nor has it been integrated into the wider circle of developmental thought.

BIOBEHAVIORAL SYNCHRONY FROM GESTATION TO WEANING AND INFANTS' EMOTIONAL DEVELOPMENT

Beginning in the first trimester of pregnancy, hormonal changes in the mother, especially in prolactin and oxytocin (OT), prepare for the initiation of maternal behavior (Nelson & Panksepp, 1998). In parallel, oscillator systems, such as the biological clock or cardiac pacemaker, consolidate in the fetus during the third trimester (Groome, Loizou, Holland, Smith, & Hoff, 1999; Mirmiran & Lunshof, 1996) and prepare for the engagement in social contingencies following birth. Measuring the biological clock and cardiac pacemaker weekly from 25 weeks' gestation to term, we found that individual trajectories in the two oscillators predicted infant neuromaturation at birth and mother–infant synchrony at 3 months (Feldman, 2006), suggesting that brainstem-mediated systems that support homeostasis and arousal modulation provide the basis for higher order social regulatory capacities (Feldman, 2009a; Geva & Feldman, 2008). At birth, mothers begin to engage in the species-typical set of maternal behavior, including gaze at infant face, "motherese" vocalizations, positive affect, and affectionate touch. As infants are biologically primed to detect social contingencies and mothers adapt the provision of social behavior to the scant moments of newborn alertness, infants may engage in the first experience of a contingent interpersonal dialogue immediately after birth. The engagement in social contingencies depends on the newborn's autonomic maturity, indexed by cardiac vagal tone, and has shown to predict the development of parent–infant synchrony (Feldman & Eidelman, 2007). Similarly, maternal OT level in the first trimester was found to predict the amount of maternal postpartum behavior and its coordination with infant state (Feldman, Weller, Zagoory-Sharon, & Levine, 2007). It thus appears that physiological support systems

44

maturing in mother and child during gestation prepare for the expression of interaction synchrony.

In humans, as in mammals, the mother's postpartum behavior and its coordination with the infant state are central for emotional growth. The expression of maternal postpartum behavior is disrupted by conditions involving physical or emotional maternal deprivation, such as premature birth or postpartum depression, and is enhanced by biomarkers of bonding, such as breastfeeding (Feldman & Eidelman, 2003, 2007). In a longitudinal study, we followed premature infants at birth, 3, 6, 12, and 24 months and at 5 and 10 years. At each time point, measures of mother–infant synchrony and child emotion regulation were collected. Beginning at birth, mother–child synchrony at each time point predicted children's emotion regulation at the next assessment. At the same time, regulatory capacities at each observation predicted synchrony at the next point. It is thus possible that mother–newborn contingencies shape emotional development not only directly but also through a series of iterations that set the child's emotional trajectory to a more optimal course.

At around 3 months of age, face-to-face synchrony in its typical form is first observed, and parent and child begin to engage in the coordination of gaze, vocal, affective, and tactile signals. Face-to-face interactions contain repetitive-rhythmic sequences of social behaviors and form a couple-specific "dance" that typically includes a time-lag, occurring in seconds, between behavioral change in one partner and parallel change in the other's (Tronick, 1989). The affective contour of infants' interactions with mother and father are parent specific, with a more rhythmic contour with mother and a more jerky, highly aroused, random contour with father (Feldman, 2003), enabling infants to engage in multiple attachments simultaneously. At this age, infants also begin to engage in triadic synchrony, adjusting their behavior not only to the interacting partner but also to the nonverbal cues between the parents (Gordon & Feldman, 2008). This ability to navigate a complex multiperson system supports the development of social skills in the "filial" attachment system and predicts toddlers' social competence during interactions with peers (Feldman & Masalha, 2010).

The experience of synchrony during its first appearance at 3–4 months of age, the most social period in human life (Stern, 1985), is an example of a critical environmental input that is required not only for the maturation of brain circuits that support social engagement (Johnson et al., 2005) but also for the infant's ultimate emotional development. Parent–infant synchrony at that age has been shown to predict infants' attachment security, self-regulation, behavior adaptation, empathy, symbolic competence, and moral internalization across childhood and up to adolescence (Feldman, 2007c, 2007d, 2009b; Feldman, Greenbaum, & Yirmiya, 1999; Jaffe, Beebe, Feldstein, Crown, & Jasnow, 2001).

During the second 6 months, with the maturation of object exploration, joint attention, intentionality, and intersubjectivity, the synchrony experience transforms into a more mutually regulated process and both partners assume responsibility for matching the other's signals. As the infant's regulatory repertoire expands, synchrony becomes tightly coupled with physiological and behavioral stress regulation systems. Conditions such as postpartum depression and anxiety disrupt both the infant's capacity for social engagement, the regulation of fear and novelty, and the functioning of the hypothalamic–pituitary–adrenal-axis stress management system (Feldman et al., 2009). With the reorganization of the brain at that age that co-occurs with the first stages of prefrontal cortex maturation, regulatory abilities as well as interpersonal synchrony consolidate into relatively stable trajectories that shape the individual's regulatory structures of the mind throughout life.

Finally, with the emergence of symbolic thought and language toward the end of the first year, the synchrony experience expands to include the concordance between the partners' affective-symbolic communication into the framework of synchrony. For instance, during symbolic play between toddlers and parents, an increase in the child's symbolic complexity is often preceded by an increase in the parent's affective reciprocity (Feldman, 2007d). With time, interactions between attachment partners, across the life span, begin to contain two parallel components: the underlying nonverbal synchrony in the gaze, touch, and affect modalities and the verbal–symbolic synchrony in the expansion of closeness between partners. Observing the interactions between romantic couples during the first 3 months of falling in love, we detected both nonverbal synchrony in the gaze, touch, and affect modalities and verbal synchrony between moments of self-disclosure in the two partners. Behavioral synchrony was related to the partners' vagal tone and OT levels, echoing the physiological precursors of the mother-newborn relationship during bond formation.

EVIDENCE FOR BIOBEHAVIORAL SYNCHRONY IN THE AUTONOMIC, HORMONAL, AND BRAIN SYSTEMS

Maternal–Infant Contact Shapes Children's Autonomic Response

In two studies, we examined the effects of maternal touch and contact on the regulation of children's autonomic reactivity, following Hofer's (1995) research on the role of maternal proximity in regulating the pup's heart rhythms. In the first study, two groups of 6-month-old infants were tested in the still-face (SF) paradigm, an experimental manipulation that simulates maternal deprivation: One group experienced the standard SF, and the other received maternal touch during the SF episode (Stack & Muir, 1992). Vagal

46

tone was measured from mother and child during the free play, SF, and reunion episodes of the paradigm. When maternal momentary unavailability was complemented by touch, infants' vagal response was milder in amplitude and the return to baseline was quicker, similar to the effects of handling on the stress response of young animals (Feldman, Singer, & Zagoory, 2010). In the second, decade-long study, mothers provided daily skin-to-skin contact (Kangaroo Care) to their preterm neonates and dyads were followed for 10 years. Children receiving maternal contact as neonates showed higher baseline vagal tone and greater vagal brake to emotional stressors at 10 years compared to a matched no-intervention group, pointing to the lasting effects of early maternal contact during periods of deprivation on the infant's physiology.

Although these data highlight the lasting impact of maternal contact on the infant's autonomic functioning, they do not demonstrate online synchrony between maternal and infant's physiology and behavior. To this end, face-to-face interactions between mothers and their 3-month-old infants were observed, while cardiac output was measured from mother and child and episodes of gaze, affect, and vocal synchrony were marked. Using bootstrap analysis, we found that mothers and infants synchronize their heart rhythms within lags of less than 1 s and the effect was specific to own infant. Moreover, during moments of vocal and affect synchrony, biological synchrony between mother and infant's heart rhythms increased substantially (Feldman, Magori-Cohen, Galili, Singer, & Louzoun, 2011). Thus, human mothers and infants coordinate their physiology and behavior through episodes of social synchrony, yet, unlike mammals, human synchrony occurs through the online matching of facial signals and does not require tactile contact.

Finally, conditions of maternal physical or emotional unavailability, such as prematurity or postpartum depression, were found to decrease both neonatal vagal tone and maternal contingent response (Feldman & Eidelman, 2003, 2007). Such findings support the hypothesis that maternal availability contributes to the emergence of bonding-related behavior, maturation of the infant's environment-dependent physiological systems, and the coupling between physiology and behavior.

Affiliation Hormones in Parent–Infant and Romantic Attachment

Bond formation is supported by a specific neuroendocrine system, and the neuropeptide OT has been shown to play a key role in processes parental bonding across mammalian species (Insel, 1997). In a series of studies, we addressed the involvement of the OT system in human bonding across the gestation-to-weaning period and beyond and its links with the partners' social synchrony. In the first study, plasma OT was measured from healthy pregnant women during the first trimester, third trimester, and first postpartum month.

OT was highly stable within individuals and levels at first trimester predicted the amount of maternal postpartum behavior and its coordination with infant state, indicating that already in the first weeks of gestation hormonal systems function to prime the mother for the expression of maternal behavior. Similar to vagal tone, maternal depression was associated with reduced OT levels at both first trimester and the postpartum (Feldman et al., 2007).

In a second study, we measured plasma OT from 160 mothers and fathers (80 couples) at the transition to parenthood and again at 6 months in relation to dyadic and triadic interactions. Surprisingly, levels of OT in fathers did not differ from those observed in mothers at both time points. Although OT has initially been implicated primarily in birth and lactation, father-infant touch and contact possibly provide additional pathways for the biological basis of fatherhood. OT was associated with maternal and paternal parent-specific behavior—affectionate play with mother and stimulatory play with father—and with parent–infant synchrony at 6 months, particularly with touch synchrony—the matching of parent affectionate touch with the parent and infant's social gaze. Consistent with the propositions of the biobehavioral model, cross-time mutual influences were found between hormones and behavior. Maternal and paternal OT in the postpartum predicted parent–infant synchrony at 6 months and vice versa; postpartum behavior predicted parental OT at 6 months, underscoring the mutual adaptation of physiology and behavior during bond formation. Interestingly, biological synchrony between attachment partners was observed and OT levels of mothers and fathers were correlated at each time point (Gordon, Zagoory-Sharon, Leckman, & Feldman, 2010a). Possibly, in the formation of affiliative bonds, partners shape each other's physiology through a variety of processes, including social synchrony during dyadic and triadic interactions.

In a second study, 122 mothers and fathers (noncouples) engaged in an episode of parent-infant "play and touch" with their 4- to 6-month-old infants and measures of plasma, salivary, and urinary OT were collected. Results indicated that salivary OT increased following parent-infant contact, but only among mothers who provided high levels of affectionate touch and among fathers who exhibited high levels of stimulatory contact. It thus appears that the parent-specific form of touch functions to stimulate OT release, highlighting both the similarities and differences between maternal and paternal care and their differential relations to the neuroendocrine foundation of bonding (Feldman, Gordon, Schneiderman, Weisman, & Zagoory-Sharon, 2010). A third study assessed salivary OT in 55 parents and their infants before and after a session of social interaction. Correlations were found between parent and infants' baseline and reactivity OT, as well as in the degree of OT increase following play. Furthermore, synchrony increased the cross-generation transmission of OT and among children growing up in the context of high synchrony, a closer link between parental and child OT was observed, similar to the

48

animal studies pointing to higher cross-generation transmission of OT in the context of environmental enrichment (Feldman , Gordon, & Zagoory-Sharon, 2010). Finally, we measured maternal and paternal plasma OT as predictors of triadic synchrony between new parents and their firstborn child. Higher triadic synchrony, defined as moments of coordination between physical proximity and affectionate touch between parents as well as between parent and infant while both parent and child are synchronizing their social gaze, was predicted by maternal and paternal OT and among mothers, also by lower cortisol (Gordon, Zagoory-Sharon, Leckman, & Feldman, 2010b). Overall, these studies point to the important links between the neurobiological basis of bonding and moments of synchronous coordination between maternal, paternal, and coparental microlevel behaviors, particularly during the first months of the infant's life and the first period of parenting.

Interestingly, OT and social behavior were associated with two additional bonding-related hormones. OT and paternal coordination of joint exploration with the infant correlated with the father's prolactin levels (Gordon, Zagoory-Sharon, Leckman, & Feldman, 2010c), similar to the associations described for fathers in biparental species (Wynne-Edwards, 2001), and with cholecystokinin (CCK), a hormone implicated in hunger and satiety that plays a role in maternal-infant bonding (Blass, 1996).

Two other studies examined OT in relation to social bonding at other points in the life cycle. OT and cortisol were sampled from single adults in relation to bonding to own parents. Levels of OT in singles were lower than those observed in parents, supporting the involvement of the OT system during periods of bond formation. OT was related to bonding to own parents and to lower depressive symptoms, further suggesting that the connection between OT and bonding-related internalizations can be observed throughout life (Gordon et al., 2008).

Finally, results from a study of romantic partners during the first 3 months of "falling in love" showed that OT levels in new lovers were higher than in singles, indicating increased activity of the oxytocinergic system during periods of bond formation across the life span. Levels of OT in new lovers, both men and women, were associated with the degree of interaction synchrony between the partners, including matched affect, positive arousal, joint social gazing, and affectionate touch, similar to the findings shown for new parents, and to the partners' preoccupations and anxieties regarding the partner and the relationship. These findings may suggest that falling in love involves a reorganization in which the partners' physiology, mental state, and synchronized behavior cohere to form the basis for the selective and enduring romantic bond (Schneiderman et al., 2012).

Based on research in animal models, a specific brain circuitry has been proposed for the development of parenting that includes hypothalamic–midbrain–limbic–paralimbic–cortical circuits. Areas rich in OT binding receptors play a critical role in parenting behavior, including the hypothalamus, medial preoptic area, the bed nucleus of the stria terminalis (BNST), substantia niagra, midbrain-pons, and superior colliculus (Leckman & Herman, 2002). Assessing the brain response of parents (fMRI) to their own versus standard infant cries and pictures in the first postpartum month and again at 3–4 months, we found that own infant cries elicited greater brain activations in this parenting networks, including the anterior cingulate, midbrain, hippocampus, basal ganglia, thalamus, and amygdala, as well as in temporal and parietal cortices, areas implicated in motivation, reward, emotional processing, habit formation, and empathy (Swain et al., 2007). Observations of parent-infant interactions were conducted at 3 months, and the parent's sensitivity, expressed in visual, vocal, tactile, and affective behaviors and their adaptation to infant cues, was coded. Greater activations in mothering-related regions to own-infant cry in the postpartum in these areas predicted greater maternal sensitivity at 3 months (Kim, Feldman, Leckman, Mayes, & Swain, 2011). In another study, we examined the brain response of synchronous mothers—those who coordinate their response with infant cues—and intrusive mothers—those who provide excessive stimulation—to videotaped vignettes of mother-infant interactions. We found that among synchronous mothers, greater activations were found in the nucleus accumbens, a central nucleus in the reward pathway, whereas intrusive mothers showed greater activation in the amygdala. Furthermore, among synchronous mothers activation in reward pathways were functionally connected to the cortical social brain circuitry, which enable the mother to read the nonverbal signals of her infant and plan for adequate parenting. Furthermore, activations of the nucleus accumbens in synchronous mothers was correlated with the level of maternal OT. Thus, mother-infant synchrony appears to be based on reward networks, affiliative hormones, and closer concordance between motivational reward and brain structures implicated in theory of mind and empathy (Atzil, Hendelr, & Feldman, 2012). Bond formation, therefore, may involve the coordination of parenting-related brain circuits with parenting behavior directed to the selective element in attachment, to "owness."

Parallel findings were observed in the infant's brain. Event-related potential response of 6-month-old infants to neutral, sad, happy, and angry facial expressions were assessed in two experiments. In the first, infants observed standard emotional faces; in the second, their own mother's emotional faces. Consistent with previous research, infants showed greater amplitudes of the Nc component to emotional compared to neutral faces, particularly to angry faces, suggesting greater allocation of attentional resources to the expression of emotions. The mother's emotional faces elicited greater activations than the unknown face, with greatest amplitudes observed to own mother's angry face. Infants of depressed mothers showed greater activations in response to maternal angry face and these were negatively related to mother–infant synchrony during interactions (Eidelman, Goldstein, Berger, & Feldman, 2010). Thus, attachment relationships may enhance the saliency, relevance, and meaning of emotions, and infants utilize the emotions and behaviors of attachment partners to perceive, encode, and learn the rules of emotional communication with social partners.

Summary

Since the 1920s, the term *synchrony* has been used to describe the process by which the physiology and behavior of mother and young during social contact are coordinated into an affiliative bond. The data presented here in the autonomic, hormonal, and brain systems point to the unique ways in which the physiology and behavior of human partners synchronize to form a selective and enduring biobehavioral attachment. Such an affiliative bond between parent and child provides an overall protective envelope that shapes the child's capacities for emotion regulation, stress management, empathy, symbol formation, and social adaptation and is observed during other periods of bond formation throughout life, such as falling in love and the transition to parenthood. Similar to other mammals, the pace, rhythms, sensory inputs, arousal contour, and interactive resonance experienced within early attachments during the critical period of gestation-to-weaning is likely to play a role in the individual's capacity to form friendships and engage in meaningful relationships throughout life.

DOMESTIC VIOLENCE AND EMOTION SOCIALIZATION

Lynn Fainsilber Katz and Tami Rigterink

Domestic violence (DV) is highly prevalent among American families, with up to 50% of married couples experiencing spousal violence at some point in their marriages (Straus & Gelles, 1990; Straus, Gelles, & Steinmetz, 1980). Not only do survivors of DV exhibit signs of significant psychological disturbance subsequent to abuse, but also there is substantial evidence that children exposed to DV may experience subsequent negative developmental outcomes (Jouriles, Norwood, McDonald, & Peters, 2001). Compared to children from nonviolent homes, children exposed to DV exhibit higher levels of anxiety, depression, and externalizing problems (Jouriles, McDonald, & Skopp, 2005), and they have greater difficulties with peers (McCloskey & Stuewig, 2001).

Our work has been focused on understanding emotional development within the context of DV. Examining the effects of severe environmental stressors such as DV can inform our understanding of how developmental processes emerge. We have examined how DV affects the biological underpinnings of emotional processes from a developmental perspective (Katz, 2007; Rigterink & Katz, 2010), examined associations between biological and social processes within the child (Leary & Katz, 2004), and studied parenting as a buffer of the effects of DV on children's adjustment (Katz & Windecker-Nelson, 2006).

A central focus of this research has been on examining children's ability to regulate emotion. The ability to successfully regulate emotional states is central to mental health (Gross & Munoz, 1995). A number of theorists and researchers have noted that diverse forms of child and adult psychopathology, encompassing both internalizing and externalizing difficulties, may reflect disturbances in the capacity to regulate emotional experiences (Beauchaine, 2001; Cole, Martin, & Dennis., 2004; Gross & Thompson, 2007).

Corresponding author: Lyn Fainsilber Katz, Ph.D., University of Washington, Department of Psychology, Box 351525, Seattle, WA 98195-1525, email: katzlf@uw.edu

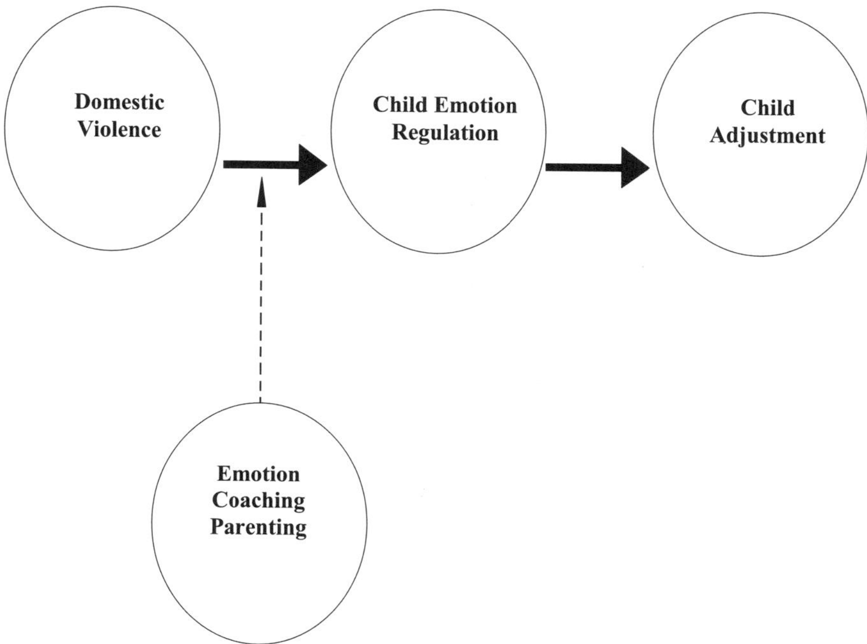

FIGURE 5.—Theoretical model.

The theoretical model underlying our work proposes that DV affects children's ability to regulate their emotions, which in turn is associated with poor child adjustment. We also suggest that parenting that shows awareness and ability to help children manage their emotions—what we have called "emotion coaching"—can buffer children from the effects of DV on child adjustment (see Figure 5). This model is consistent with results from studies of marital discord in normative, community-based samples (e.g., Davies & Forman, 2002).

There is widespread agreement among emotion theorists that the expression and regulation of emotion involves not only behavioral but also physiological systems (e.g., Thompson & Goodvin, 2007). As noted elsewhere in this volume, at the physiological level, respiratory sinus arrhythmia has received considerable attention as a psychophysiological marker of emotion regulation (Beauchaine, 2001; Porges, 2007). Although we have used a diverse array of physiological measures in our research, in this chapter we will illustrate the value-added benefit of using physiological indices by focusing on children's respiratory sinus arrhythmia, given its well-established link to emotion regulation.

DV is rarely a one-time occurrence in the life of a family. Children are often repeatedly and chronically exposed to DV (Perkins & Graham-Bermann, 2006), which can take many forms including physical, emotional, and sexual abuse. The study of physiological processes within the context of DV can provide a window into how biological processes unfold over time under adverse environmental conditions. Children and adolescents face many environmental adversities ranging from natural disasters to terrorism to family violence, and previous research has shown that these adverse environmental experiences may shape children's physiological responses concurrently and over time (e.g., Gunnar, 2006; King, Mandansky, King, Fletcher, & Brewer, 2001; Pfeffer, Altemus, Heo, & Jiang, 2007).

However, to our knowledge, there are few studies that have examined how physiological processes unfold over time by conducting longitudinal studies of the same group of children exposed to an adverse environmental event (see Pfeffer et al., 2007, for an exception). In addition, few studies have looked at the impact of adverse environmental events on physiological measures known to be related to emotional processes, such as respiratory sinus arrhythmia (RSA). In this chapter, we will review our work on DV and children's emotion regulation abilities, with a focus on how environmental influences may lead to distinct changes in physiological indices of emotion regulation over the course of development.

DOMESTIC VIOLENCE AND CHILDREN'S EMOTION REGULATION ABILITIES

Studies to date suggest that DV is associated with both behavioral and physiological aspects of emotion regulation. We focus here on recent data on physiological indices of emotion regulation. Two sets of findings from our lab may be relevant to the question of how physiological development related to emotion regulation unfolds over time in the context of DV. In general, children's ability to suppress RSA has been found to be the adaptive response to challenge. In infancy, a reduction in RSA during challenging situations is related to better state regulation, greater self-soothing, and more attentional control (DeGangi, DiPietro, Greenspan, & Porges, 1991; Huffman et al., 1998; Porges, Doussard-Roosevelt, Portales, & Greenspan, 1996). Yet some findings suggest that some children not only fail to suppress RSA but also may in fact exhibit RSA augmentation to challenge. For example, DiPietro, Porges, and Uhly (1992) found that infants who showed increases in RSA during presentation of a surprising stimulus were more attentive to the stimulus than infants who showed decreases in RSA. They interpreted their findings to suggest that RSA augmentation may reflect heightened attentiveness and the ability to detect environment change. Applying this work to the area of DV, we reasoned that although children's ability to suppress RSA is the adaptive response to

54

challenge, in family environments in which threat and hostility are habitual and salient social processes, children may learn to become hypervigilant to even mild forms of interpersonal negativity, as they portend escalation in conflict and may signal the potential for harm to themselves or family members. Children in these types of family environments may show heightened parasympathetic activation, or RSA augmentation, particularly when they are in social situations that are stressful or conflictual (Katz, 2000). Hypervigilance to negative affect has also been demonstrated in studies of physically abused children, who are quicker than typically developing children to identify anger (Pollak, Cicchetti, Hornung, & Reed, 2000), and show selective attention toward angry faces compared to faces displaying other emotions (see Strang, Hanson, & Pollak, this volume, for a review).

To address this idea, Katz (2007) examined whether individual differences in children's RSA reactivity to peer provocation was related to DV within the family. The reactions of 4- to 6-year-old children with varying levels of conduct problems, a common outcome associated with DV (Jouriles et al., 2001), were assessed during peer provocation since these types of interactions may involve negativity and hostility and may parallel the interpersonal strain that children who have experienced DV observe at home. In the peer provocation paradigm, children were expecting to interact with a difficult peer; however, instead of meeting an unfamiliar peer, the target child heard a prerecorded audiotape consisting of a staged "conversation" between the experimenter and "another child" in which the child stated his dislike for the experimenter and for any child with whom he would have to work. Physiological measures of respiratory sinus arrhythmia (RSA) were obtained under both baseline conditions and during the peer provocation.

When groups were divided into children who showed RSA augmentation versus RSA suppression to the stressful peer interaction, our findings indicated that conduct-problem children who showed vagal augmentation to interpersonal challenge came from families with the highest levels of DV. DV was not related to RSA in children with few conduct problems. Interestingly, no differences were observed with baseline measures of RSA. RSA augmentation in conduct-problem children may reflect increased attentiveness or hypervigilance to conflict in the environment. Social information processing models suggest that conduct-problem children have a hostile attributional bias, characterized by a tendency to see hostility in the environment even with ambiguous social cues (Crick & Dodge, 1994). In addition, living in a home where conflict can suddenly escalate, children may need to be hypervigilant to their surroundings, scanning their environment for cues of threat so that threat is detected early and an action plan can be developed. In this way, hypervigilance may help the children effectively monitor their own safety and support efforts necessary to prepare for danger. A related possibility is that vagal augmentation to interpersonal stress is an endophenotype

(Gottesman & Gould, 2003), or preexisting biological risk factor, of those at risk for conduct problems. Growing up in a violent environment may act as a catalyst and increase the child's likelihood of exhibiting conduct problems.

These same families were then recontacted approximately 4 years later for longitudinal follow-up. Rigterink and Katz (2010) examined the relation between DV exposure and children's regulatory functioning over time, investigating whether DV exposure was related to the trajectory of children's physiological regulatory abilities from the preschool period to middle childhood. Differences in baseline RSA were found but not in RSA to interpersonal stress, induced at this age by an in-vivo interpersonal stressor. As expected from what is known regarding normative changes in baseline RSA over the course of development (Bornstein & Suess, 2000), all children increased in baseline RSA from preschool to middle childhood. However, children exposed to DV displayed less increase in baseline RSA over time as compared to nonexposed children, independent of their level of conduct problems.

We were intrigued by the differences in findings from these two time points. During the preschool period, DV was associated with differences in reactivity to an interpersonal stressor, while over the period from preschool to middle childhood, DV was associated with differences in baseline RSA. Different stressors were used at each of these time points, which may in part explain why no differences were observed in response to the interpersonal stressor during middle childhood. In addition, RSA reactivity has been found to be relatively unstable over time. El-Sheikh (2005) found no stability in RSA reactivity during interpersonal stress (i.e., listening to an argument) but modest stability in RSA reactivity during a star-tracing task in elementary school–aged aged children and young adolescents. The lack of stability in RSA reactivity has also been observed in other samples (Bornstein & Suess, 2000; Doussard-Roosevelt, Montgomery, & Porges, 2003; Wilkinson & Howse, 2003), although modest cross-age stability has been found from age 2 to 4.5 years ($r = .17$–$.33$ across four tasks; Calkins & Keane, 2004). Environmental stress may be less likely to affect a physiological process that is itself unpredictable in its expression.

What we find interesting in our data, however, are the baseline effects. DV was not associated with baseline RSA during the preschool period but was associated with changes in baseline RSA from preschool to middle childhood. These findings raise the hypothesis that environmental stress, or more specifically in this context, DV, may affect different aspects of children's physiological regulatory abilities. Traditionally, baseline measures of physiological measures such as RSA are viewed as traitlike measures of a more stable characteristic related to the child's capacity to regulate emotional arousal. Indeed, there is evidence of moderate stability of baseline RSA over time. For example, El-Sheikh (2005) reported correlations of .36 and .49 in baseline RSA over a 2-year period in elementary school–aged children and young

56

adolescents. Field and Fox (1989) reported stability level of $r = .89$ in 3-year-olds over a 6-month period. Calkins and Keane (2004) reported stability of $r = .57$ from age 2 to 4.5. In contrast, as noted earlier, reactivity measures are typically more situationally specific and less stable over time. Our findings across these two studies, taken together, suggest that initially when children are young, the stress of living in a violent home may affect more transitory or statelike aspects of their ability to regulate emotion. That is, since emotion regulation abilities are beginning to emerge more clearly around the age of 4–6 years (Maccoby, 1980), the surfacing of this new skill may be temporarily or sporadically affected by an adverse environmental stressor such as DV. As children get older, and their regulatory capacities become more consistent, DV may be more likely to be associated with deficits in more traitlike or characterological aspects of emotion regulation. Although the true meaning of baseline measures of physiological functioning have long been a debated topic (e.g., Cacioppo, Tassinary, & Berntson, 2007), these data may reflect one of the value-added benefits of using respiratory sinus arrhythmia as a physiological measure of emotion regulation—that is, the ability to disentangle traitlike and statelike processes associated with emotion regulation.

IMPLICATIONS OF STUDIES OF PHYSIOLOGICAL MARKERS OF EMOTIONAL DEVELOPMENT

The Importance of Context: Risk and Protective Processes

Behavioral genetics studies show that individual differences in RSA are largely determined by environmental factors (Kupper et al., 2005), and increasing evidence suggests that emotion regulation is chiefly socialized within the family (Beauchaine et al., 2009). Exposure to psychological stress in the family, be it in the form of maltreatment, bereavement, DV, or parental discord or divorce, can be especially harmful during childhood when physiological regulatory mechanisms are still developing (Gunnar & Quevedo, 2007). Anda et al. (2006) point to the causal nature of childhood family adversity in the long-term development of psychological and physical disorder, identifying physiological dysregulation as a plausible pathway for the relation.

Not only is the larger family context an important factor in determining risk, but also the quality of more proximal relationships within the family, such as the parent-child relationship, plays a key role in emotion socialization. Emotion coaching, where parents provide guidance in understanding and coping with emotions, has been associated with reports of greater emotion regulation abilities (Gottman, Katz, & Hooven, 1997; Shortt, Stoolmiller, Smith-Shine, Eddy, & Sheeber, 2010; Stover, 2004), higher baseline RSA and greater RSA suppression (Gottman et al., 1997), better peer relations in children with and without conduct problems (Katz & Windecker-Nelson, 2006), and fewer internalizing and externalizing symptoms in adolescence (Shortt et al., 2010; Stocker, Richmond, Rhoades, & Kiang, 2007). Among maltreated children, maternal emotion coaching was also found to mediate the relation between maltreatment status and children's emotion regulation skills (Shipman, Schneider, Fitzgerald, Sims, Swisher, & Edwards, 2007).

While adverse family and parenting contexts can lead to compromises in emotional development, the family also serves a protective function, even when controllable or uncontrollable stressors are occurring. For example, early childhood parental loss is associated with fewer reports of minor stress and lower stress-related negative affect when the surviving parent is perceived as caring (Luecken, Kraft, Appelhans, & Enders, 2009). To expand our efforts to ameliorate the lives of children exposed to DV, studies should focus on ways to buffer violence-exposed children from negative outcomes. We have previously found that even in the context of DV, children whose parents were more emotion coaching showed fewer symptoms of aggression, withdrawal, anxiety, and depression (Katz & Windecker-Nelson, 2006), and they also exhibited fewer maladaptive behaviors during peer provocation (Katz, Hunter, & Klowden, 2008). An important next step will be to test the model displayed in Figure 5 and determine whether emotion coaching can also improve physiological regulatory indices of emotion regulation in violence-exposed children. We recently developed and are now pilot testing an emotion coaching parenting intervention for DV survivors. One goal of this study is to test whether changing mothers' emotion coaching abilities can function to increase RSA and improve children's ability to regulate strong negative affect. Increasing evidence suggests that caregivers may influence children's functioning at a biological level (Calkins & Hill, 2007). For example, recent research examining the magnitude of RSA response to challenge indicates that children display significantly greater decreases in RSA when provided with parental support during a task than when confronted with a challenge independent of support (Calkins & Keane, 2004). To the extent that environmental processes such as parenting contribute to variability in RSA (Beauchaine, Gatzke-Kopp, & Mead, 2007), then changing these environmental processes should result in changes in RSA.

Development

Animal studies suggest that adverse life circumstances early in an animal's life may have long-lasting effects. In humans, disturbances in physiological regulation have been found long after exposure to stressful life events. For example, among children who experienced the death of a parent, greater exposure to stressful events following childhood parental loss predicted lower levels of cortisol activity 6 years later (Hagan, Luecken, Sandler, & Tein, 2010). In our data, the slower growth in the trajectory of RSA over time in DV-exposed children compared to nonexposed children may be due to the early timing of the stressor (i.e., in the preschool period) or, alternately, may be due to the chronicity of stress. In either case, these data reflect a progression from state to traitlike deficits in physiological markers of emotion regulation through exposure to an adverse family context, suggesting that enduring aspects of biological development related to emotion regulation and expression can be influenced by important socialization experiences.

Specificity and Integration of Other Biological and Psychological Domains

Studies to date of emotional development within the context of DV have yet to determine whether behavioral and physiological indices of emotion regulation are related to one another and are similarly related to or affected by DV. Use of multimethod approaches, and greater integration of diverse measures of emotion regulation, may add to our understanding of the meaning and function of physiological indices of emotion regulation within the context of stressful environmental events. It may also be valuable to consider the impact of childhood family experience on other measures of neurobiological activity (e.g., neuroendocrine, serotonin) and how effects on these biological systems might interact to predict long-term psychological and health outcomes. Attenuated cortisol reactivity has been documented in kindergarten children exposed to high levels of interparental conflict (Davies et al., 2007), while poorer marital functioning has been associated with elevated basal cortisol in kindergarten-aged children as well as adolescents (Pendry & Adam, 2007). Greater integration of biological and psychological measures of emotion regulation and reactivity can also help clarify which domains of emotion regulation are most affected by environmental stressors such as DV.

CONCLUSION

It is a truism among behavioral ecologists that if an organism has a trait that has adaptive significance in terms of increased survival, natural selection will likely favor it. When faced with adverse life circumstances, children develop strategies that help them cope and survive with the stress that forms the fabric of their lives. In the context of DV, children with augmented RSA reactivity—who we suggest are hypervigilant to threat—have good reason to develop a biological adaptation to scan their environment for signs of threat. In this way, the meaning of this physiological measure is inextricably connected with the social context in which it is measured.

The data also point to a biological cost over time of DV exposure in the form of smaller gains in baseline RSA by middle childhood. The ability to regulate negative affect may be an especially important skill for children exposed to adverse family environments. When a stressful situation is controllable, problem solving or active coping methods are associated with positive adjustment in children (Compas, Connor-Smith, Saltzman, Thomsen, & Wadsworth, 2001). However, children exposed to DV are often powerless to stop the violence they witness at home. Compas et al. (2001) suggest that when a stressful situation is uncontrollable, emotion focused coping may be a superior strategy. Thus, helping children exposed to DV learn appropriate strategies for managing their strong negative affect may function to increase their feelings of control and self-efficacy in face of an uncontrollable stressor. Understanding how DV affects the biological underpinnings of emotional processes from a developmental perspective may help in the development of interventions that improve the quality of life of DV-exposed children.

THE IMPORTANCE OF BIOLOGICAL METHODS IN LINKING SOCIAL EXPERIENCE WITH SOCIAL AND EMOTIONAL DEVELOPMENT

Nicole M. Strang, Jamie L. Hanson, and Seth D. Pollak

The ability to decode and express emotions allows the developing child to assess and change many aspects of the environment. When emotional development is unfolding in a normative manner, the child's early experience within his or her family context promotes increasing abilities to successfully adapt to environmental demands. This is a critical developmental process as difficulties in emotional functioning can lead to problems in social adaptation and health. The issue of how adverse social experiences alter and shape children's social and emotional development has become a center stage for the exploration of the relative contributions of nature and nurture in child development. Our research has examined the ways in which children's developing biology is shaped in a manner that may be adaptive to their early environment but confers risk for a host of negative developmental outcomes. Here, we discuss some of the challenges that we have encountered in trying to address issues related to the influence of early social context on the development of biological processes underlying emotional development. When used thoughtfully, biological methods can enrich our understanding of emotional development by moving beyond a descriptive "biomaker" approach and excavating the mechanisms underlying developmental changes in these systems.

RESEARCH WITH AT-RISK SAMPLES OF CHILDREN

One way to understand how a system emerges is to examine perturbations in those processes. In this manner, we have studied children who have had adverse early social experiences that distinguish them from children raised in a normative family context. Specifically, we have studied children who have

---

Corresponding author: Seth D. Pollak, Ph.D., Department of Psychology, 1202 West Johnson Street, University of Wisconsin at Madison, Madison, WI 53706-8190, email: spollak@wisc.edu

been physically abused and children who were reared in understaffed international orphanages. Physically abused children are reared in an environment in which anger is an extremely salient cue. Anger is highly predictive of danger, and as such, it is adaptive for the child to be sensitized to this signal. Indeed, we have demonstrated that children who experience physical abuse are quicker than typically developing children to identify anger (Pollak, Cicchetti, Hornung, & Reed, 2000). In contrast to physically abused children, who are prominently exposed to expressions of anger, children from international orphanages have received impoverished emotional input. Children from international orphanages experienced extreme neglect. In the orphanage, a prominent lack of emotional and physical contact from caregivers is a consistent adverse feature of the environment (Human Rights Watch, 1998). Later in life, subsequent to removal from the orphanages, and adoption into typical families, many of these children experience problems in establishing social bonds and regulating social behavior. This includes a lack of developmentally appropriate wariness of strangers, atypical and disinhibited patterns of attachment, and difficulties developing close friendships (Fisher, Ames, Chrisholm, & Savoie 1997; O'Connor et al., 2003; O'Connor & Rutter, 2000). Our initial investigations underscored how these groups of children develop sets of behavioral problems that are related to specific features of their early social environment (Pollak, 2005, 2008). More recent research from our group, employing neurobiological metrics such as electrophysiological, neuroimaging, and neuroendocrine indices, has assayed potential neurobiological mediators of these apparent behavioral difficulties.

Electrophysiological Measures

Behavioral studies have indicated that physically abused children have an enhanced perceptual ability for anger detection (Pollak et al., 2000); however, the behavioral studies alone do not provide any evidence indicating how this may serve as a risk factor. We hypothesized that these behavioral features reflected that physically abused children were devoting disproportionate cognitive resources to signals of anger. Such privileged processing of anger might deflect resources from other important cognitive and emotional processes necessary for healthy social functioning. To test this hypothesis, we used an electrophysiological approach called the event-related potential (ERP). An ERP is an averaged electroencephalogram (EEG) time-locked to specific stimuli. ERPs have exquisite temporal resolution (on the order of milliseconds) but relatively poor spatial resolution. As such, ERPs can be used as an index of various cognitive processes including attention (Luck, 2005). A specific aspect of the ERP, the P3b component, is thought to reflect selective attention toward task-relevant information and is also influenced by the context and salience of attended stimuli (Isreal, Chesney, Wickens, & Donchin, 1980). As we expected, physically abused children showed an enhanced P3b in response to angry faces compared to other emotions (Pollak, Cicchetti, Klorman, & Brumaghim, 1997; Pollak, Klorman, Thatcher, & Cicchetti, 2001). Importantly, again using the P3b as an index of attention, we demonstrated that the severity of physical maltreatment was associated with the amount of attention devoted to anger (Shackman, Shackman, & Pollak, 2007).

Maltreated children also have difficulty disengaging attention from angry faces (Pollak & Tolley-Schell, 2003) and show impaired regulation of goal-directed attention (Shackman et al., 2007). Research using the N2 ERP component, an index of conflict processing (Nieuwenhuis, Yeung, van den Wildenberg, & Ridderinkhof, 2003), has revealed that physically abused children attend to facial signals of anger, even when instructed to ignore them (Shackman et al., 2007), and that the degree of cognitive conflict experienced in response to task-irrelevant angry faces predicts poorer task performance (i.e., slower reaction times; Shackman, Shackman, Jenness, & Pollak, 2010). In this series of investigations, ERPs provided us with insight into an aspect of maltreated children's social development—attention to anger—something that could not have been observed by behavioral methods alone. The severity of the maltreatment predicted attention to anger, and the more attention devoted to anger, the worse the children performed on the task.

Hormonal Measures

Hormonal systems play an important role in social behavior, and animal studies have provided a great deal of evidence that they can be altered through early experience (Sanchez et al., 2005). In our lab we have investigated the effects of early adverse experience on the neuropeptide oxytocin (OT) and the stress-related hormone cortisol. OT is produced in the hypothalamus and released centrally and peripherally into the blood stream via axon terminals in the posterior pituitary (Kendrick, Keverne, Baldwin, & Sharman, 1986) and appears to be part of the neural system of reward circuitry that includes the nucleus accumbens (Lovic & Fleming, 2004). For example, in nonhuman animals and humans alike, higher levels of OT are associated with decreases in stress hormones, such as cortisol, and increases in positive social interactions and attachment behaviors (Kosfeld, Heinrichs, Zak, Fischbacher, & Fehr, 2005; Witt, Carter, & Walton, 1990; for review see Carter, 1998). Cortisol, the end product of the hypothalatic–pituitary axis (HPA), modulates a wide range of biological responses such as energy release, cardiovascular function, immune activity, growth, emotion, and cognition (Diorio, Viau, & Meaney, 1993; Sapolsky, Romero, & Munck, 2000; Takahashi et al., 2004).

These hormonal changes allow the organism to adapt and cope effectively with current stressors. However, chronic elevation of cortisol impairs behavioral adaptation and has been associated with emotion regulation difficulties and psychopathology (Goodyer, Park, Netherton, & Herbert, 2001; Gunnar & Vazquez, 2001; Heim, Owens, Plotsky, & Nemeroff, 1997; Sapolsky et al., 2000).

The behavioral problems of postinstitutionalized children are consistent with dysregulation in the OT system and the HPA. To examine these questions, we investigated the response of OT and cortisol to a social game with their mother and a stranger. Our investigation demonstrated that, unlike typically developing children, postinstitutionalized children have an abnormally muted OT response after interacting with their mother (Fries, Ziegler, Kurian, Jacoris, & Pollak, 2005). Furthermore, postinstitutionalized children showed prolonged elevations in cortisol levels following the interaction with their mother, but not the stranger. More severe neglect was associated with the highest basal cortisol levels and the most impaired cortisol regulation following the mother interaction (Fries, Shirtcliff, & Pollak, 2008). These results suggest that early social deprivation may disrupt the function of the OT system and the HPA. The use of hormonal measures provided us with insight into postinstitutionalized children's experience of a social interaction with their mother. The disrupted response of the OT system and the HPA suggests that for postinstitutionalized children, interactions with their mother may be stressful, rather than calming and comforting. If this is the case, it is easy to infer how such experiences could interfere with the development of adaptive social relationships.

Structural MRI Methodology

Evidence from our ERP studies suggests that physically abused and typically developing children have differences in their neural responses to anger. To investigate whether maltreatment was related to structural brain changes, we employed structural magnetic resonance imaging (sMRI), which provides detailed anatomical images. Considering maltreated children's difficulties with social and emotional functioning, we investigated brain regions that have previously been implicated in these processes. The orbitofrontal cortex (oFC) has important implications for socioemotional development and behavioral regulation (Bachevalier & Loveland, 2006; Schore, 1996). Furthermore, longitudinal neuroimaging research in child, adolescent, and adult populations implicates the oFC as one of the last regions in the brain to fully develop (Gogtay et al., 2004), with changes in the oFC seen well into the third decade of life. The protracted development of the oFC suggests that it may be particularly vulnerable to postnatal experience. Our data revealed that maltreated children had smaller oFC volumes compared to nonmaltreated children and that the size of the child's oFC region predicted the amount of stress that children reported experiencing (Hanson et al., 2010).

Based on the social and behavioral deficits demonstrated by postinstitutionalized children, we further examined the question of whether there were structural brain differences based on early care experience. In this study, we focused specifically on the cerebellum. The cerebellum is a brain region that is highly influenced by experience rather then genetic endowment (Giedd, Schmitt, & Neale, 2007). Furthermore, subregions of this structure have been implicated in cognitive and social behavior (Riva & Giorgi, 2000; Schmahmann, Weilburg, & Sherman, 2007; Tavano et al., 2007).

We found that the posterior–superior lobe of the cerebellum was smaller in the postinstitutionalized children as compared to typically developing children; this region was also associated with children's performance on a task of executive function. Children with a smaller superior–posterior lobe volume showed poor executive control (Bauer, Hanson, Pierson, Davidson, & Pollak, 2009). The results of this study suggest a mechanism by which the early experience of deprivation could exert lasting consequences on social regulation.

THINKING CLEARLY ABOUT BIOLOGICAL METHODS IN DEVELOPMENTAL SCIENCE

As detailed thus far, integration of biological methods to the study of emotional and social development can provide important evidence that enriches our understanding of the development of emotional and social processes. There are, however, important conceptual, methodological, and statistical challenges that must be considered.

Impact of Biological Measure on Emotion

Unlike simple behavioral tasks, some biological methods are invasive. A challenge in employing such a measure is that the experimenter must consider the contribution of the experimental context to the biological signal. For instance, in a large-scale sMRI study in our lab, which included 160 adolescents who ranged from 9 to 14 years of age, we found an increase in the stress hormone cortisol in response to the MRI environment (Eatough, Shirtcliff, Hanson, & Pollak, 2009). This issue is particularly salient for investigations directed at emotional and social processes, where the experimental context elicits an emotional response. As such, it is important to include measures, such as baseline samples collected prior to the experimental manipulation, to determine the response to the experimental manipulation. It is also essential to remember that the laboratory context is itself a social context that may influence dependent variables of interest.

Group Differences in the Baseline Measure

Another important challenge to consider when employing biological methods is that there is a great deal of interindividual variation, even in typically developing populations. As a result, control conditions or regions are often included in experimental designs, and this is true of all the methods described in this review. The studies using hormonal and ERP methodologies compared a signal change between groups relative to a baseline, and the sMRI investigations compared specific regions while controlling for differences in the whole brain volume. A challenge for developmental and clinical investigations is that groups often differ in the baseline measure, which adds a level of complexity to the interpretation of any results. Consider the previously described study with OT which demonstrated a difference between postinstitutionalized and typically developing children while interacting with their caregiver (Fries et al., 2005). In order for us to suggest that social interactions with their mother were different experiences for postinstitutionalized, as compared to typically developing, children, it was important to demonstrate that their OT systems responded similarly when interacting with a stranger (control condition). Without the control condition, which demonstrated that the behavior of the OT system differed only when the children were interacting with their mother, we would not have been able to link the dysregulation to a specific social experience. If possible, it is important to determine the specificity of differences in the response of a biological system.

CONCLUSIONS

This chapter was an attempt to illustrate the rich evidence that can be gleaned from the use of biological methodologies on social and emotional development. We also strove to identify some of the challenges one must consider when using these methods. We also recommend recent papers detailing the broad limitations of employing electrophysiological (Cacioppo, Tassinary, & Berntson, 2007; Luck, 2005), hormonal (Dickerson & Kemeny, 2004), and neuroimaging measures (Aue, Lavelle, & Cacioppo, 2009; Logothetis, 2008). While use of these methodologies does require careful consideration, they also offer untold promise in unpacking the mechanisms driving developmental trajectories in social and emotional development.

INTRODUCTION TO SECTION THREE: PHYSIOLOGY AND AFFECTIVE PSYCHOPATHOLOGY

Kristin A. Buss, Paul D. Hastings, and Tracy A. Dennis

The focus of the third section, "Physiology and Affective Psychopathology," is on the interplay of physiological and emotional systems that underlie or impact the development of adaptive and maladaptive outcomes. Most of the monograph themes—developmental timing, context, integration across physiological systems and specificity—are touched on in each of these contributions. Although these chapters only scratch the surface of the vast literature on developmental psychopathology, these authors' contributions represent advances in integrating biological measures to advance understanding of maladaptive behavior.

In the first chapter, Dahl, Silk, and Siegle discuss a set of conceptual and methodological issues to move research in the area of affective dysregulation forward—highlighting the monograph themes of context, specificity, and integration. They point out that emotions are influenced by the social context as much as they are by internal states; thus an important implication for conceptual model and research design is capturing the naturally occurring emotional behaviors within the contexts that elicit them—mainly social in nature. Dahl and colleagues call for greater specificity in conceptual models and link these to comprehensive designs that integrate across disciplines: "We must move beyond general approaches seeking 'biological' evidence in support of vague models of 'dysregulated' emotions." This call sets the stage for the subsequent two chapters in this section.

Next, Beauchaine summarizes his program of research on externalizing pathology and autonomic nervous system regulation. His work is an outstanding example of the ways in which the integration of physiological measures can be used to identify the mechanisms underlying specific aspects of disorder such as emotion dysregulation and impulsivity in children and adolescents at risk for externalizing pathology. In his model, these biomarkers—

Corresponding author: Kristin A. Buss, Ph.D., The Pennsylvania State University, Child Study Center, 163 USBI, University Park, PA 16802, email: kbuss@psu.edu

PEP as a marker for central dopamine responsivity and RSA as a marker for emotion regulation in externalizing pathology—are woven into a developmental model of biosocial risk. His work highlights the importance of the eliciting context for the emotion or behavior that is being correlated with the physiological measures. The extant literature is rife with evidence that RSA (either suppression or augmentation) to various challenges is not uniformly associated with emotional reactivity, emotion regulation, attention and performance, and social engagement at the behavioral level. The importance of context and specificity are critical to this line of work. Moreover, as many of the authors point out, a one-to-one correspondence between physiological measures and group differences cannot be expected, nor is it the right question to ask.

In the final chapter, Cicchetti and Rogosch discuss developing emotional systems and neuroendocrine regulation in emotionally vulnerable children within the context of maltreatment. Much like the chapters in Section One, individual differences and the notion of developmental pathways are highlighted. That is, not all maltreated children develop maladaptive behaviors and dysregulated HPA functioning. Cicchetti and Rogosch make the point that the link between HPA axis dysregulation and maladaptive behaviors may not be fully explained by chronic stress and maltreatment models that do not take a developmental approach. This point is best captured by their findings related to the developmental timing of maltreatment. More so than later-occurring abuse, sexual abuse prior to age 5 was shown to be related to increased internalizing disorder symptoms and dysregulation of the HPA axis, suggesting an early vulnerability in neurodevelopment. Finally, this contribution highlights how the developing brain and biological systems are affected by adverse contexts and events.

Together, these chapters serve as examples and guidelines for how to effectively incorporate physiological measures into our understanding of the roles of emotion in developmental psychopathology. More than reflecting the state of the science, they highlight the directions that researchers must take to advance the science. By recognizing contributing factors of biological, social, and developmental contexts within which emotion and emotion regulation are embedded, these authors bring a striking new perspective to the study of children's maladjustment. As so eloquently stated by Cicchetti and Rogosch, "The field can no longer afford to continue the artificial distinction among genetics, neurobiology, and behavior in research on the determinants of psychopathology and resilience." Thus, we must, as a field, adhere to this edict if we are to gain ground in our understanding of biopsychosocial causes of maladjustment.

PHYSIOLOGICAL MEASURES OF EMOTION DYSREGULATION: INVESTIGATING THE DEVELOPMENT OF AFFECTIVE DISORDERS

Ronald E. Dahl, Jennifer S. Silk, and Greg J. Siegle

In this chapter, we discuss the use of physiological measures of emotion to investigate clinically relevant questions regarding the development of affect dysregulation. The primary focus is on the consideration of promising approaches to advance understanding of affective disorders in children and adolescents in ways that can provide new insights into the development, etiology, and treatment of these disorders. We discuss several conceptual and methodological issues. These include the importance of interdisciplinary teams of clinical, developmental, and basic scientists working together—in an integrated manner—to develop and refine conceptual models which include greater specificity regarding the particular aspects of emotion that are hypothesized to be dysregulated. We also recognize the *inherently social* nature of emotion and its regulation in children and adolescents and the importance of this social dimension to investigations into clinically relevant aspects of emotion regulation.

A major point of emphasis is the need for a better integration of social, developmental, cognitive, and affective neuroscience with clinical research. Not only does this interface present exciting opportunities for scientific advances, but also it has enormous relevance from a clinical and public health perspective. Problems with the control of emotion (and emotional influences on risky behavior) are major sources of the morbidity and mortality that increases dramatically between childhood and early adulthood. That is, the majority of the serious health consequences that emerge in adolescence, including accidents, suicide, homicide, depression, and substance abuse, reflect problems with the

Corresponding author: Ronald E. Dahl, Community Health and Human Development and Joint Medical Program, School of Public Health, University of California, Berkeley, Berkeley, CA 94720-1190, email: rondahl@berkeley.edu

control of emotion and behavior (Dahl & Gunnar, 2009). Moreover, many of the most costly, chronic, and impairing disorders of adulthood—including mood disorders, anxiety disorders, and drug and alcohol abuse—typically begin in adolescence (Alpert, Maddocks, Rosenbaum, & Fava, 1994; Chung, Martin, & Winters, 2006; Pine, Cohen, Gurley, Brook, & Ma, 1998). Thus, there is a compelling need to advance understanding of how emotional reactivity and regulation contribute (negatively and positively) to the *development* of these high-impact health problems. A particularly important goal is to gain insights that can inform early intervention and prevention efforts.

One promising approach to making progress toward this goal is to advance etiologic understanding through the use of physiological measures and neuroimaging—particularly with respect to mechanistic understanding as to what specifically goes awry regarding emotion and its regulation and at what point in development. These types of mechanistic insights into the neurobehavioral underpinnings of affective dysregulation at key points along the developmental trajectory can inform opportunities for targeted and well-timed interventions. These points will be illustrated with specific examples later.

Yet it is equally important to emphasize the clinical relevance of pursuing such mechanistic understanding in light of the *social and contextual influences on emotion regulation*—factors of particular importance to the development of affective disorders. Taken together these complexities can create formidable challenges. Designing well-controlled studies that aim at mechanistic understanding as well as consideration of ecological validity and the importance of social context, combined with the difficulties of recruiting and studying clinical samples of children and adolescents, represent an enormous set of challenges.

In this chapter, we propose several strategies to help meet these challenges. In particular we emphasize the need for (1) developing and refining conceptual models that aim for greater specificity regarding which aspects of emotion are hypothesized to be dysregulated, and in what specific ways, in particular disorders; (2) thoughtfully and creatively using the rapidly advancing toolbox of social affective neuroscience (including a range of physiological and neuroimaging measures of emotion) to test key features of these models in well-designed clinically relevant studies, within a strong developmental framework; and (3) developing truly transdisciplinary teams that include developmental psychologists, clinicians, and scientists with expertise in social, affective, and cognitive neuroscience, working together to address mechanistic questions at the level of developmental cognitive and affective neuroscience, with sufficient consideration of ecological validity and relevant social and clinical contexts.

DEVELOPING AND REFINING CONCEPTUAL MODELS: WHAT ARE THE IMPORTANT QUESTIONS TO BE TARGETED?

Prior to discussing how best to use physiological measures to investigate emotion and its regulation in the development of affective disorders, there are important conceptual issues to consider. It is important to acknowledge that some of the easiest approaches—simply collecting the most accessible physiological measures in samples of convenience and looking for differences associated with symptoms—have relatively limited capacity to advance understanding in ways that will truly inform clinically relevant questions. We must move beyond general approaches seeking "biological" evidence in support of vague models of "dysregulated" emotions. Instead there is a need to further develop and refine conceptual models that lead to focused questions—and ultimately to testable hypotheses regarding the specific aspects of emotion regulation that underlie the development of specific disorders of emotion.

To illustrate this point more fully, let us take the example of childhood anxiety disorders. First, it is important to consider the differences between a typically functioning child who reports higher than average levels of fears or worries and a child with an impairing anxiety disorder. It is equally important to consider differences across disorders (e.g., generalized anxiety disorder vs. obsessive-compulsive disorder vs. post-traumatic anxiety given the evidence for differentiation among these disorders at a biological level as well as in symptom presentations). However, even if we focus in on one disorder (e.g., generalized anxiety disorder), there is a wide range of possible mechanisms contributing to the functional impairment. At the simplest level, we can conceptualize the problem as an increased or inappropriate activation of threat and arousal that results in functional impairments in that child's life (typically social and academic impairments secondary to the anxiety). Yet at a more mechanistic level there are several different ways this might occur: (a) altered attention to detect threat; (b) lower threshold to activate fear or worry; (c) increased intensity of fear or worry once they are activated; (d) difficulties terminating fear or worry once they are activated; (e) normal fear activated in inappropriate contexts; (f) greater awareness/monitoring of internal state; (g) lower distress tolerance to feelings of fear; (h) maladaptive patterns of avoidance in response to minor fears; and (i) a perseverative style of coping with affect. Any one or more of these hypotheses could be relevant to the clinical path toward developing an impairing generalized anxiety disorder. However, each could lead to different targets/predictions in affective neuroscience studies, different ways of using physiological measures of emotion, different study design, and ultimately each could lead to very different approaches to early intervention. In a similar way, we could consider several different models focusing on the development of depression or the development of bipolar disorder.

Several research groups around the world that are interested in the development of affective disorders are actively engaged in research programs that seek to build and refine these types of models. Many emphasize the promise of neuroimaging with fMRI as the central tool to test key features of these models; there appear, however, to be increasing opportunities to use a range of other physiological measures of emotion that permit the use of more flexible social paradigms integrating methods popular outside the realms of clinical psychology and psychiatry. These are particularly relevant to addressing questions that include consideration of social context and ecologically valid measures. Given these complexities and challenges outlined, we believe that that truly integrated approaches—transdisciplinary teams working across levels—represent particularly promising strategies. The development and refinement of conceptual models can synergistically link controlled laboratory studies aimed at mechanism, clinical studies aimed at intervention, consideration of social context, and a strong developmental frameworks of understanding.

DEVELOPMENTAL SOCIAL AFFECTIVE NEUROSCIENCE: A TRANSDISCIPLINARY APPROACH TO CLINICALLY RELEVANT QUESTIONS

A developmentally informed social affective neuroscience perspective offers promise for developing synergistic methodologies to test cross-level interactions (see Figure 6 and later text) in the development of emotion regulation relevant to clinical questions. This type of approach provides a novel integration of the fields of developmental psychopathology, social neuroscience, and affective neuroscience. These fields represent recent integrations of more traditional disciplines, such as clinical and developmental psychology, child psychiatry, pediatrics, social psychology, and basic and cognitive neuroscience. In our research group, for example, key concepts and methods from each discipline are incorporated: From developmental psychopathology, we take an ecological perspective on development (Bronfenbrenner, 1979), a framework that seeks to understand individual differences in adaptation across the life course by integrating perspectives on typical and atypical development (Cicchetti, 1993). Developmental psychopathology offers observational methods for studying social interactions, as well as recent advances in ecological assessments of adolescent behaviors. From the emerging field of social neuroscience, we take the view that multilevel analyses can foster understanding of the mechanisms underlying human behavior and that there are bidirectional relationships between social contextual and neurobiological influences on development (Cacioppo, Berntson, Sheridan, & McClintock, 2000). For example, from affective neuroscience, we take an understanding of emotions as brain states associated with rewards and

72

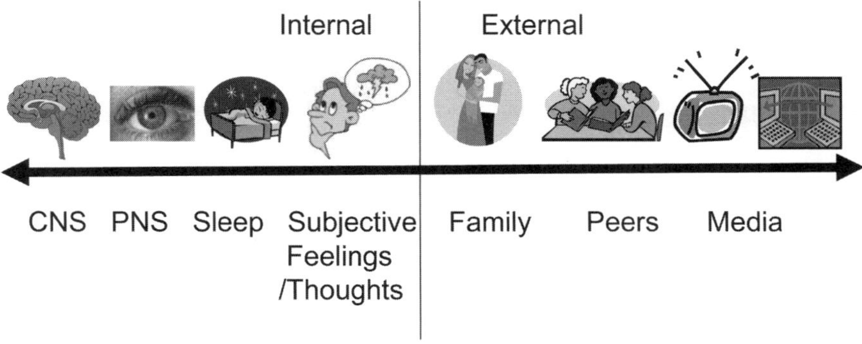

FIGURE 6.—Internal and external influences on adolescents' emotional reactivity and regulation.

punishments (Rolls, 1999), and from social neuroscience, an increasing recognition that for humans, these neural systems of rewards and punishments are inherently intertwined with social goals. Similarly, from affective neuroscience, we attend to the importance of the chronometry of reactions to affective stimuli (Davidson, Jackson, & Kalin, 2000) and from social psychology the interplay of social information processing styles and affect over time. Neuroscience perspectives also offer experimental laboratory methods for measuring social and emotional experience. A better integration of the concepts and methods across these disciplines will facilitate advances in the ability to test key features of models relevant to understanding developmental pathways to clinical disorders.

THE DEVELOPMENT OF EMOTION REGULATION (AND DYSREGULATION) INVOLVES CROSS-LEVEL INTERACTIONS ACROSS BIOLOGICAL AND SOCIAL CONTEXTS

As shown in Figure 6, we recognize that emotion regulation—particularly during development—likely involves interactions across several levels of biological and social influences. These range from internal neurobiological processes to external social influences from family, school, peers, and media. Even broader influences, such as culture, are also important but are beyond the scope of this discussion. The social environment also has the potential to buffer or amplify the effects of biological vulnerabilities on the development of disorders such as depression (e.g., Caspi et al., 2003). Understanding *how* the social environment interacts with biological vulnerabilities is particularly important because social influences can be modified through family, school, and community-based interventions and public policies. However, few studies have integrated neurobiological and social measures of emotion regulation in developmental populations, and there is a need for methods that can uncover brain-behavior–social environment interactions at key intervals of development (Silk, Vanderbilt-Adriance et al., 2007).

Tools to Examine Social Influences on Emotion Regulation

Social contexts can contribute in both positive and negative ways to adolescents' emotional reactivity and regulation. Parents and peers are frequent sources of emotional arousal in adolescence (Larson & Asmussen, 1991), but they also can contribute in adaptive ways to adolescents' emotion regulation by modeling or teaching skills, assisting in problem solving, and offering emotional support. Although most studies of parental socialization of emotion regulation have focused on young children, parental support of affective processes remains crucial as youth navigate the emotional challenges of adolescence (Bell & Calkins, 2000). Obtaining status with peers becomes a central motivating factor for most adolescents, and peer acceptance or rejection carries strong emotional significance, although particular adolescents may vary in their sensitivity to social status concerns (Rudolph & Conley, 2005). Little is known about how peers help each other in managing emotion, although there is evidence that adolescents (especially girls) spend considerable time discussing emotional issues with each other (Gottman & Mettetal, 1986) and some evidence that such "corumination" can be associated with depression and anxiety (Rose, 2002). Media (e.g., television, music, Internet), another domain, serves to up-regulate or down-regulate adolescents' emotions (Zillman, 1988). The average adolescent spends 6 hours a day using some type of commercial media (Brown & Cantor, 2000), yet little is understood about how adolescents use media to regulate emotion. Sleep is another important (yet rarely studied) contributor to emotion regulation that influences adolescents' ability to integrate cognitive processing with social and emotional demands (Dahl, 1996; Horne, 1993). Dramatic reductions in sleep as a result of social and circadian influences toward staying up later could pose serious challenges for regulatory control of emotions during this period (Dahl & Lewin, 2002). Despite the potential influences of parents, peers, media, and sleep on adolescent emotional reactivity and regulation, few methods exist for examining the impact of these domains on daily affective experience. In particular, there is a need for measures in home settings in which adolescents can self-select their environments and have access to naturally occurring regulatory resources. Emerging technologies, such as cell-phone based ecological momentary assessment (EMA) and ambulatory physiological monitoring, represent one ecologically valid method of gathering real-time data on affect and behavior in natural environments yielding the potential to advance understanding of how adolescents experience and regulate emotions in daily life (see Silk, Steinberg, & Morris 2003; Silk et al., 2011).

Incorporating Physiological Measures of Emotion Regulation

Across all of these social contexts, there are promising opportunities to use and integrate physiological measures. Whether these involve distributed systems useful for imaging activity throughout the brain, such as near-infra-red imaging or high-density event-related potential assessments, or single sources, such as, cardiac measures, sleep measures, autonomic, or stress measures—or as illustrated later, measures of pupil response to emotional information—physiological measures can provide insights into the interactions between internal neurobehavioral processes and external social influences in ways that are critical to understanding the normal and abnormal development of emotion regulation.

To illustrate the potential to use well-understood physiological measures in social contexts, in the following sections we describe our laboratory's use of pupillometry to create a synergistic set of links across these different levels of investigation. Pupil diameter—measured in real time through infra-red videography—provides a quantitative index of the temporal pattern of neural activity to emotional stimuli. More specifically, pupillary reactivity represents an exciting tool for social affective neuroscience because it (a) reflects activity in neural systems known to be involved in emotional reactivity and regulation (Koikegami & Yoshida, 1953; Siegle, Steinhauer, Stenger, Konecky, & Carter, 2003; Urry et al., 2006) and (b) through the use of emerging technologies, can be measured nonintrusively during naturalistic social interactions. We have specifically observed sustained pupil dilation in response to affective stimuli in adult depression (Siegle, Granholm, Ingram, & Matt, 2001), particularly depressed individuals who ruminate (Siegle, Steinhauer, Carter, Ramel, & Thase, 2003). The clinical utility of this measure is further supported by its ability to predict treatment outcome for depression (Siegle, Steinhauer, Friedman, & Thase, in press).

Currently, our research group is using pupil measures to examine several interrelated questions focusing on adolescence. For example, we recently reported evidence for puberty-specific changes in emotional reactivity (Silk, Siegle et al., 2009); altered affective responses in youth with affective disorders (Silk, Dahl et al., 2007); and changes in pupil response among youth at high risk for affective disorders (Silk, Dahl, & Siegle, 2009). Currently we are exploring the use of pupil responses to examine social interactions among youth, including peer rejection and parent-child interactions. Recently, we began to use this technology to examine the *synchrony* of affective responses between parents and children during an interaction task. In brief, pupil dilation and eye gaze are obtained synchronously for both the adolescent and his or her mother during a live parent-child interaction. Adolescents and their mothers participate in a 20-min series of parent-child interaction tasks designed to reveal styles of emotional reactivity and regulation among parent-adolescent dyads, while wearing head-mounted pupilometers. Data were gathered from 33 mother-child dyads who completed discussions on themes of support, conflict, and planning of a fun activity during pupillometric assessment. Data from representative participants were subjected to smoothed lagged cross-correlation and vector-autoregressive analyses, and evaluated on a case-by-case basis to understand dyad-wise differences in reactivity during mother-child interactions. In general, correlations between mother and child pupillary motility were of moderate magnitude ($\sim$0.3); however, there appear to be some very interesting differences across dyads. For example, in some cases a strong relationship was observed in the direction of mothers' pupils dilating in a pattern that followed reactivity in the child, while in others, the child's pupil was positively or negatively related to the changes in the mother's pupil.

These data provide preliminary evidence for observable dyad-wise differences in the nature of mother-child interactions at the level of real-time physiological measures of emotion reactivity in the midst of ecologically valid social interactions. Moreover, this example illustrates how these types of measures can be used to investigate specific (mechanistic) hypotheses about pathways toward the development of affective disorders—for example, to examine patterns of negative affect among dyads of depressed mothers and high-risk adolescents. This type of approach allows quantification of specific components of social behavior and a very promising way to quantify specific aspects of emotional responses (intensity, timing, and duration) in ecologically valid social and developmental studies. These types of investigations can provide insights that could be extremely important to understanding clinically relevant aspects of emotion-regulation in naturalistic environments—including links to other measures from affective neuroscience, as well as measures obtained in natural environments.

We also explored how these pupil measures correlate with real-world (EMA) measures of emotion and behavior as well as with neural correlates of emotion in fMRI tasks. For example, diminished late pupil dilation to negative words (observed in adolescents with depression) was strongly associated with children's reports of higher negative affect ($r = -.49, p < .01$) and lower positive affect ($r = .41, p < .05$) in the naturalistic environment collected via EMA ($N = 42$) (Silk, Dahl et al., 2007). To better illustrate how this type of approach can advance understanding of clinically relevant questions about the development and treatment of affective disorders requires consideration of specific models—as discussed in the next section of this chapter. Moreover, we (and other research groups) can also obtain the same types of pupil responses concurrent with MRI to elucidate the specific neural underpinnings. Thus, the affective pupil response measures can bridge between the neuroimaging studies and measures obtained in more naturalistic social contexts. In this way, the pupil measures provide a critical link between mechanistic questions at the level of underlying neural systems, and measures of emotion in real-world social contexts.

DEVELOPMENT, TRAJECTORIES, AND WINDOWS OF OPPORTUNITY FOR INTERVENTION

To go back to the original framework, one of the most important dimensions of the work to advance this field is not simply how to develop and refine the methods and apply them to developmental clinical problems but also how to frame and focus the questions. It can be valuable to step back and consider—from a clinical and public health perspective—how these types of mechanistic and physiological questions might best contribute early intervention and prevention efforts. To illustrate how this may occur, we offer a few examples:

- A deeper understanding of the neural underpinnings underlying specific risk factors, risk groups, effects of risk environments, and risky periods of maturation could inform targeted strategies for early intervention (e.g., identifying an attentional bias to detect and respond to threat as a risk factor for developing anxiety disorders that could be altered by early attentional training programs).

- Identifying periods of neural plasticity during which targeted treatments may have more enduring effects throughout the life span could inform the optimal developmental timing for behavioral interventions, specialized learning programs, or techniques to promote specific skill acquisitions in ways that improve developmental trajectories at vulnerable points (e.g., a cognitive behavioral treatment targeting negative cognitive biases during a maturational interval in which these biases are beginning to become more deeply ensconced in other levels of behavior, emotion, sense of self; or identifying a sensitive window for teaching and developing social cognitive capacities).

- Helping to parse complex developmental processes (e.g., development of emotion regulation, cognitive control, development of "self") into quantifiable components could provide a framework for identifying specific targets for early intervention (e.g., identifying specific maturational changes in reward-seeking at puberty relevant to adolescent-onset depression that could be altered through cognitive-behavioral interventions in early adolescence).

Clearly, we are very early in the curve of progress in the field of developmental social affective neuroscience and its application to clinical questions about the development of healthy and unhealthy emotion regulation. Yet, there appear to be many reasons to be optimistic. The future and its potential impact on human health and well-being look exciting.

PHYSIOLOGICAL MARKERS OF EMOTION AND BEHAVIOR DYSREGULATION IN EXTERNALIZING PSYCHOPATHOLOGY

Theodore P. Beauchaine

Much of the research conducted in our lab over the past decade has focused on identifying peripheral and central nervous system (CNS) markers of both trait impulsivity and emotion dysregulation in preschoolers (e.g., Crowell et al., 2006), middle schoolers (e.g., Shannon, Beauchaine, Brenner, Neuhaus & Gatzke-Kopp 2007), and adolescents (e.g., Crowell et al., 2005). This body of work includes studies of boys with attention-deficit/hyperactivity disorder (ADHD), boys with conduct disorder (CD; e.g., Beauchaine, Katkin, Strassberg, & Snarr, 2001), and girls with borderline personality traits (e.g., Crowell, Beauchaine et al., 2008). One key assumption of this work is that inherited impulsivity interacts across development with socialized deficiencies in emotion regulation (ER) to promote the development of conduct problems among boys and borderline traits among girls. Although space constraints preclude a full description of the theoretical bases of this assumption, in writing this chapter, I summarize how the use of autonomic nervous system (ANS) markers, neuroimaging, and genetic data have led my research group to our current thinking about the roles of impulsivity and emotion dysregulation in the development of externalizing psychopathology. I note at the outset that my discussion of environmental risk is limited given the objectives of this monograph. However, I consider such risk factors to be as important in the development of psychopathology as biological vulnerabilities (see Beauchaine, Hinshaw, & Pang, 2010). Furthermore, although not discussed in this chapter, and not difficult to identify in humans, epigenetic alterations in the DNA structure that are brought about through adverse life events are also likely to potentiate psychopathology (Mead, Beauchaine, & Shannon, 2010; Tremblay, 2005).

Corresponding author: Theodore P. Beauchaine, Department of Psychology, Washington State University, Pullman, WA 99164, email ted.beauchaine@wsu.edu

The conceptual model that informs my research on the development of externalizing behaviors and borderline personality traits has been described in several recent reviews (Beauchaine, Gatzke-Kopp, & Mead, 2007; Beauchaine, Klein, Crowell, Derbidge, Gatzke-Kopp, 2009; Beauchaine, Crowell, & Linehan, 2009). Broadly speaking, this model can be summarized as follows (Beauchaine et al., 2009, 2010): (1) trait impulsivity, derived largely from heritable compromises in central dopamine (DA) function, is a principal predisposing vulnerability to externalizing behavior disorders, including borderline pathology; (2) impulsive individuals are especially vulnerable to developing externalizing behavior disorders within high-risk family environments in which emotional lability is shaped by operant reinforcement contingencies; and (3) over time, these reinforcement contingencies result in enduring patterns of emotion dysregulation, culminating in antisocial and borderline personality development among impulsive individuals.

TRAIT IMPULSIVITY AND EXTERNALIZING BEHAVIOR DISORDERS

Although definitions of impulsivity abound, my research group defines the construct as "behavior that is socially inappropriate or maladaptive and is emitted without forethought" (Oas, 1985, p. 142). This trait is common to all disorders along the externalizing spectrum, including ADHD, oppositional defiant disorder (ODD), CD, antisocial personality disorder (ASPD), and many drug and alcohol dependencies (Beauchaine & Neuhaus, 2008; Beauchaine et al., 2010). Behavioral genetics research indicates that these disorders share a common latent vulnerability (Tuvblad, Zheng, Raine, & Baker, 2009), which is over 80% heritable (Krueger et al., 2002) and is best described as trait impulsivity. One challenge we have faced is identifying a biological marker of impulsivity that can be used across a broad age range. Though neuroimaging can be used to identify the CNS substrates of impulsivity among adolescents (Beauchaine, Sauder, Gatzke, Kopp, Shannon, & Aylward, in press), it is difficult to use it with externalizing preschoolers and middle schoolers. Thus, my research group has developed alternative means for assessing biological markers of impulsivity. Achieving this goal requires knowledge of structural and functional relations between the CNS and ANS (Beauchaine, 2009).

CENTRAL DOPAMINE FUNCTIONING AND TRAIT IMPULSIVITY

It has long been known that impulsive individuals, including those with ADHD, ODD, CD, ASPD, and various addictive disorders respond differently to rewards than do controls. Across a number of monetary incentive paradigms, males with these disorders perseverate in reward responding for much longer than their peers both (a) when contingencies turn against them and they begin to lose money and (b) when incentives are discontinued entirely (e.g., Giancola, Peterson, & Pihl, 2006; Matthys, van Goozen, Snoek, & van Engeland, 2004). A core CNS substrate of aberrant reward responding is underactivation in the ventral striatum, an evolutionarily old network of interconnected neural structures that subserves approach motivation in mammals, including nonhuman primates and humans. This brain region is rich in dopaminergic projections, which are less responsive to reward—including monetary incentives—among impulsive individuals than among controls (see Durston, 2003; Sagvolden, Johansen, Aase, & Russell, 2005). Consistent with theories of underarousal (e.g., Gatzke-Kopp, Raine, Loeber, Stouthamer-Loeber, & Steinhauer, 2004), my research group argued that those with impulse control disorders engage in excessive reward-seeking behaviors in part to upregulate a chronically underactive mesolimbic DA system, which is experienced psychologically as an aversive and irritable mood state (e.g., Laakso et al., 2003).

CARDIAC PRE-EJECTION PERIOD: A MARKER OF CENTRAL DA RESPONDING?

Several sources of evidence now suggest that cardiac pre-ejection period (PEP)—indexed as the time interval between left ventricular depolarization and ejection of blood into the aorta—marks striatal DA responding during approach behaviors, including those elicited by monetary incentives (Brenner, Beauchaine, & Sylvers, 2005). PEP is controlled by the sympathetic nervous system (SNS), with shorter intervals indicating a stronger sympathetic response. The argument that PEP shortening marks central DA reactivity to reward is based on several considerations. First, behavioral approach requires expenditure of energy, and an important function of the SNS is to mobilize resources to meet metabolic demands. Furthermore, increases in cardiac output required for motivated behavior are mediated by SNS-induced changes in the contractile force of the left ventricle (Sherwood, Allen, Obrist, & Langer 1986). Finally, infusions of DA agonists into striatal structures produce SNS-mediated increases in cardiac output (van den Buuse, 1998), which are similar to those observed when normal controls participate in reward tasks. Taken together, these observations suggest that reduced SNS-linked cardiac reactivity to incentives is a likely marker attenuated DA responding. This argument is supported further by research indicating that PEP shortening among controls is *specific* to conditions of reward and is not observed during extinction (Brenner et al., 2005).

My research group and others (e.g., Bubier & Drabick, 2008) have now examined PEP responses to incentives among externalizing preschoolers, middle schoolers, and adolescents, ages 4–18 (Beauchaine et al., 2001;

Beauchaine, Hong, & Marsh, 2008; Brenner & Beauchaine, 2011; Crowell et al., 2006; Mead et al., 2004). These samples have included individuals with ADHD, ODD, CD, and antisocial personality traits. In each of our studies, male externalizers exhibited less PEP reactivity to rewards than controls. In fact, in most of our studies, *no* PEP reactivity to incentives has been observed among the externalizing groups. These findings suggest that the neural substrates of impulsivity may be established by age 4. This would be expected if (a) disorders across the externalizing spectrum, including ADHD, share a heritable etiological substrate (see above) and (b) PEP reactivity to incentives marks the biobehavioral expression of this trait.

EMOTION REGULATION AS A MODERATOR OF EXTERNALIZING VULNERABILITY

Recall from the model presented earlier that impulsivity develops into more severe behavior problems only when coupled with deficient ER. Emotion regulation comprises the processes through which emotional experience and expression are shaped—whether volitionally or automatically—in the service of adaptive behavior (Thompson, 1990). Following from this definition, emotion *dysregulation* might best be described as a pattern of emotional experience or expression that interferes with appropriate goal directed behavior. In most forms of psychopathology, one or more negative emotions (sadness, panic, rage) is experienced either too intensely or for too long to be adaptive (Beauchaine et al., 2007). Thus, emotion dysregulation is a broad risk factor for psychopathology (Beauchaine, 2001).

Much has been learned about the CNS substrates of ER in the past decade. Key neural structures that subserve ER include the amygdala and the ventromedial prefrontal cortex (VMPFC; see Goldsmith, Pollak, & Davidson, 2008). The VMPFC inhibits amygdala activation when individuals purposefully regulate negative emotions. Furthermore, lesions to the VMPFC impair ANS responses to emotional stimuli (Verbane & Owens, 1998). Much has also been written about the modulatory effects of certain brainstem nuclei—particularly the nucleus ambiguus—on emotional expression (see Porges, 2007). These nuclei serve as final common pathways—via the vagus nerve—from the central nervous system to the cardiovascular system.

RESPIRATORY SINUS ARRHYTHMIA AND EMOTION REGULATION

At the parasympathetic nervous system (PNS) level, the ability to regulate emotions is often marked by respiratory sinus arrhythmia (RSA), a quantification of cyclic increases and decreases in heart rate across the respiratory cycle (see Beauchaine, 2001; Obradović & Boyce, this volume; Porges, 2007).

Under appropriate stimulus conditions, RSA indexes neural traffic through the vagus nerve (Porges, 1995). Since publication of Porges's polyvagal theory describing relations between PNS responding and emotional expression, a consistent body of research has emerged linking deficiencies in RSA to emotion dysregulation and psychopathology (see Beauchaine et al., 2007; Hastings et al., 2008; Porges, 2007). As we have reviewed elsewhere, low baseline RSA and excessive RSA withdrawal in response to emotionally evocative stimuli have been linked to conduct problems, trait hostility, eating disorders, anxiety disorders, depression, and panic—among other adverse outcomes (see Beauchaine, 2001).

Although some researchers have suggested that impulsivity is a direct manifestation of emotion dysregulation, the two traits derive from very different etiological and neural substrates, as described previously. Accordingly, in the model presented above, I view impulsivity and ER as distinct behavioral constructs. Indeed, in contrast to impulsivity, which is almost entirely heritable, emotion dysregulation is largely socialized within families (Beauchaine et al., 2007; Beauchaine et al., 2009; Snyder, Schrepferman, & St. Peter, 1997). Consistent with this assertion, behavioral genetics studies indicate that individual differences in RSA are in large part determined by environmental factors (Kupper et al., 2005).

My research group typically measures RSA both at baseline and in response to emotionally evocative (e.g., sadness-inducing) stimuli. In fact, in each of the studies cited earlier in which PEP responding to reward was assessed, RSA data were also collected during negative emotion induction. Interestingly, among externalizers, attenuated baseline RSA and excessive RSA reactivity to emotion evocation were observed only in the conduct-disordered middle school and adolescent samples (Beauchaine et al., 2001; Beauchaine, Hong, & Marsh, 2008; Mead et al., 2004). In contrast, neither RSA nor RSA reactivity discriminated externalizing preschoolers with ADHD and ODD from controls (Crowell et al., 2006). At first, we found this perplexing because these preschoolers are at very high risk for later conduct problems and delinquency (Campbell, Shaw, & Gilliom, 2000). However, others have demonstrated that ADHD progresses to more serious conduct problems only for children in families where emotional lability is negatively reinforced (e.g., Patterson, DeGarmo, & Knutson, 2000). Accordingly, our current thinking is that impulsivity may be "regulated"—expressed as pure ADHD—or "dysregulated"—expressed as more serious externalizing outcomes—depending on ER strategies that are socialized through recurring parent–child interactions. In the case of externalizing preschoolers, it may be too soon for familial negative reinforcement processes to have fully shaped emotional lability, with consequential deficiencies in RSA (see Beauchaine et al., 2007).

As noted earlier, our model specifies that trait impulsivity confers risk for serious externalizing conduct only when *coupled with* familial socialization of emotion dysregulation. According to this perspective, one would expect that adolescents with pure ADHD would exhibit less emotional lability, as indexed by RSA reactivity to emotion evocation, than adolescents with ADHD and CD. In one of our studies contrasting adolescents with pure ADHD versus those with ADHD and CD, this is exactly what we found (Beauchaine et al., 2001).

RSA AS A MODERATOR OF EXTERNALIZING VULNERABILITY

Given that emotion dysregulation and associated RSA deficiencies confer risk for psychopathology—especially among impulsive children and adolescents—well socialized ER skills, reflected both behaviorally and in high RSA, should *buffer* children from some of the adverse effects of trait impulsivity. In our own research, we have demonstrated buffering effects of RSA on relations between paternal ASPD and adolescent conduct problems (Shannon et al., 2007). Children with low baseline RSA tended toward conduct problems regardless of the level of paternal ASPD symptoms, whereas children high in RSA were partially protected from their father's antisociality. Moreover, an accumulating body of literature links high RSA to children's positive adjustment in the face of diverse familial risk factors for psychopathology, including interparental conflict, parental drinking, and parental divorce (El-Sheikh, 2005; El-Sheikh, Harger, & Whitson, 2001; Katz & Gottman, 1995).

THE IMPORTANCE OF STIMULUS CONDITIONS

It is not unusual for social scientists to mistakenly equate behavioral constructs and traits such as impulsivity with psychophysiological markers such as cardiac PEP. When this mistake is made, authors often expect the psychophysiological marker—in this case PEP—to discriminate between impulsive and nonimpulsive children—regardless of stimulus conditions (Beauchaine, 2009). However, our data show quite clearly that PEP reactivity is not observed during extinction or emotion evocation in impulsive individuals *or* controls. Rather, it is only during reward tasks that group differences emerge. Accordingly, our choice to use stimulus conditions of reward to assess PEP responding as a marker of impulsivity is based on strong theoretical considerations regarding the function of SNS-linked cardiac reactivity during approach behaviors, as outlined above (Beauchaine, 2001; Beauchaine et al., 2001, 2007). A similar argument can be advanced for RSA reactivity as a marker of emotional lability (see also Hastings et al., 2008). Here, one would expect better differentiation between labile individuals and controls during conditions of emotion evocation than during conditions of reward. Again, our data support this assertion. Unfortunately, researchers often expect to find group differences in psychophysiological markers across all of their stimulus conditions. When they do not, results are often interpreted as null findings. This illustrates how atheoretical choices of stimulus conditions can lead to considerable confusion in the literature (Beauchaine, 2009). Researchers should therefore select their stimuli carefully, based on the specific physiological process that they seek to mark (Cole, Martin, & Dennis, 2004; Fox, Kirwan, & Reeb-Sutherland, this volume; Goldsmith & Davidson, 2004).

FUTURE DIRECTIONS: BIOLOGY × ENVIRONMENT INTERACTIONS

Following from my discussion thus far, it has become increasingly clear that certain biological vulnerabilities interact with contextual risk to potentiate psychopathology (see also Bubier, Breiner, & Drabick, 2009). In addition to psychophysiological markers of vulnerability, a number of Gene × Environment interactions have been reported in the etiology of externalizing disorders. Perhaps the most famous of these was reported by Caspi et al. (2002), who found that the combination of child maltreatment and a polymorphism in the monoamine oxidase-A (MAOA) gene predicted antisocial behavior. Those who experienced maltreatment *and* inherited the low MAOA activity gene were at much higher risk for antisocial behavior than those who experienced maltreatment but did not inherit the low MAOA activity gene.

Importantly, biological vulnerabilities and environmental risk factors are often synergistic rather than additive (Crowell, Beauchaine, & Lenzenweger, 2008; Raine, 2002). Furthermore, significant Biology × Environment interactions are sometimes observed in the absence of main effects (Beauchaine, Neuhaus, Brenner, & Gatzke-Kopp, 2008). Thus, it is critical that the joint effects of vulnerabilities and risk factors be explored—even when each in isolation is only weakly associated with adverse outcomes. For example, in a recent study of biological and behavioral correlates of self-injury among adolescent females, we reported that peripheral serotonin was reduced among self-injuring teens (Crowell et al., 2005). Independently, however, peripheral serotonin was only a weak predictor of lifetime self-injurious events. Moreover, observational ratings of negativity within mother–daughter dyads failed to predict self-injury. Nevertheless, the Serotonin × Negativity interaction accounted for a remarkable 64% of the variance in self-injurious behaviors, including suicide attempts (Crowell et al., 2008).

In addition to such moderating effects, mediational models linking genes, neural responses, and behavior are now emerging. For example, Buckholtz et al. (2008) recently reported that stronger neural coupling between the amygdala and VMPFC mediated links between MAOA alleles and personality. This finding is particularly exciting because the mediational model spanned genes → brain → behavior. It has often been noted that genes do not affect behavior directly (see, e.g., Beauchaine, Gatzke-Kopp, & Hinshaw, 2008). Mediational models specifying neural processes through which genes influence behavior are therefore an extremely important development. These models take us one step closer to understanding the complexities of behavioral dysfunction. In our view, these studies mark a new generation in behavioral research. It is our hope that the specification of causal pathways from genes to behavior will answer important questions that behavioral scientists have been pondering for generations.

In this brief chapter, I have summarized my thinking about how heritable trait impulsivity can be amplified across development through socialization mechanisms that occur within families. I have also explained how psychophysiological variables, and to a lesser extent genetics and neuroimaging, have informed research. Though my focus has been on adverse effects of interactions between impulsivity and emotion dysregulation, our model also implies that interventions that focus on teaching strong ER skills to impulsive children and their parents may prevent the development of conduct problems as children mature. Thankfully, such interventions already appear to be effective (see, e.g., Beauchaine, Reid, & Webster-Stratton, 2005). Through careful use of ANS and CNS markers, we are learning more about the brain bases of behavior and behavioral change.

NEUROENDOCRINE REGULATION AND EMOTIONAL ADAPTATION IN THE CONTEXT OF CHILD MALTREATMENT

Dante Cicchetti and Fred A. Rogosch

The empirical study of the emotions has significant implications for comprehending the complexity of normal and abnormal development (Cicchetti & Hesse, 1983; Hesse & Cicchetti, 1982; Izard & Harris, 1995; Pollak, 2008). One of the theoretical consequences of the examination of normal emotional processes is that it underscores the necessity of constructing a model of the ontogenesis of the emotions that can distinguish between well-adjusted and psychopathological emotional development (Cicchetti & Schneider-Rosen, 1984; Hesse & Cicchetti, 1982; Sroufe, 1979, 1996). The investigation of the emotions is also essential with respect to the formulation of an integrated theory of development that can account for both typical and atypical ontogenesis and epigenesis. Thus, it is critical that we possess information about how the emotions relate to other domains of the human mind in order to specify the experiences and conditions necessary to bring about changes in the emotional domain. In addition, the study of atypical populations can enhance our understanding of the processes involved in normal emotional development (Cicchetti & Schneider-Rosen, 1984; Hesse & Cicchetti, 1982). To theorize about development without considering the deviations that might be expected from prominent and pervasive intra- and extraorganismic disturbances, as well as the transactions that occur among them, would result in incomplete and ambiguous accounts of the developmental process (Cicchetti, 1990).

Many lessons about developmental processes can be learned from the study of maltreated children (Cicchetti & Lynch, 1995; Cicchetti & Toth, 2005). By investigating the effects of severe environmental disturbances (such as child sexual, physical, and emotional abuse, and neglect; Cicchetti & Barnett, 1991) on individual development, it may be possible to examine

This work was supported by grants from the National Institute of Drug Abuse, DA12903 and DA017741, and the Spunk Fund, Inc.

Corresponding author: Dante Cicchetti, Institute of Child Development, University of Minnesota, 51 E. River Rd., Minneapolis, MN 55455, email: cicchett@umn.edu

processes that are so subtle and gradual that they are not observed or detected in the study of normal development (Chomsky, 1968; Cicchetti, 1996). For example, through investigating the nature and course of development in children who have not grown up in a benign rearing environment, researchers are in a position to elucidate the impact that caregiving experiences exert on brain circuitry, structure, and function (Cicchetti, 2002a, 2002b; De Bellis, 2001, 2005; Pollak, 2008; Teicher, 2002). Furthermore, there is evidence for various sensitive periods in development associated with different caregiving experiences, as supported by the finding of different experience-dependent effects that emerge when maltreatment occurs at different points in development (Black, Jones, Nelson, & Greenough, 1998; Cicchetti, Rogosch, Gunnar, & Toth, 2010; Heim, Newport, Mietzko, Miller, & Nemeroff, 2008; Kim, Cicchetti, Rogosch, & Manly, 2009; Manly, Kim, Rogosch, & Cicchetti, 2001).

Growing up under conditions of child maltreatment constitutes a profound immersion in severe stress that challenges and frequently impairs development across diverse domains of functioning (Cicchetti & Valentino, 2006). Not only is psychological development often compromised, but also biological consequences ensue (Cicchetti, 2002a, 2002b; DeBellis, 2001, 2005; Pollak, Cicchetti, Klorman, & Brumaghim, 1997; Teicher, 2002). Nevertheless, not all maltreated children succumb to extreme adversity (Cicchetti & Rogosch, 1997). Multilevel investigations of how some maltreated children cope adaptively with significant stressful experiences provide an opportunity to discover processes at multiple levels of analysis that may be germane to understanding emotional development yet are less readily detectible under more normative stress exposure.

Stress engenders both biological and psychological responses. The biological response to stress includes the activation of specific neural circuits and neuroendocrine systems (Cicchetti & Walker, 2001; Kaufman & Charney, 2001). Psychological responses to stressful experiences show variability among individuals, ranging from active coping to depression, suggesting variation in emotion processes. Although the experience of ongoing chronic stress is typically associated with deleterious outcomes, such as neurobiological dysfunction, immunological difficulties, neuroendocrine dysregulation, and increases in autonomic activity, as well as with maladaptation and mental disorder (Gunnar & Adam, in this volume; Gunnar & Vazquez, 2006), not all individuals who are persistently exposed to stressful experiences are affected in a uniform fashion.

In keeping with the systems theory concepts of multifinality and equifinality (Cicchetti & Rogosch, 1996), similar stressful experiences do not necessarily exert the same effects on biological and psychological functioning in all individuals; conversely, pathways from different stressful experiences may eventuate in the same biological or psychological outcome. There are multiple converging processes that determine the neural and psychological responses to stressors. These include the neural circuits that are activated by physiological and psychological stressors, as well as the influences of genetic makeup, prior experience, and ongoing life events (Sapolsky, 1994). Stressful or threatening experiences, such as child abuse and neglect, create adaptational challenges. The hypothalamic–pituitary–adrenal (HPA) axis is one of the physiological systems that has evolved in mammals to help direct and sustain emotional, cognitive, behavioral, and metabolic activity in response to threat. The capacity to elevate cortisol in response to acute trauma is critical for survival. Brief elevations in corticosteroids appear to enhance the individual's ability to manage and adapt to stressful experiences effectively. However, both chronic hyperactivity of the HPA axis and reduced cortisol secretion, known as hypercortisolism and hypocortisolism, respectively, exert negative impacts on the brain and impede an individual's ability to cope with stress.

NEUROENDOCRINE REGULATION IN THE CONTEXT OF CHILD MALTREATMENT

During the past decade, we have conducted a number of investigations on cortisol regulation in maltreated children. Each of our investigations has been conducted in the context of a research summer day camp (Cicchetti & Manly, 1990). Unless otherwise noted, cortisol was collected at 9 a.m. and 4 p.m. each day throughout the camp week. Given the approximately 45-min transportation from the home to the camp and the time spent being greeted by camp staff, children had been awake at least 1 hr prior to providing the morning saliva samples, thus avoiding the dynamic cortisol awakening response (Susman et al., 2007).

Maltreated children were recruited from the local County Department of Human Services (DHS), and, with parental consent, each family's DHS record was examined and maltreatment information was coded using the *Maltreatment Classification System* (Barnett, Manly, & Cicchetti, 1993). Most of the maltreated children were from low socioeconomic (SES) backgrounds; thus, demographically comparable nonmaltreated comparison children were recruited from families receiving Temporary Assistance for Needy Families. To verify nonmaltreatment status, we interviewed each family about child maltreatment experiences and inspected the state child abuse registry for absence of incidents.

Because maltreatment is a multifaceted stressor, in our first study, we sought to examine aspects of child maltreatment that might differentially relate to neuroendocrine functioning (Cicchetti & Rogosch, 2001a). Overall group differences between maltreated and nonmaltreated children were not found for average morning or average afternoon cortisol levels. However, significant variations were found that were based on the subtypes of maltreatment that the children had experienced. Maltreated children who had been physically and sexually abused (as well as neglected or emotionally maltreated) exhibited substantial elevations in morning cortisol levels; children who had high cortisol levels in both the morning and afternoon were also overrepresented in the multiple abuse group. Developmental timing of maltreatment did not account for these group differences, whereas the severity of sexual abuse was implicated.

In contrast to the multiple abuse group, a subgroup of physically abused children evidenced a trend toward lower morning cortisol relative to nonmaltreated children; the physically abused subgroup also displayed a significantly smaller decrease in cortisol levels from morning to afternoon. Thus, among maltreated children, different subgroups exhibited widely divergent patterns of neuroendocrine regulation. The sexually and physically abused group appeared to resemble children who evidence hypercortisolism, whereas children in the physically abused subgroup displayed evidence of cortisol suppression and significantly less diurnal variation—a pattern that was akin to hypocortisolism. These findings were important because they demonstrated that maltreated children do not display uniform patterns of cortisol regulation.

Subsequently, we investigated the impact of child maltreatment and psychopathology on neuroendocrine functioning (Cicchetti & Rogosch, 2001b). Children who exhibited clinical-level internalizing problems only, clinical-level externalizing problems only, and comorbid clinical-level internalizing and externalizing problems were identified. Clinical-level cases were more prevalent among the maltreated children. Maltreated children with internalizing problems were distinguished by higher morning, afternoon, and average daily cortisol levels. In contrast, nonmaltreated boys with externalizing problems emerged as distinct in terms of exhibiting low levels of morning and average daily levels of cortisol. Maltreated children with comorbid internalizing and externalizing problems were more likely not to show the expected diurnal decrease in cortisol. The results suggested that associations between different forms of psychopathology and neuroendocrine dysregulation varied by maltreatment experience. As in the Cicchetti and Rogosch (2001a) study, the differential patterns of cortisol regulation observed in this investigation provide further evidence that the neurobiological functioning of all children who have experienced maltreatment is not affected in a similar fashion (Cicchetti, 2002a, 2002b).

Further research examined neuroendocrine regulation and physical and relational aggression (Murray-Close, Han, Cicchetti, Crick, & Rogosch, 2008). Salivary cortisol was assessed at 9 a.m., 12:30 p.m., and 4:00 p.m. daily. We found that physical aggression was associated with heightened morning cortisol and relatively steep declines in cortisol over the day, whereas relational aggression was associated with lower morning cortisol and a more blunted diurnal change in cortisol. In addition, maltreatment was a significant moderator of this relationship such that aggression was more strongly related to cortisol dysregulation among nonmaltreated than among maltreated children. The findings suggest that physiological correlates of aggression may differ for physical and relational forms of aggression and among maltreated versus nonmaltreated children. These results are congruent with the "social push" perspective, in which biological contributors to involvement in aggression are thought to be more influential among children who have a less strong social push toward conduct disturbance (Raine, 2002). In the Murray-Close et al. (2008) study, the maltreated and nonmaltreated children all experienced SES adversity. Yet in the absence of maltreatment, the association between neuroendocrine functioning and various forms of aggression was more evident among nonmaltreated children who by definition had less intrafamilial risk.

Although dysregulation of the HPA axis appears to be associated with maltreatment for children who are high in internalizing problems or who are clinically depressed (Hart, Gunnar, & Cicchetti, 1996; Kaufman, 1991), it remains unclear whether this is due to the type, severity, or developmental timing of the maltreatment. The relevant published studies have either focused on physical or sexual abuse, or both, or have not examined a specific subtype of maltreatment. Strikingly, few published investigations include a measure of developmental timing (Fox, Kirwan, & Reeb-Sutherland, in this volume), a critical variable in neuroendocrinology (Tarullo & Gunnar, 2006). Indeed the empirical evidence gleaned from rodent and nonhuman primate investigation indicates that adverse or maltreating (i.e., neglectful and abusive) care early in an animal's life has long-lasting effects.

In an attempt to reduce this significant gap in the literature, Cicchetti et al. (2010) conducted a study that was designed to examine the hypothesis that children who were physically or sexually abused prior to age 5 (early physical abuse/sexual abuse) and who expressed high depressive and internalizing symptoms would exhibit a more dysregulated pattern of diurnal cortisol activity (less decline; flatter slope) than would other maltreated children (no early physical or sexual abuse) or nonmaltreated children. We chose the infancy, toddler, and preschool periods as our index of early maltreatment for two reasons. First, national epidemiological studies of child maltreatment highlight this period as a critical time for the emergence of abuse and neglect (Cicchetti & Toth, 2003). Second, despite the fact that the neural systems underlying stress reactivity/regulation and internalizing problems undergo a prolonged period of development, components of the limbic system, such as the hippocampus, the amygdala, and the pathways to the prefrontal cortex from these structures develop rapidly over the first years of life (Thompson & Nelson, 2001).

Consistent with our predictions, we found that children experiencing abuse in the first 5 years of life exhibited more internalizing symptoms than maltreated children without early abuse and nonmaltreated children of the same SES level. In addition, children experiencing early abuse who had high internalizing symptoms exhibited an atypical flattening of cortisol production over the daytime hours. Not all children with depression exhibited cortisol dysregulation; Cicchetti et al. (2010) found it only for the physically/sexually abused children with high internalizing/depressive symptomatology—a group that is more likely to have dysfunctions in early neurobiological development through the high allostatic load caused by abuse.

Early abuse may be more damaging to developing emotion and stress systems because it occurs during periods of rapid neurodevelopment (Cicchetti & Walker, 2001; Gunnar & Vazquez, 2006). Very young children also may be less able than older children to discern the emotional cues predictive of an abusive episode, and this lack of predictability may engender chronic stress and hypervigilance to aggression in these youngsters, even when abusive events are not occurring (Rieder & Cicchetti, 1989; Teisl & Cicchetti, 2008). School-aged children with a history of physical abuse, on the other hand, have been shown to be highly sensitive to even very degraded signals of emotional threat. Although potentially maladaptive in some contexts, such hypervigilance may be adaptive in the abusive home environment (Pollak, Cicchetti, & Klorman, 1998; Pollak & Sinha, 2002; Shackman, Shackman, & Pollak, 2007).

The impact of early physical/sexual abuse on developing brain systems may be especially pernicious because it occurs during a period when the child is nearly wholly dependent on parents for survival. For the abused infant, toddler, or preschooler, a hypervigilant state of mind and chronic stress with respect to unpredictable parental abuse may shift neurobiological development onto pathways leading to depression and neuroendocrine dysregulation.

It is also important to note that not all of the children who have experienced physical/sexual abuse had high depressive symptoms (Cicchetti et al., 2010). Why is the HPA axis functioning of this group of early abused children better regulated than that of early abused and depressed children with the attenuated diurnal decrease in cortisol? It is likely that there are genes that increase the probability of depression/internalizing problems under conditions of high stress, such as early physical/sexual abuse (see, e.g., Caspi et al., 2003; Cicchetti, Rogosch, & Sturge-Apple, 2007). Conversely, genetic elements also may confer a protective function by decreasing the probability that individuals experiencing severe maltreatment will develop depression.

We also have embarked on empirical studies of the processes contributing to resilience in an attempt to redress the unitary emphasis on psychosocial factors that has predominated in the literature. In a multilevel investigation, Cicchetti and Rogosch (2007) focused on the contribution that the personality factors ego control and ego resiliency and the regulation of two stress-responsive adrenal steroid hormones, cortisol and dehydroepiandrosterone (DHEA), make to adaptive functioning under stressful and adverse conditions in a sample of maltreated and nonmaltreated children. Ego control refers to the degree to which individuals express their emotional impulses, varying between spontaneous and immediate to constrained and inhibited; ego resiliency involves the dynamic capacity to modify one's modal level of ego control in adapting flexibly to meet environmental contextual demands. The steroid hormones cortisol and DHEA are the two primary adreno-cortical products of secretory activity of the HPA axis. The capacity of individuals to elevate cortisol levels in response to exposure to acute trauma is important for survival (Gunnar & Vazquez, 2006). DHEA exerts an impact upon a diverse array of biological actions, including effects on the immune, cardiovascular, endocrine, metabolic, and central nervous systems (Majewska, 1995).

Our measure of resilient adaptation included multimethod, multi-informant assessments of competent peer relations, school success, and low levels of internalizing and externalizing symptomatology. We found that ego resiliency, the degree of relative flexibility in regulating affect and behavior to meet situational demands, and ego control, the ability to monitor and control impulses and regulate affect, and the adrenal steroid hormones associated with stress (i.e., cortisol and DHEA) made independent and noninteractive contributions to resilience. Although operating at different levels of analysis, behavioral/psychological and biological factors each made unique contributions to resilience. For both maltreated and nonmaltreated children, a more reserved, restrained, and rational style of interacting with peers and adults contributed to these children being more attuned to behave in ways that were critical for adapting successfully to their stress-laden environments.

Prolonged stress, as is often the case in child maltreatment, can lead to allostatic load, characterized by cumulative physiological dysregulation across multiple biological systems, through a cascade of causes and sequelae that can change the brain, organ systems, and the neurochemical balance that undergirds cognition, emotion, mood, personality, and behavior (Lupien et al., 2006). In a seminal article, McEwen and Stellar (1993) proffered the concept of allostatic load to refer to the cost the body pays for repeatedly using allostatic responses to adapt to stress; allostatic load is thought to occur when the adaptation to stress necessitates that the responses must be maintained over sustained time periods. As described by Lupien et al. (2006), allostasis and allostatic load can be conceived as embodying a general biological principle—namely, that the systems that help the body adapt to stress and serve a protective function in the short term also may take part in the development of pathophysiological processes when overused or managed ineffectively.

In our study (Cicchetti & Rogosch, 2007), we found that higher morning cortisol levels were related to lower levels of resilient strivings for the nonmaltreated children. High basal cortisol may indicate that nonmaltreated children are experiencing greater stress exposure and, consequently, are constrained in their ability to adapt competently. Within the group of maltreated children, differences in cortisol regulation were found as a function of the subtype(s) of maltreatment experienced. Physically abused children with high morning cortisol had higher resilient functioning than physically abused children with lower levels of morning cortisol. The positive role of increased cortisol for physically abused children is divergent from the more general pattern of higher cortisol being related to lower resilient functioning as we discovered in the nonmaltreated and sexually abused children.

Prior research on neuroendocrine regulation has indicated that physically abused children generally exhibit lower levels of morning cortisol secretion (Cicchetti & Rogosch, 2001a). It may be that the subgroup of physically abused children who were able to elevate cortisol to cope with the life stressors was demonstrating a greater striving for resilient adaptation. In contrast, the larger subgroup of physically abused children with lower levels of morning cortisol may have developed hypocortisolism over time in response to chronic stress exposure. As a result, for these children there may be a diminished capacity to mobilize the HPA axis to promote positive adaptation under conditions of ongoing stress. Additionally, Cicchetti and Rogosch (2007) found that the very low level of resilience among sexually abused children with high basal cortisol may be a product of their different traumatic experiences and the consequences of chronic excessive vigilance and preoccupation, with commensurate HPA axis hyperarousal.

Notably, we also discovered that maltreated children with high resilient functioning exhibited a unique atypical pattern of a relative DHEA diurnal increase (Cicchetti & Rogosch, 2007). Maltreated children who have the capacity to increase DHEA over the day may be better equipped to cope with the demands of high chronic exposure to stress and to adapt competently. In contrast, the nonmaltreated children who functioned resiliently did not exhibit the pattern of diurnal DHEA increase; instead they manifested the lowest levels of DHEA across the day.

CONCLUSIONS AND FUTURE DIRECTIONS

The study of neuroendocrine regulation in relation to emotional development and diverse psychopathologies linked to emotion processes is brought into relief when children experiencing very atypical and adverse rearing environments are considered. Our findings highlight the lack of uniformity, both psychological and biological, with which maltreated children adapt to trauma and deprivation in their lives. Rather than exhibiting a common pattern of neuroendocrine dysregulation, maltreated children display a diversity of neuroendocrine regulatory patterns that are differentially linked to internalizing and externalizing disturbances, as well as resilient adaptations. These relations also have been shown to differ for maltreated children and their peers who have had less exposure to chronic stress. That seemingly atypical patterns of neuroendocrine regulation are related to resilience in highly stressed maltreated children challenges unitary conceptualizations of how physiology and emotions are related and necessitates that both typical and atypical populations be considered in tandem for a more comprehensive understanding of emotional development.

In addition to our investigations of neuroendocrine regulation, emotion, and psychopathology in maltreated children, we have conducted studies utilizing other physiological measures of emotion and psychopathology in abused and neglected children. These include studies of gene–environment interaction and the development of psychopathology (Cicchetti et al., 2007; Cicchetti et al., 2010), event-related potentials (ERP) in response to a range of emotion stimuli (Cicchetti & Curtis, 2005; Pollak et al., 1997), and the contribution of electroencephalographic (EEG) hemispheric activation asymmetries and emotion regulation to resilient functioning (Curtis & Cicchetti, 2007).

At this stage of our research, findings have revealed that the varied physiological and psychological measures of emotion have demonstrated a relatively independent influence on psychopathological and resilient outcomes in maltreated children. In the future, we will begin to decipher co-actions across multiple levels of analysis through incorporating genetic and multiple physiological measures of emotion in our multilevel research on pathways to psychopathology and resilience in abused and neglected children. For example, in a longitudinal investigation that is currently underway in our laboratory, we will be employing a multiple-levels-of-analysis approach to examine the course of trauma-related psychopathology in maltreated children, as well as the multilevel processes that contribute to resilient outcomes. In addition to genotyping relevant candidate genes, we plan to incorporate multiple measures of neurophysiological (e.g., EEG hemispheric activation asymmetry, ERP responses to classes of emotion stimuli, and emotion-potentiated startle), hormonal, neurocognitive, and behavioral functioning. The field can no longer afford to continue the artificial distinction among genetics, neurobiology, and behavior in research on the determinants of psychopathology and resilience. The pathways to either psychopathology or resilience are influenced, in part, by a complex matrix of the individual's level of biological and psychological organization, experience, social context, timing of adverse events and experiences, and developmental history.

INTRODUCTION TO SECTION FOUR: OVERARCHING ISSUES AND METHODOLOGICAL CONSIDERATIONS: WHAT CAN PHYSIOLOGICAL MEASURES REVEAL ABOUT EMOTION?

Tracy A. Dennis, Paul D. Hastings, and Kristin A. Buss

The goals of the fourth section, "Overarching Issues and Methodological Considerations: What Can Physiological Measures Reveal About Emotion?," are to take a step back after the first three sections to provide an overview of several core physiological measures used in studies of emotional development, articulate what each measure can reveal about emotion, and describe state-of-the-art methods and statistical techniques for working with physiological data. The chapters in this section do not represent an exhaustive review of physiological measures described in this monograph, but highlight key methodological challenges and themes facing the field as a whole. These challenges reflect the five themes of time, context, specificity, integration, and development highlighted throughout the monograph.

Fox and colleagues discuss the use of EEG/ERP and the startle response in developmental psychophysiological studies of emotion. They present a list of desiderata, including a careful consideration of developing systems and of individual differences. As is clear by their title, they also highlight that "timing is everything" and that measures with millisecond precision can reveal much about the importance of temporal dynamics in understanding emotion.

Gunnar and Adam also discuss the importance of timing, here on the order of minutes and hours and in the context of the hypothalamic-pituitary-adrenocortical (HPA) system. As a central arm of the stress response system, HPA activity can be used to examine emotions and emotion regulation in children who are both typically developing and are at risk for emotional disorders. The authors provide practical measurement and methodological guidelines and highlight key conceptual issues, such as developmental shifts in the coupling between the HPA system and behavior, chronic versus acute stress, and

---

Corresponding author: Tracy A. Dennis, Department of Psychology, Doctoral Program in Biopsychology and Behavioral Neuroscience, Hunter College, The City University of New York, 695 Park Avenue, New York, NY 10065, email: tracy.dennis@hunter.cuny.edu

what HPA activity can reveal about the effectiveness of social support and self-regulation in reducing stress.

In the next chapter, Obradović and Boyce focus on another arm of the stress response system, the sympathetic-adrenomedulary (SAM) system. This chapter describes sympathetic nervous system responses that are triggered in the context of an emotional event, along with methods and methodological challenges in the assessment of these physiological correlates of emotion reactivity and regulation in children. The authors also consider the integration of sympathetic and parasympathetic activation, suggesting that distinct profiles of activation and withdrawal differentially relate to specific behavioral symptoms and vulnerabilities for psychopathology. Importantly, these profiles may vary with context and the nature of stimuli, as well as across time with maturation. Moreover, there is a need to understand how such associations differ based on age, gender, and race. This chapter both summarizes the state of the science in this area and articulates directions for future research.

Complementing these three chapters, the fourth chapter in this section by Molenaar and Gates describes considerations in statistical analyses and modeling when working with neuroimaging data. The authors argue that the statistical methods used to analyze these data are often inadequate for capturing the complexity of the underlying dynamic and system-level processes. There is a focus on two key analytic techniques—the estimation of coherency maps based on multivariate EEG and the estimation of connectivity maps based on fMRI time series. These state-of-the-art analytic approaches provide unique information about the functional relationships among brain regions during cognitive and affective tasks.

Taken together, these chapters provide a tantalizing glimpse into the complexities and benefits of using psychophysiology to study emotional development and psychopathology. The work described here represents the cutting edge of recent research, united by a focus on dynamic and interactive affective processes and by methodologically rigorous measurement approaches. The emphasis on environmental context and multiple, integrated psychobiological systems heralds a new decade of research that will explore how physiological responses influence behavior while also articulating how emotional experiences and contexts in turn shape biological sensitivities and vulnerabilities across development.

MEASURING THE PHYSIOLOGY OF EMOTION AND EMOTION REGULATION—TIMING IS EVERYTHING

Nathan A. Fox, Michael Kirwan, and Bethany Reeb-Sutherland

The study of emotion has an intimate relationship to the measurement of physiological activity. The definition of an emotion has been debated for some time in the psychological literature (e.g., Ekman & Davidson, 1994). Ekman (Ekman 1992; Ekman & Davidson, 1994) defined emotion as a psychological state that has a defined and often rapid onset, a defined and usually brief duration, and a set of defined changes in facial muscle activity. Emotions have been described with physiological terms, and theories of emotion incorporate physiological change. For example, in Ekman's definition of emotion, he argues that certain emotions have distinct patterns of autonomic activity and consequently that different emotion states may be the result of autonomic appraisal (often with little conscious awareness). Thus, measurement of physiological activity during the expression and experience of emotion has been the goal of a good deal of psychological research. Finally, there has been a good deal of discussion regarding a definition of emotion regulation. Emotion regulation may best be viewed as the modulation of behaviors that underlie a present emotion state. In this chapter, we discuss one central area for the use of physiological measurement in the study of emotion: the importance of temporal dynamics in measuring physiology and emotion. Prior to that discussion, we present five desiderata that are important to consider when studying psychophysiology in general, and emotion and psychophysiology in particular, from a developmental perspective. For more in-depth discussions of the issues in measurement of emotion, interested readers are referred to important chapters by Davidson (1994b) and our own work (Fox, Schmidt, Henderson, & Marshall, 2006; Schmidt & Fox, 1998a), as well as edited volumes such as that by Schmidt and Segalowitz (2008).

Corresponding author: Nathan A. Fox, University of Maryland, 3304 Benjamin Building, College Park, MD 20742-1131, email: fox@umd.edu

DESIDERATA FOR DEVELOPMENTAL PSYCHOPHYSIOLOGICAL STUDIES

It Is Critical to Link Behavior to Physiology

It is often appealing to measure physiological responses to a stimulus or experimental manipulation, identify change in physiology, and infer psychological processes as a function of that manipulation. However, we would argue that the physiological data require concordant behavioral observation and measurement so as to accurately interpret physiological effects. It is certainly the case that behavioral response and physiology do not always "correlate." This may be a result of the fineness of the behavioral assessment, or it may reveal an important dissociation between particular behaviors and their underlying physiology. The optimum situation is one in which both levels of measurement are acquired. Measurement of concurrent behavior is important for multiple reasons, particularly with child populations. Infants and children move, vocalize, or do not attend to stimulus presentation. Movement or vocalization can affect physiology, and physiological measurement during periods of inattention can be misleading. It is best to measure behavior when measuring biology in developmental studies, as this allows one to synchronize the acquisition of behavior and physiology. In doing so, one can later code behavior and extract physiology from those periods of time that reflect a particular emotional response or state. An example of this work can be found in a study by Davidson and Fox (1989) who recorded electroencephalography (EEG) while 10-month-old infants' behavior was videotaped during both maternal separation and the approach of an unfamiliar adult. Periods in which infants expressed discrete emotions were identified and these time epochs were used to define periods of EEG that were extracted, processed, and analyzed to examine the concordance of physiology and behavior.

Physiological Systems Change With Development

There are obvious changes in the physiology of the peripheral and central nervous systems with development, and these changes *will* affect the interpretation of physiological data. For example, measurement of brain electrical activity via EEG has utilized frequency bands to reflect different cognitive states and states of consciousness. The alpha frequency band, often associated with attention and relaxation, is characterized as falling between 8 and 13 Hz in adults. However, the frequency band for alpha changes as a function of age, beginning around 3–5 Hz in early infancy and moving upward with development (Marshall, Bar-Haim, & Fox, 2002). Similarly, vagal tone, a measure of parasympathetic influence on heart rate akin to respiratory sinus arrhythmia (RSA), is computed as a function of respiratory influences on heart rate. This also changes as a function of age as children's respiratory rates and heart rates change with development (Bar-Haim, Marshall, & Fox, 2000; Goto et al., 1997). The morphology of the event-related potential (ERP) also changes with age. In infancy and early childhood, responses to novel or low-frequency events elicit a negative component called the Nc. This deflection changes with age, actually becoming positive and reflecting the more common adultlike P3 component in late childhood (Courchesne, 1978). Finally, experience interacts with development to shape both structure and physiology. This topic is explored later in this monograph in the chapter by Strang, Hanson, and Pollak. Thus, one must be cognizant that the physiological systems being measured are themselves maturing and hence their measurement must take into account developmental status.

Attempt to Determine the Origin of the Signals Being Measured

Modern technology and computers have made it easy to measure the electrocardiogram (ECG) or to record brain electrical activity from participants. Using these methods, one can obtain reliable changes in measures as a function of stimulus presentation or experimental manipulation. What is more difficult is the interpretation of the meaning or underlying source of the signal. For example, heart rate is a multidetermined signal arising from the confluence of both sympathetic and parasympathetic systems, as well as physical movement and thermoregulatory inputs. Researchers have attempted to derive "pure" measures of sympathetic (e.g., preejection phase) or parasympathetic (RSA and vagal tone) activity to more directly interpret links between physiology and behavior. The problem is more complex when dealing with brain electrical activity measures like EEG and ERP. Since electrical activity is being measured at a distance from the source (somewhere in the head), one must identify the source from the output. This problem in electrophysiology, called "the inverse problem," has led to a number of computational solutions to identify sources of EEG/ERP activity. These solutions are not perfect and necessitate high-density, multilead EEG acquisition. A conservative approach for both EEG and ERP is to refer to activity as scalp derived and nonspecific to any single source in the brain.

Individual Differences Play an Important Role in Understanding Physiology-Behavior Links

As in other areas of psychological research, individual differences have often been viewed as a nuisance, clouding the effects of a particular experimental manipulation. Conversely, psychophysiological studies, and developmental psychophysiology in particular, have long appreciated the importance of both individual variability in response and individual differences in subject characteristics. Close to 40 years ago, Stephen Porges noted that some infants displayed cardiac deceleration to a visual or auditory stimulus reflecting their attention to the presentation while others did not. Closer inspection of their prestimulus baseline ECG patterns revealed that infants who displayed decelerated responses had more variable heart rates prior to stimulus presentation, while those who did not display deceleration had less variable and more stable heart rates. Porges went on to model these individual differences based on the degree of parasympathetic influence on infant heart rate and the role they played in attention (Porges, 1974; Porges, McCabe, & Yongue, 1982).

Using the difference in EEG power between left and right frontal scalp locations (i.e., EEG asymmetry), Davidson and Fox (1989) found that the pattern of resting frontal asymmetry in 10-month-old infants predicted their affective response to maternal separation. Infants exhibiting right frontal EEG asymmetry were more likely to cry and show distress to separation compared to those with a resting pattern of left frontal EEG asymmetry. These two examples suggest that measuring baseline or resting physiology may contain important information regarding the subject's pattern of behavioral and physiological response to stimulation.

Investigating the Specificity of Discrete Emotions

The argument that emotions have distinct patterns of facial expression that can be measured is based, in part, on Ekman's study of different facial muscles and their actions, which create patterns of facial expression that can be identified across cultures (Ekman, Sorenson, & Friesen, 1969). There have been a number of debates in the field of emotion research about whether this is the case, or whether emotions are less categorical and can be located across dimensions such as arousal and valence. The history of this debate goes back to the suggestion by James (1890) that emotions have different patterns of autonomic activity and, in some models, that this autonomic activity feeds back to the central nervous system for the experience of a particular emotion. Much of this debate has centered on the measurement of autonomic activity using directed facial action tasks (Ekman, Levenson, & Friesen, 1983). Less work has attempted to utilize measures of central nervous system activity such as EEG.

The exception is work by Davidson and colleagues (Davidson, Ekman, Saron, Senulis, & Friesen, 1990; Tomarken, Davidson, & Henriques, 1990), who attempted to elicit discrete emotions in adult subjects using film clips while simultaneously recording EEG. EEG was then extracted during the expression of particular emotions. The results were suggestive of a dichotomy between emotions associated with approach and those associated more with withdrawal. On the other hand, there was no evidence with the EEG for distinctive patterns for specific discrete emotions. Similarly, Davidson and Fox (1989) examined 10-month-old infant facial expressions in response to maternal separation and approach of an unfamiliar adult while simultaneously recording EEG. Periods of discrete emotion were identified and EEG was extracted during those periods of time. Again, while there was evidence for differences in EEG pattern as a function of motivational state (approach versus withdrawal), there was no evidence for specificity of EEG patterns for discrete emotions.

The Importance of Temporal Dynamics in the Measurement of Emotion—Timing Is Everything

The experience of emotion involves many qualities, including the intensity of the expression, the degree to which the emotion is overtly expressed either facially or vocally, the success (or lack thereof) in communication or signaling, and, lastly, its duration. While each of these qualities is important for understanding the signal value of the emotion (the intent of the person expressing the emotion as well as the success of communication), the duration provides an opportunity to differentiate those emotions that are momentary from those that reflect more enduring mood states. This is particularly important when considering the task of modulating or regulating an emotion or mood. The temporal dynamics of the expression and experience of the emotion, the latency to reach its peak intensity, the duration during which that intensity is maintained, and the time required to return to baseline are all critical components of the regulatory process. Successful regulation of emotion most probably involves mechanisms of attention and cognition that alter the temporal dynamics of emotion experience, and often the lack of success in modulating this temporal picture can lead to disruptive patterns of behavior. Thus, measurement of this dynamic is of critical importance.

Paul Ekman, one of the most important and influential current psychologists involved in the study of emotion, laid out a precise vocabulary and conceptualization of emotion: what it is, what its parameters are, and how to approach its measurement. In a chapter published in 1984, titled "Expression and the Nature of Emotion" (Ekman, Sorenson, & Friesen, 1984), he outlined 10 characteristics of emotion. Among these are the suggestions that there are limits on the duration of an emotion, the timing of an emotion expression reveals information about the experience of that emotion, and specific changes in autonomic and central nervous system activity are related to different emotions. Ekman argued that emotions vary in their onset, offset, and duration and that these parameters inform the psychological experience of the emotion. For example, most emotions are short in duration compared to mood states. Thus, the experience of emotion is short lived compared to enduring mood states that may not share the same facial, behavioral, or physiological characteristics. Although an emotion can vary in its timing parameters, it is more likely that each emotion possesses central tendencies in onset, offset, and duration. Fear may have a sudden onset and a brief duration, whereas anger may have a longer latency but also longer duration of expression. The temporal dynamics of emotion fit well within a structure for viewing emotions as biological signals, since physiology itself is not static but dynamically changing with the psychological state of the individual. Ekman's approach thus provided a foundation for linking physiological activity to the experience and expression of emotion. Indeed, he postulated that there should be distinct signatures in autonomic activity associated with different emotions. One of the reasons for differentiation of autonomic signals for different emotions involves their adaptive functions; fear requires immediate attention, mobilization of energy, and necessity to withdraw, while anger requires mobilization of energy and behavioral approach. Thus, fear should be accompanied by increased heart rate and low skin temperature, whereas anger would involve increased heart rate but high skin temperature, and happiness would involve low heart rate responses. The ability to empirically identify the presence of emotion using precise methods of behavioral coding opened the door for psychophysiologists to link ongoing physiological activity to the presence of emotion.

Most physiological and biological responses change dynamically over time. One can thus examine this dynamic signal as a function of response to a stimulus, or average its fluctuations over time to derive a mean-level response. The use of heart rate in emotion research is a good example. Heart rate is measured via recording of the ECG. The ECG signal is a complex waveform reflecting electrical activity of the heart muscle as it goes through the process of pumping blood to the body and brain. The different components of this waveform reflect changes in electrical muscle activity, with the most prominent components, known as the QRS complex, reflecting ventricular depolarization. The R wave is usually the largest amplitude wave or spike in the complex. The interval between two R waves in milliseconds is a measure of heart period (the inverse is heart rate, so a 500 ms heart period corresponds to 120 beats per minute). The ECG is easy to measure from and use with infants and young children making it a popular measure with developmental samples. In one study, van IJzendoorn and colleagues presented young children with movie clips selected to elicit different emotions (fear, happiness, and neutral affect) and measured ECG as the children watched the movies (Gilissen, Koolstra, van IJzendoorn, Bakermans-Kranenburg, & van der Veer, 2007). They found increased heart rate during the clips designed to elicit fear compared to clips designed to elicit neutral or positive affect. This is but one example of work that has examined dynamically changing patterns of heart rate during the elicitation of different emotions. Indeed, there is a good deal of work with this approach that has confirmed the presence of emotion responses in children. Another body of work has attempted to distinguish different emotion regulation responses to certain affective challenges. In one such example, Forbes, Fox, Cohn, Galles, and Kovacs (2006) presented a disappointment paradigm to 4-year-old children and measured heart rate during presentation of the "disappointing" toy as well as behavioral response. Some children who displayed little behavioral change to the presentation of the disappointing toy nevertheless exhibited increased heart rate responses, suggesting these children were able to regulate the expression of overt affect while still displaying an internal physiological response to the event.

Similar to the aforementioned heart rate research, there is also a history of studies examining temporal changes in brain activity during the expression and experience of emotion. In order to monitor dynamic changes in brain activity with a high degree of temporal resolution, researchers utilize computation of an ERP from the ongoing EEG brain electrical activity. Unlike EEG, an ERP is computed in the time domain rather than frequency domain by time-locking brain electrical activity to the presentation of specific stimuli.

A given ERP waveform carries with it several defining characteristics: its polarity, latency, amplitude, scalp distribution, and potential source (Otten & Rugg, 2004), the last of which has become increasingly important given the imperfect relationship between scalp topography and actual brain structure (Key, Dove, & Maguire, 2005). Methods such as cortical source analysis (Scherg & Berg, 1991; Scherg & Picton, 1991) can be used to estimate the locations of current dipoles, a process that can be further improved by combining structural magnetic resonance imaging with ERP to generate individual brain maps as replacements for average brains or Talaraich coordinates (Richards, submitted).

ERP components are generally classified based on their polarity (P for positive, N for negative) and either their order (i.e., N1, P2) or their peak latency after stimulus onset or response (i.e., N170, P300; Key et al., 2005). Shorter latency waveforms have previously been assumed to represent more endogenous, automatic responses to stimuli, with longer latency waveforms representing exogenous components or information processing (Donchin, 1978). In other words, a given ERP component's latency after stimulus onset may reflect its place in the stream of information processing for that stimulus.

ERP methods have been important in the study of emotion in multiple ways. First, there is a long history of examining the neural bases of face processing and particularly faces of different emotions using ERP. One of the most studied ERP components related to face processing is the N170, a negative deflection that is observed between 156 and 189 ms after visual stimulus presentation of faces in adults and is significantly larger in amplitude in response to human faces compared to other stimuli (Bentin, Allison, Puce,

Perez, & McCarthy, 1996). Rudimentary forms of the N170, the N290, and the P400 have been extensively studied in infants and children as young as one year of age (de Haan & Nelson, 1999; Halit, de Haan, & Johnson, 2003). In addition, its development is continuous and gradual through adolescence. Specifically, Taylor, Batty, and Itier (2004) found that, by midadolescence, children still differ from adults in the pattern of their N170 despite developing a recognizable N170 as early as age 4. The N170 can also be modulated by emotion, such that fearful faces elicit an enhanced ERP compared to neutral, happy, or angry faces in 7-month-olds (Leppanen, Moulson, Vogel-Farley, & Nelson, 2007; Nelson & de Haan, 1996) as well as in adults (Blau, Maurer, Tottenham, & McCandliss, 2007; Leppanen et al., 2007).

Second, there are a number of studies that have examined differences in ERP and information processing between tasks with and without an affective component. For example, Pérez-Edgar and Fox (2003) presented 11-year-olds with both a traditional and emotion Stroop task. The emotion Stroop task involved words that had affective significance (e.g., socially threatening words) and subjects were asked to name the color of these words as well as words reflecting neutral or positive meanings. The authors report differences in ERP components as a function of the affective valence of the word. In another study, 7-year-old children selected for temperamental fearfulness heard words of positive, negative, and socially threatening meaning and had to report whether the speaker was a male or female (Pérez-Edgar & Fox, 2007). Again, ERPs time locked to the word presentation were computed, and differences were found between temperamentally fearful and nonfearful children in the morphology of the ERP components as a function of word meaning.

A third approach to the use of ERP methods in assessing emotion response has been to utilize traditional cognitive tasks and manipulate subject affect during the task. For example, Pérez-Edgar and Fox (2005a) presented children with a traditional Posner spatial cuing task under two different conditions. In one condition, the task was presented as a standard attention-spatial cuing task, while children in the second condition were told that they would be playing for points and were given feedback regarding their performance. In actuality, feedback was random and noncontingent on their actual responses. ERP measures of attention differed as a function of the affective manipulation, with the amplitude of specific components reflecting children's attempts to regulate their attention in the face of emotional demands.

In another series of studies, Lewis and colleagues induced negative emotional states during a go/no-go task while recording high-density EEG (Lewis et al., 2008; Lewis, Lamm, Segalowitz, Stieben, & Zelazo, 2006; Lewis & Stieben, 2004; Stieben et al., 2007). Using a sample of 5- to 16-year-old children, they found that the amplitudes of both the frontal N2 and P3 ERPs showed effects of negative emotion induction during the middle block of the task (Lewis et al., 2006; Lewis & Stieben, 2004). During this block, a change in the game's point-adjustment algorithm caused the subjects to lose all of their points earned from the previous block, with the effects of negative emotion persisting into the third block despite regaining their points for a prize. Increased N2 amplitudes for no-go versus go trials after emotion induction at all ages were taken to represent an effect of negative emotional states on effortful response inhibition. This task design has also been used to highlight different underlying mechanisms for externalizing and comorbid externalizing–internalizing subtypes of behavior problems in a sample of 8- to 12-year-old boys (Stieben et al., 2007). In the same go/no-go task, the comorbid children showed a significant increase in N2 amplitude in response to emotion induction, while externalizing children displayed consistently lower N2 amplitudes than both comorbid and control children across all blocks. Using the same sample, this task has also been used to identify changes in these mechanisms between pre- and postassessment during a 14-week community-based treatment program for the children and their parents (Lewis et al., 2008). Though children who showed improvement did not display differences in their N2 amplitude, they did show reductions in ventral prefrontal activation during the same time window of the N2 as determined by source modeling software. These results both differentiated them from nonimprovers and brought their activation levels in line with those of nonclinical children. For a more in-depth discussion of EEG/ERP and the emotion-cognition interface, interested readers should refer to the chapter by Bell and Diaz in this monograph.

Yet another approach to studying the temporal dynamics of emotion experience is to measure electromyographic (EMG) activity produced by the eyeblink startle response that is elicited by the sudden onset of an intense stimulus (i.e., startle probe). The potentiated startle response has been associated with amygdala activation (Davis, 2006; Lang, Bradley, & Cuthbert, 1998) and has been shown to be modulated by both emotionally valenced pictures (Cuthbert, Bradley, & Lang, 1996) as well as threat of an aversive stimulus, such as a shock (Grillon & Davis, 1997). Specifically, increased startle magnitude is observed when viewing unpleasant scenes (Lang et al., 1998) or negative facial expressions (Springer, Rosas, McGetrick, & Bowers, 2007), and in the presence of the threat (Grillon & Baas, 2003). In contrast, startle magnitude is attenuated during the presentation of pleasant stimuli (Lang et al., 1998). In addition, startle magnitude has been shown to be modulated by emotion regulation, such that it is decreased when participants are asked to suppress their emotions to unpleasant pictures and increased when asked to enhance their emotions to unpleasant pictures (Jackson, Malmstadt, Larson, & Davidson, 2000; Lee, Shackman, Jackson, & Davidson, 2009). Furthermore, startle magnitude is greatest during anticipation of viewing affective stimuli compared to either during the stimulus presentation or after the stimulus presentation (Dichter, Tomarken, & Baucom, 2002; Sabatinelli, Bradley, & Lang, 2001).

The startle response has been examined in both infants and children as measure of emotion. Balaban (1995) found that 5-month-old infants display a potentiated startle response while viewing angry faces and an attenuated startle to happy faces. Similar potentiated startle responses to aversive compared to pleasant pictures have been demonstrated in children (McManis, Bradley, Berg, Cuthbert, & Lang, 2001) and adolescents (Quevedo, Benning, Gunnar, & Dahl, 2009). Several studies have also examined individual differences in startle potentiation among infants (Schmidt & Fox, 1998b), children (Waters, Neumann, Henry, Craske, & Ornitz, 2008), and adolescents (Grillon, Dierker, & Merikangas, 1998; Merikangas, Avenevoli, Dierker, & Grillon, 1999; Reeb-Sutherland et al., 2009). Schmidt and Fox (1998b) found that negative reactive 9-month-old infants showed greater baseline startle and fear-potentiated startle to an approaching stranger than positive reactive infants. In addition, high anxious children have been shown to exhibit an increased startle response to the presentation of neutral and angry faces compared to nonanxious children (Waters et al., 2008). Grillon's research group (Grillon et al., 1998; Merikangas et al., 1999) demonstrated that adolescent girls with a family history for anxiety disorders showed increased startle response during safe cues, while boys showed an increased startle response during threat cues. Similarly, Reeb-Sutherland and colleagues (2009) found that anxious adolescents were high on measures of behavioral inhibition throughout early and middle childhood and showed a potentiated startle response to safety cues compared to nonanxious behaviorally inhibited adolescents and non-inhibited adolescents. Together, these studies suggest that examining the eye-blink startle response may be another useful measure for understanding the processing of emotional information over the course of development.

SUMMARY

In this brief paper, we have presented five principles that are important for utilizing physiological signals when assessing emotion in infants and young children. We have also argued that one of the critical qualities of emotion is its dynamic temporal pattern, and that physiological measures may be uniquely positioned to assess this pattern over time. While researchers often utilize static images to assess subjects' responses, evaluations, or appraisals of emotion, the real-life quality of emotion experience and expression is that of a dynamically changing signal and of a dynamically changing experience over time. Measurement thus requires an approach that can assess the time course, the information processing flow, and the changes that occur to affect the experience of emotion or success in its communication. Since physiological signals change dynamically, and often will track the temporal changes of emotion, they remain ideally suited for assessing emotion and its regulation over time.

THE HYPOTHALAMIC–PITUITARY–ADRENOCORTICAL SYSTEM AND EMOTION: CURRENT WISDOM AND FUTURE DIRECTIONS

Megan R. Gunnar and Emma K. Adam

Measures of the hypothalamic–pituitary–adrenocortical (HPA) axis can help us understand emotional development. However, to use these measures effectively, we must remember that the HPA system evolved to serve multiple essential functions, including regulation of glucose and carbohydrate metabolism and modulation of the immune and cardiovascular systems (Sapolsky, Romero, & Munck, 2000; Schulkin, 1999). While emotions do influence the HPA axis, this system is also capable of responding when the individual is comatose. Emotions are, thus, neither necessary nor often sufficient to account for increases and decreases in HPA activity. Nonetheless, when approached with an understanding of the complexity of its regulation, HPA activity can provide insights into emotions and their role in neurobehavioral development. This chapter provides an overview of some of the critical issues and current advances in using measures of HPA activity, particularly cortisol, in developmental studies of emotion. Because the HPA axis forms one arm of the mammalian stress system, this chapter should be read in conjunction with the chapter by Obradović and Boyce in this volume, which includes discussion of the other major arm, the sympathetic-adrenomedullary system.

The basic anatomy and physiology of the HPA axis and of the extra-hypothalamic corticotrophin-releasing hormone (CRH) system are covered in detail in other reviews (Gunnar & Quevedo, 2007; Joëls & Baram, 2009; Korosi & Baram, 2008; Papadimitriou & Priftis, 2009; Ulrich-Lai & Herman, 2009) and will not be covered here. The remainder of the chapter is written as if the reader has a full grasp of this information. Indeed, we argue that without grounding in the biology of these systems, researchers will be unable to make much headway in using activity of the HPA axis to illuminate understanding of emotional development.

Corresponding author: Megan R. Gunnar, Institute of Child Development, 51 East River Road, University of Minnesota, Minneapolis, MN 55455, email: Gunnar@umn.edu

With this caveat in mind, we first turn to a discussion of advances in methodological issues in the study of the HPA axis and emotion, followed by a discussion of new directions in HPA axis–emotion research. Throughout we highlight cross-cutting themes of this monograph, by paying close attention to: the time course of emotion–HPA associations; the importance of social context in contributing to and modifying HPA axis responses; examining the specificity of associations between HPA axis activity and emotion; and considering how the coordination of, and interactions between, multiple stress-sensitive systems might help us to better understand associations between HPA axis activity and both typical and atypical emotional functioning.

ADVANCES IN ASSESSING STRESS REACTIVITY OF THE HPA AXIS

Many studies of emotion and stress focus on relations between the dynamics of cortisol production in response to acute stressors. There have been a number of advances recently in understanding how to measure, analyze and interpret such acute responses.

What Activates the HPA Axis?

The literature on stress and the HPA axis is replete with laboratory paradigms in adults (Dickerson & Kemeny, 2004) and children (Gunnar, Talge, & Herrera, 2009) that while effective in provoking emotional responses fail to provoke increases in cortisol. Dickerson and Kemeny (2004) argued that these paradigms address the wrong emotion–motivational system, that the HPA axis evolved to respond to threats to self. Situations that create a significant threat to the physical self are difficult to create in the laboratory and, in any case, would not be ethical to use with children. Threats to the social self, they argued, engage the HPA axis, especially if the threat is perceived as uncontrollable and unpredictable. Their meta-analysis of the adult literature supported their contention. No similar meta-analysis has been performed on the child literature; however, there is evidence that situations that elicit self-evaluative emotions (embarrassment, shame) do produce elevations in cortisol among even in very young children (reviewed in Gunnar, Talge et al., 2009). Social rejection, another form of threat to the social self, also increases cortisol activity in young children (Gunnar, Sebanc, Tout, Donzella, & van Dulmen, 2003) and adolescents (Stroud et al., 2009). Identifying the correct emotion–motivational system to activate the HPA axis is critical in stress–emotion research. Given developmental changes in the self-system, further research is needed to identify developmentally appropriate situations that ethically create threats to the social self.

Creating situations that activate the axis can be challenging in the laboratory, hence researchers have sought to capture naturally occurring stressors by assessing the axis as children go about their everyday lives. Measurement in naturalistic environments allows an assessment of how typical social and emotional experiences relate to basal cortisol rhythms, and also cortisol reactivity to specific social or affective events. Several naturalistic studies have identified family conflict, parent marital problems, and parenting styles as potent influences on children's and adolescents' average cortisol levels in the home setting (Flinn & England, 1995; Pendry & Adam, 2007). Other studies relating diary reports of adolescent mood across the day to cortisol levels measured shortly thereafter have found that cortisol levels are significantly higher following adolescents' experiences of negative mood states, such as anger, worry, and loneliness (Adam, 2006; Doane & Adam, 2010). Thus, naturalistic studies support the notion that the HPA axis is strongly regulated by social emotions and social experience.

Researchers need to ensure they are assessing the correct emotion–motivational system to examine cortisol–emotion relationships and should move beyond considering cortisol as a general stress hormone responding to all levels and types of perceived stress and emotional experiences. Future research needs to continue to hone in on the specific socio-affective dimensions that contribute to the cortisol stress response at various ages.

Advances in Thinking About Baseline

In laboratory studies, the magnitude of the cortisol stress response is typically determined by comparison of poststressor values to measures of prestress baseline. Unfortunately, simply coming to the laboratory perturbs the system such that levels are either lower (often in infants and very young children; e.g., Larson, Gunnar, & Hertsgaard, 1991) or higher than the individual's nonstimulated levels. Because of negative feedback regulation, when levels are initially elevated, mild activation typically does not override negative feedback control, and as a result cortisol levels decrease over the stressor period. One way of overcoming this problem is to adapt the participant to the laboratory for a prolonged period (e.g., 30 to 60 min) and sample several times during that period to assure that cortisol levels have recovered to baseline prior to the imposition of the stressor task. Another method is to use a control day when the participants return to the laboratory knowing that they will only engage in nonchallenging activities (Lovallo, Farag, & Vincent, 2010; Stroud et al., 2009). Yet a third way to identify baseline is to collect a home baseline over the same time period as the laboratory assessments (Gunnar, Wewerka, Frenn, Long, & Griggs, 2009).

The bottom line is that without carefully identifying baseline activity of the system, measures of stress reactivity will not likely reflect the true reactivity of the system to whatever stressor the researcher is interested in. When most of the participants show declining values over a brief period in the laboratory, it is highly unlikely that this simply reflects the normal diurnal decrease and much more likely that the laboratory stressor was imposed on an already activated system.

Advances in Quantifying the Cortisol Stress Response

Early studies of the cortisol response to stressors in children and adolescents often relied on two measures: pre and post. Newer work involves multiple measures allowing much richer examination of the dynamics of cortisol reactivity and regulation. The use of multiple measures, though, requires attention to the timecourse of the HPA system in order to relate these measures to dynamic changes in emotion. Once the hypothalamus has received signals to produce a response, it takes about 5 min to observe elevations in ACTH and about 20–25 min to observe peak cortisol levels in plasma, with about 2 more min before levels peak in saliva (Gunnar & Tagle, 2007). *Thus, emotion–cortisol associations in response to acute stressors should be offset by about 20–25 min, with cortisol levels measured at a particular time reflecting affective experiences occurring roughly 20–25 min earlier.* Moreover, once produced, it takes time to clear cortisol from circulation, and, because of negative feedback regulation of the axis, once a significant response has been produced, the system is resistant to further responding, making it difficult to differentiate the impact of multiple stressors in the context of the same experimental session. Simply sampling one pretest and one posttest measure of response is inadequate to fully examine the response pattern of this system, as individuals differ in both rise time and time to return to baseline (Ramsay & Lewis, 2003). *Whenever possible, multiple samples leading up to the onset of the emotional stressor event and multiple samples following it, obtained at 10- to 20-min intervals, are advisable.*

When multiple measures were obtained, researchers used to rely on examining the total amount of cortisol produced in response to a stressor by calculating the area under the curve either with respect to ground or to initial level (Pruessner, Kirschbaum, Meinlschmid, & Hellhammer, 2003). Because interest has risen in examining the dynamics of changes over time in cortisol, newer studies have taken advantage of multilevel growth curve approaches and group-based trajectory modeling. While these statistical procedures have most often been applied to studying changes in cortisol across the waking day, they are equally applicable to studying the stress response and its relation to emotional reactions and coping processes. Briefly, in multilevel growth curve approaches, the investigator models an expected pattern of cortisol change over time, and examines whether variables chosen apriori cause deviations from that expected pattern (e.g., Doane & Adam, 2010). By contrast, group-based trajectory models identify and describe the patterns of cortisol change that exist within the data and then identify which variables are most associated with membership in each (e.g., Van Ryzin, Chatham, Kryzer, Kertes, & Gunnar, 2009). Both these approaches, unlike ANOVA (e.g., Van Goozen Matthys, Cohen-Kettenis, Buitelaar, & van Engeland, 2000), use maximum likelihood techniques that allow for missing observations and unequal spacing of observations.

Social Support and Self-Regulation

Relevant to both laboratory and fieldwork, and illustrating a major theme of this monograph (the importance of context), is evidence that social support, or its lack of, moderates relations between stressor exposure and HPA activity. Especially in young children who use their emotional behavior to solicit support from attachment figures and other adults, the presence of an adult with whom the child has a secure or trusting relationship may buffer or block elevations in cortisol even when the child appears to be quite emotionally frightened or otherwise distraught (see review, Gunnar & Donzella, 2002). With the development of self-regulatory competence, associations between individuals' emotional appraisals of stressful situations and their HPA responses begin to reflect regulatory strategies and competencies (Smeekens, Riksen-Walraven, & van Bakel, 2007). Indeed, cognitive-behavioral stress management training can produce dissociations between emotional appraisals of threat and HPA responding (e.g., Gaab, Sonderegger, Scherrer, & Ehlert, 2006). *Thus, children's social contexts, and their internalization of those contexts in the form of self-regulatory strategies, play an important role in modifying associations between emotion and HPA axis activity. Indeed, measures of HPA activity can provide a way of assessing the effectiveness of social support and self-regulatory competencies in preventing or reducing HPA responses to emotionally evocative and threatening situations.*

Recent Work on Chronic Stress and HPA Reactivity

Past or recent exposure to chronic stress can modify the impact of current or acute stress on HPA axis activity. This is because in response to chronic elevations in cortisol activity, the axis undergoes modifications that tend to bring activity to lower levels (Fries, Ziegler, Kurian, Jacoris, & Pollak, 2005; Miller, Chen, & Zhou, 2007). For example, chronic elevations in cortisol can down-regulate or reduce CRH activity in the hypothalamus, reducing ACTH and cortisol reactivity, while these same elevations produce an up-regulation or increase of CRH activity in the amygdala potentially increasing fearful or anxious responses to threat (Makino, Gold & Schulkin, 1994a, 1994b). As a result, chronic stress can produce heightened autonomic activity, accompanied by blunted HPA activity (Evans & Kim, 2007). Not all individuals respond to chronic stress with a blunting of the HPA system; some appear to increase the HPA set point exhibiting increased basal levels and larger stress responses. Lower basal and response levels following chronic childhood stress appear to be more commonly observed among psychiatrically healthy individuals (Carpenter et al., 2007; Elzinga et al., 2008); elevated basal levels and hyper-responsivity are more often observed among individuals with depression or internalizing problems (Ashman, Dawson, Panagiotides, Yamada, & Wilkinson, 2002; Heim & Nemeroff, 2001). Extreme blunting of the HPA axis to chronic stress, however, is associated with a variety of somatic disorders (Fries et al., 2005) and post-traumatic stress disorder (Yehuda, 2002). These patterns are noted among adults, and may be related early life stressors altering the development of the axis (Heim, Plotsky, & Nemeroff, 2004). Their expression may vary with the developmental period of assessment and duration of stressor exposure (De Bellis, 2001; Gunnar & Quevedo, 2007). Thus, without awareness of developmental histories of stress exposure (particularly exposure to severely stressful conditions), the current behavior of the HPA axis in relation to emotion is more difficult to explain. This theme is mirrored throughout this monograph, with multiple other chapters making note of the importance of developmental histories as modifiers of current emotion–biology associations (see, e.g., chapters in this volume by Adam; Feldman; Strang, Hanson, and Pollack; and Cicchetti and Rogosch). *The bottom line is that researchers interested in studying emotion–HPA axis relations in chronically stressed populations should be aware that chronic stress alters both basal activity and acute reactivity to stress.*

NEW DIRECTIONS IN HPA AXIS RESEARCH

There are a number of new directions in research on the HPA axis and emotions. Here we highlight several that we believe are likely to have the largest impact on developmental research on emotion and emotion regulation.

ADVANCES IN MEASUREMENT

Salivary and plasma cortisol reflect moment to moment changes in cortisol production. When questions of chronic stress are the focus, the researcher is interested in cortisol production over a longer time frame. The production of cortisol over longer time frames can be measured in hair. Cortisol and other endogenous substances accumulate in hair with their location on the hair shaft reflecting their production levels at the time the hair was formed. This has allowed researchers to collect hair, divide the hair shaft into lengths (e.g., 3 cm to assess every 3 months of cortisol production; 50 mg per segment needed), and use hair analysis as a way of creating a calendar of cortisol production (see Kirschbaum, Tietze, Skoluda, & Dettenborn, 2009). Recent evidence suggests that variables such as hair color, curvature, or number of washes per week do not confound measurement (Kirschbaum et al., 2009). Furthermore, studies in rhesus macaques have shown high correlations between hair measures and repeated samples of cortisol collected over a chronic stress period (Davenport, Tiefenbacher, Lutz, Novak, & Meyer, 2006). To our knowledge, so far the only published report using hair cortisol measures in children was an analysis of stress in the neonatal nursery (Yamada et al., 2007). Nonetheless, this technique is highly promising for the study of longer periods of stress–emotion exposure.

PUBERTY AND PLASTICITY

Activity of the HPA axis changes with development (Gunnar & Quevedo, 2007). While changes during infancy and early development are certainly of import, there is increasing interest in the changes that occur during puberty. With puberty, basal cortisol levels begin to rise and there is increasing evidence that over the pubertal transition, pubertal maturity is associated with heightened cortisol reactivity (Gunnar, Wewerka et al., 2009; Stroud et al., 2009). Animal studies suggest that marked changes in HPA axis reactivity during pubertal development open up a second sensitive period, with prenatal and infancy being the first one (see discussion of epigenetics, later), when the HPA axis is especially sensitive to being programmed or reprogrammed by experience (Romeo, 2010). Puberty is also associated with marked alterations in the functioning of neural systems involved in emotional responses to threat and reward (Dahl, 2004; Dahl & Gunnar, 2009). The confluence of developmental changes in neuroendocrine and emotion systems over the course of puberty may help explain why puberty is associated with marked increases in stress-related psychological and behavioral disorders. This confluence, plus the opportunity to use neuroimaging techniques to study the developing brain in later childhood and adolescence, provides a unique opportunity to study HPA axis–brain–emotion dynamics across a period of great significance for the understanding of developmental psychopathology. Furthermore, there is increasing interest in understanding how early experience effects on the developing stress–emotion system interact with experiences during the pubertal period to influence both adolescent and adult outcomes (e.g., Halligan, Herbert, Goodyer, & Murray, 2007).

With advances in neuroimaging, there has been a rise in interest in using functional imaging to interrogate the relations between HPA axis activity and emotion. Some of this work focuses on the impact of stress on emotional learning and memory (van Stegeren, 2009), while other work focuses on developing a better understanding of the neural correlates of cortisol regulation in response to stress (Dedovic, Duchesne, Andrews, Engert, & Pruessner, 2009). To our knowledge, none of this work has involved children or adolescents, although some of the procedures would be highly appropriate for use in these populations, with appropriate attention to the methodological issues in hormone-imaging studies (King & Liberzon, 2009). Key findings from stress-imaging research include evidence that activity of the HPA axis, in conjunction with central (brain produced) norepinephrine (NE), plays complex roles in emotional learning that may vary with age and gender (Stark et al., 2006; van Stegeren, 2009). The amygdala, hippocampus, and several regions of the prefrontal cortex are targets of NE and cortisol in producing these effects. Findings from this literature reveal differential impacts of stress on emotional learning by gender (Merz et al., 2010; Stark et al., 2006) that may have significant implications for our understanding of adolescent-emergent sex differences in affective pathology (see also, Goldstein, Jerram, Abbs, Whitfield-Gabrieli, & Makris, 2010).

Studies attempting to understand the correlates of brain activity during a stressor and activity of the HPA axis (Dedovic et al., 2009; Dedovic, Wadiwalla, Engert, & Pruessner, 2009) have also highlighted the importance of gender, puberty, and the impact of stressor type and stress anticipation, on the neural correlates of stress experiences and HPA axis activity. There is also growing interest and some evidence that experiences in early in life, at least when retrospectively reported, influence both the patterning of neural activity and the magnitude of response to stressor tasks in adulthood (Buss et al., 2007).

Genetics and Epigenetics

Examining genetic variations relevant to HPA axis functioning and their interactions with experience is a noninvasive approach to moving "beyond cortisol" to gain insights into the role of other levels of the axis in emotional functioning. HPA axis polymorphisms, such as CRH receptor, and glucocorticoid and mineralocorticoid receptor polymorphisms have been linked to individual differences in reactivity to laboratory-based stressors (Thode et al., 2008; Wüst et al., 2004; Wüst, Federenko, Hellhammer, & Kirschbaum, 2000) and to individual differences in risk for development of depression and posttraumatic stress disorder (Gillespie, Phifer, Bradley, & Ressler, 2009). Recent studies have found that interactions between HPA axis polymorphisms and measures of early life adversity provide the best prediction to stress reactivity, depression, and PTSD (Binder et al., 2008; Gillespie et al., 2009; Tyrka et al., 2009).

Additional genetic approaches have focused on epigenetic changes, rather than differences in gene sequence. Epigenetic changes are experience-driven, semipermanent alterations to portions of the DNA that can serve to either turn up or turn down expression of particular genes. Recent research supports the possibility of experience-based epigenetic programming of the GR gene in humans. Epigenetic changes to the GR promoter region have been observed in postmortem hippocampal tissues of suicide victims exposed to child abuse, and in lymphocytes in the cord blood of infants exposed to prenatal maternal depressed mood (McGowan et al., 2009; Oberlander et al., 2008). In the latter study, the observed epigenetic changes had functional consequences, predicting greater infant cortisol reactivity to a challenge task at 3 months of age. Epigenetic changes are however tissue specific, such that changes seen in peripheral cells may not reflect epigenetic changes and gene expression in other sites of interest, such as cortico-limbic circuits involved in emotion. As a result, interpretations of epigenetic data need to be specific to the particular cell type (e.g., lymphocytes) examined. *Genetic and epigenetic approaches, particularly when used in combination with functional measures of HPA axis activity and examined in relation to histories of stress exposure, are likely provide important insights into how activity at multiple levels of the HPA axis relate to typical and atypical emotional functioning.*

INTERACTIONS BETWEEN HPA AXIS ACTIVITY AND OTHER STRESS-SENSITIVE BIOLOGICAL SYSTEMS

Another new direction for research on the HPA axis research and emotion is to examine interactions between the HPA axis and other stress-sensitive biological systems. A key theme of this monograph is that no one biological system acts in isolation. Newer research, rather than simply giving a nod to the fact that we know multiple systems are involved, attempts to measure multiple systems, examine cross-system interactions, and consider their implications for understanding emotional processes.

HPA/ANS Interactions

One set of studies includes simultaneous measures of autonomic nervous system activity (sympathetic and parasympathetic activity; see Obradović & Boyce and Fox et al. chapters in this volume) and HPA axis activity and examines how these systems interact to predict internalizing and externalizing disorders in children and adolescents (Bauer, Quas, & Boyce, 2002). For example, Gordis and colleagues found that low cortisol reactivity predicted higher levels of aggressive behavior in adolescents, but only in the presence of low sympathetic reactivity, as indicated by lower reactivity of salivary alpha amylase (a proposed surrogate marker for sympathetic activation) (Gordis, Granger, Susman, & Trickett, 2006). Attenuated responses of both the HPA and SAM are hypothesized to reflect low arousal, and low inhibition, fear, and anxiety, making risk taking and aggression more likely (Gordis et al., 2006). In a study of 8- to 9-year-olds El-Sheikh, Erath, Buckhalt, Granger, and Mize (2008) found that the combination of *high* basal SNS activity (alpha amylase or skin conductance) and high basal cortisol was associated with higher levels of internalizing and externalizing symptoms; on its own, without consideration of level of SNS activity, cortisol was not a significant predictor of child adjustment. Thus, in several studies, consideration of HPA/SNS interactions shed greater light than considering either variable alone.

HPA Interactions With Immune/Inflammatory Activity

Another set of studies examines interactions between emotion, HPA axis activity, and immune/inflammatory system activity. For example, studies of children examine the impact of day care and school experiences on cortisol levels and, in turn, the impact of variations in cortisol for immune function and illness (see, e.g., Boyce & Ellis, 2005; Watamura, Coe, Laudenslager, & Robertson, 2010). Other adolescent research examines the impact of early adverse experience on the ability of glucocorticoids to regulate inflammatory responses to stress (see Miller & Chen, 2010). Collectively, these studies show a strong impact of social context and emotional experience on both HPA axis activity and inflammation. On the other side of the causal coin, the potential *impact* of stress-related alterations in immune functioning and inflammation on emotion needs attention. Theoretical models and meta-analytic findings suggest that elevations in cytokines such as IL6 contribute to "sickness behavior" and elevated depressive symptoms and diagnoses in adults (Dowlati et al., 2010). The extent to which stress-related alterations in inflammatory processes contribute to internalizing symptoms and behaviors in child and adolescent populations remains to be examined. *These studies suggest that the HPA-axis/inflammation interplay is a potential mechanism by which socioemotional experiences may be translated into health outcomes and raise the possibility that immune and inflammatory activity, and individual differences in the ability of the HPA axis to contain such activity, may also be important contributors to individual differences in emotional experience.*

118

CONCLUSIONS

Measuring cortisol does not provide a simple read-out of child and adolescent emotional states. As Seymour Levine cautioned years ago (Levine & Wiener, 1989), it is not the "emotion juice." Yet the activity of the HPA axis can be used to examine emotions and emotion-regulatory functioning when the research is conducted with attention to the neurobiology of the system, its development, and the regulatory systems that impact its activity. Studies incorporating measures of this system have burgeoned in recent years. We are, however, just beginning to tap the potential of what we can learn by close examination of how this endocrine system functions in both typically developing, low-risk children and those at risk for developing emotional disorders. We are also just beginning to understand how the HPA axis interacts with other stress systems to help explain both normal and atypical emotional functioning. While many of the new directions in HPA–emotion research so far have involved primarily adult populations, this work offers promising avenues for developmental studies of stress and emotion.

DEVELOPMENTAL PSYCHOPHYSIOLOGY OF EMOTION PROCESSES

Jelena Obradović and W. Thomas Boyce

Children's bodies respond to emotional stimuli and events with a set of highly integrated neurobiological responses that are related to the experience, expression, and regulation of emotions. This chapter addresses how the physiological activity of the *autonomic nervous system* (ANS) relates to various components of emotion processing. Researchers have linked ANS activity to emotion by examining (1) how ANS activity changes in response to emotional stimuli, (2) how ANS reactivity relates to concurrent displays of emotion expression or behavioral regulation strategies, and (3) how individual differences in ANS reactivity to laboratory stressors relate to the variability of behavioral problems associated with emotion dysregulation. This chapter will review recent and cutting-edge research, discuss conceptual and methodological issues that still need to be addressed, and identify important directions for future work.

PHYSIOLOGICAL PROCESSES AND MEASURES OF AUTONOMIC REACTIVITY

Psychological, emotionally laden stressors are assessed initially within cortico-limbic structures, including the orbital prefrontal cortex, anterior cingulate cortex, amygdala, and hippocampus. The brain responds rapidly to stressful environmental stimuli, primarily via the *locus coeruleus*, a brainstem nucleus with noradrenergic projections to the hypothalamus that initiates and

Preparation of this chapter was supported in part by a research grant from the Canadian Institute for Advanced Research (CIFAR) to Dr. Obradović. Dr. Obradović is the Great-West Life Junior Fellow in the CIFAR's Experience-based Brain and Biological Development Program and Junior Fellow Academy. Dr. Boyce is a Fellow of the CIFAR and holds the Sunny Hill Health Centre/BC Leadership Chair in Child Development at the University of British Columbia.

Corresponding author: Jelena Obradović, Stanford University, School of Education, 485 Lasuen Mall, Stanford, CA 94305-3096, email: jelena.obradovic@stanford.edu

120

regulates the ANS response. Specifically, the *sympathetic nervous system*'s (SNS) neurons secrete norepinephrine and epinephrine, which bind to receptors in various target tissues and facilitate a fight-or-flight response by increasing heart rate (HR), diverting blood flow from the skin and stomach to the muscles and brain, stimulating production of glucose, dilating pupils, raising cardiac output, and launching other preparatory physiologic processes (Sapolsky, Romero, & Munck, 2000). *Pre-ejection period* (PEP) is a noninvasive cardiac measure of pure SNS activation (Cacioppo et al., 1994). It represents the period of isovolumetric contraction indexed by the time in milliseconds from left ventricular depolarization to the opening of the aortic valve and the passage of blood into the aortic outflow tract from the left ventricle. Shorter PEP intervals indicate higher SNS activation and are correlated with faster HR and increased cardiac output. Some SNS postganglionic neurons stimulate the eccrine glands of the skin by releasing the neurotransmitter acetylcholine (ACH), so the levels of sweat in eccrine gland ducts can be used to measure peripheral SNS activity (Dawson, Shell, & Fillion, 2007). Elevated *skin conductance level* (SCL) indicates higher SNS activation, as increased sweat causes the skin's surface to be less resistant and more conductive.

At the same time, the *parasympathetic nervous system*'s (PNS) neurons secrete ACH, which serves to restore homeostasis by countering and curtailing SNS activation. The only noninvasive measure of PNS stress response is *respiratory sinus arrhythmia* (RSA), which refers to high frequency HR variation controlled by efferent fibers of the vagus nerve during the respiratory cycle (Porges, 2001). A decrease in RSA (i.e., vagal withdrawal) generates a faster HR and allows an increase in SNS input to the heart, whereas an increase in RSA (i.e., vagal augmentation) slows the HR and inhibits SNS input (Porges, 1995, 2003, 2007). Many researchers also employ integrative, summative indices of overall autonomic reactivity, such as HR and blood pressure (BP), which are influenced by both SNS and PNS activity (Berntson, Cacioppo, & Quigley, 1995; Berntson, Quigly, & Lozano, 2007) and thus can be used only broadly in examining how ANS psychophysiology relates to emotion processes. For a more detailed description of ANS responses to stress and measurement approaches, as well as other indices, see Berntson et al. (2007), Dawson et al. (2007), Obradović and Boyce (in press), Porges (2007), and Sapolsky et al. (2000).

ASSOCIATIONS BETWEEN ANS ACTIVITY AND EMOTIONS

Even after decades of research on psychophysiology of emotions in adults, the physiological profiles associated with discrete emotions are still not clearly delineated. A meta-analysis revealed that the most robust physiological difference is between positive and negative emotions (Cacioppo, Berntson, Larsen,

Poehlmann, & Ito, 2000). ANS reactivity, as indexed by measures such as HR, BP, and PEP, is significantly higher during negative emotional states than during positive emotional states. Increases in ANS reactivity in response to negative stimuli have also been noted in children (Cole, Zahn-Waxler, Fox, Usher, & Welsh, 1996; Gilissen, Koolstra, Van IJzendoorn, Bakermans-Kranenburg, & Van der Veer, 2007). In addition, increases in HR during emotional challenges have been linked to concurrent expressions of negative affect in toddlers, as indexed by facial distress and crying (Buss, Goldmsmith, & Davidson, 2005). However, significant associations between ANS reactivity and concurrent expression of distress have not been consistently reported (see Brooker & Buss, 2010; Quas, Hong, Alkon, & Boyce, 2000). Ascertaining the physiology of discrete emotional states in children has been hindered by the practice of averaging physiological responses across displays of fear, anger, and sadness to create an index of overall negative affectivity that may obscure important differences. Studies show that in adults, anger was more strongly linked to vascular reactivity than fear and less strongly linked to cardiac reactivity (Cacioppo et al., 2000). In infants, an expression of anger, but not sadness, was uniquely related to ANS reactivity (Lewis, Ramsay, & Sullivan, 2006).

Further, it is difficult to isolate ANS correlates of emotion expression from individual differences in the physiological responses that underpin processes of emotion reactivity and regulation. Generally, both hypo- and hyper-arousal to laboratory challenges have been linked to behaviors associated with maladaptive emotion reactivity and regulation (Beauchaine, Gatzke-Kopp, & Mead, 2007; Boyce et al., 2001; Calkins & Dedmon, 2000; Calkins & Keane, 2004). Children who show high levels of fearfulness, behavioral inhibition, and internalizing symptoms tend to exhibit heightened levels of SNS and PNS reactivity (Boyce et al., 2001; Kagan, Snidman, Zentner, & Peterson, 1999; Weems, Zakem, Costa, Cannon, & Watts, 2005), whereas children who show high levels of impulsivity, disinhibition, emotional lability, and other externalizing symptoms tend to show low SNS reactivity and, less consistently, low PNS reactivity (Boyce et al., 2001; Calkins & Dedmon, 2000; Crowell et al., 2006; Herpertz et al., 2003; Gatzke-Kopp et al., 2002; Lorber, 2004). However, excessive RSA withdrawal has also been associated with externalizing symptoms (see the Beauchaine chapter in this volume; Beauchaine, Hong, & Marsh, 2008). Recent work indicates that the association between ANS physiology and developmental psychopathology may additionally vary with the severity and comorbidity of behavioral and emotional problems (Boyce et al., 2001; Calkins, Graziano, & Keane, 2007; Kibler, Prosser, & Ma, 2004). Both externalizing and internalizing symptoms comprise numerous disorders that may be linked to different physiologic and emotion processes (see the Dahl, Silk, & Siegle chapter in this volume for a review of emotional mechanisms that could yield functional impairments). Thus, more work is needed to delineate how variability in ANS responsivity across different systems and variability in emotion processes jointly contribute to the development and maintenance of symptoms associated with over- and under-controlled affect.

Although biological systems respond to environmental threats, demands, and challenges in a highly integrated manner, with their primary function to protect the organism and promote active coping, emerging evidence suggests a possible degree of specificity across different indices of ANS activity. Since SCL reactivity can be elicited by the threat of punishment, some researchers propose that it may reflect individual differences in passive avoidance tendencies (Fowles, Kochanska, & Murray, 2000; Shannon, Beauchaine, Brenner, Neuhaus, & Gatzke-Kopp, 2007). In contrast, PEP seems to be particularly sensitive to rewards or anticipation of rewards, leading researchers to conceptualize it as an index of behavioral approach tendencies and reward sensitivity (Beauchaine, 2001; Brenner, Beauchaine, & Sylvers, 2005; Crowell et al., 2005, 2006). Since PNS modulates the activation of SNS stress response, RSA has been regarded as a measure of children's capacity for regulatory responses to positive and negative environmental demands (Beauchaine, 2001; Beauchaine et al., 2007; Porges, 2001, 2007). High RSA reactivity to challenges and stressors has been linked to more adaptive emotion regulation strategies, self-soothing behaviors, better social skills, and lower levels of emotional behavior problems and negative reactivity (Calkins, 1997, Calkins, Blandon, Williford, & Keane, 2007; Calkins, Graziano, & Keane, 2007; Calkins & Keane, 2004). These possibly unique relations between different indices of ANS reactivity and behavioral regulation need to be further tested by controlling for the interplay of the two branches (see El-Sheikh et al., 2009).

TIMING AND DEVELOPMENTAL COURSE OF EMOTION EXPRESSION AND REGULATION

Since emotion expression and regulation are dynamic processes (see the Fox, Kirwan, & Reeb-Sutherland chapter for discussion of onset, offset, and duration of emotions), it is important to be cognizant of issues related to the time course of ANS activity. First, measures of PEP and RSA are better suited to capture instantaneous responses to emotional stimuli than SCL, which can be assessed 1 to 3 s after the stimuli presentation (Dawson et al., 2007). Second, a visit to a laboratory setting can elicit fear, anxiety, frustration, or excitement and pleasure in children, further complicating the onset of emotional experience and measures of baseline ANS activity. A recent study shows that a high baseline measure of adrenocortical activity collected at the beginning of the study protocol, possibly indexing high levels of children's anticipation, exacerbated the risk for rumination and depressive symptoms in victimized children (Rudolph, Troop-Gordon, & Granger, 2010). Moreover, Hinnant and El-Sheikh (2009) reported that the interaction between children's baseline RSA value and RSA regulation in response to an interpersonal stressor predicted later emotional disturbances. It is thus important that future research address the role of the individual's physiological and emotional state prior to the onset of discrete emotional stimuli in order to understand consequent emotional responses. Third, researchers need to move beyond analyzing a single indicator of ANS reactivity in order to capture onset, offset, and duration of the emotional experience. For example, Santucci et al. (2008) found that lower RSA recovery, but not reactivity, following an emotional challenge was associated with poor emotion regulation strategies in response to frustration. Thus, it is important to examine not only how initial or peak ANS levels relate to emotions but also how long changes in ANS activation persist following an emotional experience. Future studies may benefit from using trajectory analyses to examine how the time course of ANS activation relates to concurrent facial, bodily, or vocal displays of emotions. In a recent study, Brooker and Buss (2010) found that both dynamic and static measures of RSA change during a fear-inducing challenge were important in understanding toddlers' affect and emotion behaviors. Growth curve modeling would also enable researchers to examine the dynamic covariation of PNS and SNS activity in the context of emotion processing.

In addition to considering the time course of the acute emotional experience, it is important to examine the longitudinal interplay of emotional and physiological development. There is a need for more systematic study of the longitudinal stability and variability of physiological responses to emotionally charged stimuli across different indices and developmental periods. Maturational changes in respiratory and heart rates (Bar-Haim, Marshall, & Fox, 2000), as well as the development of regulatory capabilities during early childhood, must be taken into account. For example, high levels of basal RSA have been associated with negative emotionality in infancy (Porges, Doussard-Roosevelt, & Maiti, 1994; Stifter & Fox, 1990), whereas later in childhood high levels of basal RSA have been linked to better emotion regulation (Beauchaine, 2001; Blair & Peters, 2003; Fabes, Eisenberg, & Eisenbud, 1993). Furthermore, as suggested by Quigley and Stifter (2006), young children may be incapable of producing a phasic sympathetic cardiac response; may have no physiological need for sympathetic reactivity, given that they show effective parasympathetic regulation; or may have sufficiently low basal PEPs to preclude any additional shortening. However, as children develop, this branch of ANS may become more responsive (Buss et al., 2005; Talge, Donzela, & Gunnar, 2008). Yet there is a lack of studies examining how ANS activity changes in the same children over distinct developmental periods (see the Katz & Rigterink chapter in this volume for an exception).

THE CONTEXT OF PHYSIOLOGICAL MEASUREMENT

As interest in the physiology of emotion processes continues to grow, researchers will need to address some important measurement issues. First, there is very little consistency in the stimuli used to elicit ANS reactivity in children. Many researchers employ various tasks and challenges—physical, sensory, social, emotional, and cognitive—in order to capture an overall measure of children's ANS reactivity (Alkon et al., 2003; Boyce et al., 2001). ANS reactivity is often averaged across the tasks to create a single index, despite the fact that these different tasks may induce diverse emotions and opposing physiological responses. Although this approach can provide a broad index of the child's ANS reactivity, it may obscure our understanding of physiological correlates of specific emotional experiences. Thus, it is important that researchers more closely scrutinize how physiological responses are elicited and measured. Recent studies have begun to examine how the effect of ANS reactivity on adaptation varies across the nature of the laboratory challenge (see Chen, Matthews, Salomon, & Ewart, 2002; El-Sheikh et al., 2009; Hinnant & El-Sheikh, 2009; Obradović, Bush, & Boyce, 2011). For example, our recent work suggests that ANS reactivity to cognitive versus interpersonal stressors may represent different markers of biological sensitivity to marital conflict exposure (Obradović et al., 2011). In addition, there is a need to determine what types of stimuli are best at measuring the variability in psychophysiological responses in children. Buss and colleagues suggested that individual differences in fear responses may be best captured in a situation of mild threat, since the most dysregulated children may exhibit exaggerated and maladaptive fear responses (Buss, Davidson, Kalin, & Goldsmith, 2004).

Similarly, since the nature of the tasks vary greatly, it is important to determine that the assessed physiological responses reflect emotional experiences rather than task characteristics. Emotions in preverbal children may be evoked by frustration tasks, object denial, or the presence of a stranger, whereas emotions in verbal children may be elicited by watching emotionally laden films, listening to audio-taped conflicts, recalling personal events, or verbally responding to situational vignettes. Regardless of the nature of the emotional task, baseline ANS activity levels are generally measured while children are relaxed, resting, or attending to a calming story or video, as a means of keeping them still. This is potentially problematic, because ANS response can be activated by simple motor activity, such as gesturing and speaking, or by focused attention and nonchallenging social engagement (Bazhenova & Porges, 1997; Bernardi et al., 2000; Kamarck & Lovallo, 2003; Porges et al., 2007). Studies should thus include control tasks designed to parallel the motor and engagement demands of challenge tasks, in order to isolate ANS responses elicited by emotional or stressful experiences from peripheral triggers of cardiovascular activation (Bush, Alkon, Obradović, Stamperdahl, & Boyce, 2011).

The lack of a standardized set of stimuli that can be used to elicit emotions and physiological responses across different ANS systems and developmental periods also undermines longitudinal research. For example, PEP reactivity can be difficult to elicit in young children using challenges that are known to generate HR and PNS reactivity (Alkon et al., 2003; Buss et al., 2005; Quigley & Stifter, 2006; Talge et al., 2008). Further, tasks known to elicit emotions and physiological responses in infants may be ineffective with older children, raising additional concerns regarding measurement equivalence and the sources of longitudinal change. Thus, developing a standardized battery of challenge and control tasks would facilitate more rigorous assessments, as well as comparisons across different developmental periods and populations.

MULTIPLE LEVELS OF ANALYSIS

Emotionally stressful or challenging experiences trigger a set of highly integrated physiological responses that implicate multiple systems. However, only a few studies have examined concurrent SNS and PNS activity within the same child, identifying four distinct ANS reactivity profiles: (1) *coactivation*, as indexed by SNS and PNS activation; (2) *coinhibition*, as indexed by SNS and PNS withdrawal; (3) *reciprocal parasympathetic activation*, as indexed by SNS withdrawal and PNS activation; and (4) *reciprocal sympathetic activation*, as indexed by SNS activation and PNS withdrawal (see Alkon et al., 2003; Berntson, Cacioppo, & Quigley, 1993; Salomon, Matthews, & Allen, 2000). Recent studies suggest that examining the concurrent activity and interaction of the two ANS branches has potential to better differentiate groups of children who show distinct patterns of behavioral symptoms and susceptibilities to contextual influences (Boyce et al., 2001; El-Sheikh et al., 2009). However, the prevalences of the four ANS profiles seem to vary across age and tasks (Alkon et al., 2003; Salomon et al., 2000), suggesting that activation of the two ANS branches may change with the nature of stimuli and maturation. ANS reactivity profiles need to be further studied in response to varying emotional challenges and across time.

Similarly, examining associations between ANS reactivity and the hypothalamic–pituitary–adrenocortical (HPA) axis response (see the Gunnar & Adam chapter in this volume for review) may reveal distinct roles that the two systems play in processing various emotional stressors. For example, Lewis and colleagues (2006) found that ANS reactivity was uniquely associated with anger, whereas HPA reactivity was uniquely related to sadness. Moreover, a few studies have shown that children who exhibit either concurrently low or high activation of both the ANS and HPA axis may be at highest risk for emotional

126

behavior problems (El-Sheikh, Erath, Buckhalt, Granger, & Mize, 2008; Gordis et al., 2006), providing initial evidence for an additive model of physiological vulnerability proposed by Bauer, Quas, and Boyce (2002).

More studies of children's physiological reactivity should also examine the co-occurrence of behavioral and physiological responses to emotional stimuli. Although both elevated temperamental reactivity (i.e., negative emotionality) and physiological reactivity have been found to index children's susceptibility to contextual influences (Belsky, Bakermans-Kranenburg, van IJzendoorn, 2007; Belsky & Pluess, 2009), it is unclear whether behavioral indices of emotion reactivity mirror concurrent physiological reactivity, suggesting representation of the same phenomena at different levels of analysis, or whether the two systems operate in an independent fashion (Obradović & Boyce, 2009). Similarly, studies relating genetic variation to physiological reactivity phenotypes (Out, Pieper, Bakermans-Kranenburg, & van IJzendoorn, 2010; Wang et al., 2009; Wu, Snieder, & de Geus, 2010) suggest a current research frontier with the potential to advance our understanding of emotion processing at molecular level.

Identifying physiological processes that underlie emotion expression, reactivity, and regulation across multiple levels of analysis can provide only a partial understanding of how children negotiate emotional challenges and stressors in real life. Researchers must also consider the environmental influences that affect variability among children's physiological responses, as well as their implications for adaptation. Recent studies have shown that temperamentally fearful children with low-quality parent-child relationships demonstrate high SCL reactivity to fear-inducing films, whereas fearful children with high-quality relationships demonstrate low SCL reactivity (Gilissen et al., 2007; Gilissen, Bakermans-Kranenburg, Van IJzendoorn, & Van der Veer, 2008). Similarly, Blandon, Calkins, Keane, and O'Brien (2008) reported that children with high basal RSA had lower levels of emotion regulation only if they were also exposed to high levels of maternal depressive symptoms.

A growing number of studies show that ANS reactivity can also moderate the effect of family adversity, such as marital conflict, harsh parenting, and parental psychopathology, on children's emotional and behavioral adaptation. For example, high SNS reactivity has been linked to higher levels of social and emotional problems, but only in contexts of high adversity (Cummings, El-Sheikh, Kouros, & Keller, 2007; El-Sheikh, Keller, & Erath, 2007; Shannon et al., 2007). Similarly, we recently reported that high RSA reactivity exacerbated the effects of high family adversity on adaptive functioning but promoted better adaptive functioning in the context of low family adversity (Obradović, Bush, Stamperdahl, Adler, & Boyce, 2010). In contrast, several studies suggest that high PNS reactivity buffers children against the deleterious effects of marital conflict and hostile-withdrawn parenting (El-Sheikh, Harger, & Whitson, 2001; El-Sheikh & Whitson, 2006; Katz, 2007;

Katz & Rigterink chapter in this volume). Examining emotion processes related to ANS reactivity during laboratory challenges may shed more light on when heightened arousal indicates higher susceptibility to environmental influences and when it buffers children from those effects (Obradović et al., 2011).

With recent advances in measuring variability in gene expression and epigenetic modifications, researchers have an opportunity to discover how social context shapes children's neurobiological reactivity across development. Emerging evidence suggests that experiences of early family disadvantage or abuse may play an important role in "programming" individuals' stress responsivity (Chen, Miller, Kobor, & Cole, 2010; McGowan et al., 2009; Miller et al., 2009; Oberlander et al., 2008). A recent study showed that the interplay between genetic polymorphisms and the degree of promoter region DNA methylation significantly predicted unresolved emotional state of mind regarding early experiences of loss and trauma (van IJzendoorn, Caspers, Bakermans-Kranenburg, Beach, & Philibert, 2010). Researchers interested in studying ANS correlates of emotion processing should also consider how early experiences influence the development of different ANS responsivity phenotypes.

CONCLUSION

In sum, extant psychophysiological studies chart some basic associations among ANS activity, emotion expression, emotion regulation strategies, and behavioral problems associated with emotional dysregulation. Presently, a growing interest in the complexities that underlie the physiology of emotion processes is ushering a new wave of studies characterized by more dynamic and methodologically rigorous approaches to measuring associations between ANS activity and emotions across multiple systems and levels of analysis. Researchers are also increasingly focused on the role that environmental contexts play in moderating the association between physiology and adaptation. Future research will also provide exciting opportunities to examine how early emotional experiences influence the development of children's physiological activity.

ASPECTS OF PSYCHOPHYSIOLOGICAL DATA ANALYSIS: EEG COHERENCY AND fMRI CONNECTIVITY MAPPING

Peter C. M. Molenaar and Kathleen M. Gates

The field of cognitive and affective neuroscience has flourished in the past decades. The increased use of brain imaging techniques, in particular, the mapping of functional connections between brain regions based on electroencephalographic (EEG) and functional magnetic resonance (fMRI) registrations (cf. Friston, Ashburner, Kiebel, Nichols, & Penny, 2008), contributed significantly to this development. Brain imaging has been very instrumental in identifying cortical regions associated with emotional states, showing for instance that approach-related positive emotions and withdrawal-related negative emotions are correlated with distinct patterns of asymmetrical activity of prefrontal regions (cf. Fox, 2008, for a comprehensive review of these and many other findings). EEG and fMRI studies have also been essential in uncovering the neural bases of emotional development, in particular, the development of processing emotion in the face (cf. de Haan & Matheson, 2009; Nelson, de Haan, & Thomas, 2006).

In what follows, we present an overview of a few key aspects of psychophysiological data analysis that are important in applied brain imaging, in particular, the estimation of coherency and connectivity maps based on, respectively, multivariate EEG and fMRI time series. Coherency and connectivity maps constitute the state of the art in functional brain imaging. Thus, the focus of this chapter is somewhat distinct from those in the rest of this monograph. We seek to introduce the reader interested in developmental affective neurophysiology to some leading-edge approaches to analyzing data on neural activity that can be used to generate new insights into affective and cognitive processes. The presentation will be heuristic and general, focusing on relevant statistical models and their interpretation. Illustrative findings are offered as examples. However, the focus remains on methods and the reader interested in developmental affective neuroscience theory is referred to the excellent

---

Corresponding author: Peter C. M. Molenaar, 113 Henderson Building, The Pennsylvania State University, University Park, PA 16802, email: pxm21@psu.edu

monograph by Nelson et al. (2006) as well as the edited volume by de Haan and Matheson (2009). Where relevant, insight into issues specifically related to research with children or standard aspects of experimental psychophysiogical designs is given. Even with these limitations, it will be impossible to cover all important aspects within the confines of a single chapter. Therefore, ample references to the published literature will be given where the reader can find more complete coverage.

ANALYSIS OF MULTILEAD EEG

EEG registrations obtained with multilead montages are standard in psychophysiological research. Often the aim is twofold. First, researchers wish to derive topographic maps displaying the dynamic interaction of the activity of different neocortical areas. Second, researchers seek to identify the neural sources underlying this activity. For instance, as mentioned in the introduction, asymmetry has been linked to emotional regulation and appears to influence the development of emotion regulation and tendencies. In terms of absolute activity, increased levels of right frontal activity have consistently been associated with withdrawal and negative affect at both the trait (Fox, 1994; Tomarken, Davidson, & Henriques, 1990) and state levels (Allen, Harmon-Jones, & Cavender, 2001).

This section outlines the use of topographic coherency maps and modeling approaches to multilead EEG that serve both these aims. Prior to discussing these approaches, two aspects of the initial analysis of EEG time series require brief mentioning because they have given rise to longstanding discussion in the published literature. The first aspect is the choice of the reference electrode. The second aspect concerns correction for ocular motion artifacts.

Reference Electrode

EEG is a measure of quasistatic electric activity of the brain. An arbitrary constant can be added to the electric potential field without changing the measured electric activity. Consequently, only differences in potential can be measured, independent of the arbitrary constant (cf. Geselowitz, 1998). The EEG potential differences at each lead are defined with respect to a reference electrode which ideally should be neutral. Various references have been used, such as tip of the nose (e.g., Essl & Rappelsberger, 1998), ear (e.g., Thatcher et al., 2001), linked mastoids (e.g., Gevins & Smith, 2000), and average (e.g., Nunez, Wingeier, & Silberstein, 2001). None of these references will be entirely neutral, although this does not affect source localization under noiseless conditions. The reference which perhaps best approaches neutrality is the so-called infinity reference (Yao, 2001; Yao et al., 2005). The infinity reference depends on the head model, the electrode montage, and the neural source distribution model (Yao, 2001); it has been shown to outperform alternative choices of reference electrode in spectral analysis of multilead EEG (Yao et al., 2005).

Ocular Motion Artifacts

The front of the eye (cornea) is positively charged with respect to the back (retina), thus constituting a dipolar configuration. Rotation of this dipole due to eye motion will induce electric field changes that are picked up by EEG registrations. This defines the ocular motion artifact in EEG. In addition, eye blinks generate related motion artifacts. Conversely, electrooculographic (EOG) electrodes positioned close to the eyes will not only register EOG activity but also pick up EEG activity. These "crossover" signals are the main reason why correction of ocular motion artifacts is difficult.

Various methods have been used to correct for ocular motion artifacts. Early methods include linear regression analysis in the time domain (Gratton, Coles, & Donchin, 1983), regression in the frequency domain (Kenemans, Molenaar, Verbaten, & Slangen, 1991), and equivalent dipole modeling (Berg & Scherg, 1991; Elbert, Lutzenberger, Rockstroh, & Birbaumer, 1985). See Croft and Barry (2000) for an authoritative review of these methods. Recently, methods based on component analysis (e.g., Jung et al., 2000) as well as dynamic systems modeling and adaptive filtering (e.g., Haas et al., 2003; Shooshtari, Mohamadi, Arkedani, & Shamsollahi, 2006) have been applied. Recent comparative studies of some of these methods are reported in Wallstrom, Kass, Miller, Cohn, and Fox (2004) and Kierkels, van Boxtel, and Vogten (2006). Both studies reported suboptimal results obtained with independent component analysis approaches to remove ocular motion artifacts. Kierkels et al. (2006) indicated that multiple regression approaches yield good performance in case only two EOG electrodes are used. Hoffmann and Falkenstein (2008) reported good performance of independent component analysis when used to remove eye blink artifacts.

EEG COHERENCY MAPS

Topographic EEG coherency maps have been a prominent tool to assess functional associations between the activities of different brain regions. Coherency is essentially a correlation measure in the frequency domain. High levels of coherence suggest increased neuronal coupling across spatially separate regions and coherence patterns have been associated with cognitive functioning (Thatcher, North, & Biver, 2005), basic emotions (Hinrichs & Machleidt, 1992), and aggression (Peterson, Shackman, & Harmon-Jones, 2007). Atypical coherence patterns have also been associated with maltreatment history in a sample of children (Teicher et al., 1997). Oftentimes, coherence within a region or hemisphere is compared to that of its lateral counterpart to assess the degree of asymmetry. Miskovic and Schmidt (in this volume) discuss the laterialization of multiple biological systems including EEG, with some of this work also reviewed by Fox (in this volume), highlighting the power of examining asymmetry for understanding affective processes. For example, increased levels of left hemispheric coherence mediated the association between maltreatment and psychiatric symptoms in a sample of female adolescents (Miskovic, Schmidt, Georgiades, Boyle, & Macmillian, 2010). Greater levels of cohesion are thought to indicate higher degrees of spatial disorganization. Coherence estimates come from analysis of two electrodes at a time. Let $y_k(t)$ denote the EEG measured at the kth electrode (lead) in a montage of K electrodes positioned across the scalp. It is assumed that the analog EEG signal at each lead $k = 1, 2, \ldots, K$ has been sampled at $T + 1$ equidistant time points $t = 0, 1, \ldots, T$, spanning a time interval of 1 s.

The first step in determining the topographic coherency map is to apply the discrete Fourier transform (DFT) to the EEG obtained at each lead $k = 1, 2, \ldots, K$. This yields $y_k(\omega_n)$, where $\omega_n = n/(T + 1)$, $n = 0, 1, \ldots, T$, denotes the frequency. Notice that $y_k(\omega_n)$ is complex valued: $y_k(\omega_n) = |y_k(\omega_n)| \exp[j\phi_k(\omega_n)]$, where $j = \sqrt{-1}$ denotes the imaginary unit. $|y_k(\omega_n)|$ is the absolute value of $y_k(\omega_n)$ and $\phi_k(\omega_n)$ is the phase of $y_k(\omega_n)$. An important property of the DFT is that, under certain regularity conditions, $y_k(\omega_n)$ and $y_k(\omega_m)$ for different frequencies ω_n and ω_m are asymptotically independent random variables.

The next step is to determine the coherency $C_{km}(\omega_n) = \text{cor}[y_k(\omega_n), y_m(\omega_n)]$ between each pair of leads $k, m \in \{1, 2, \ldots, K\}$ at each frequency ω_n. Notice again that $C_{km}(\omega_n)$ is complex valued: $C_{km}(\omega_n) = |C_{km}(\omega_n)| \exp[j\phi_{km}(\omega_n)]$. The absolute value $|C_{km}(\omega_n)|$ is called the coherence between leads k and m at frequency ω_n; $\phi_{km}(\omega_n)$ is called the phase angle between leads k and m at frequency ω_n. Brillinger (2001) presents an in-depth discussion of the sampling theory of coherency estimators.

A different topographic EEG coherence map is defined for each different frequency (see, e.g., Nunez et al., 1999, for interesting examples). As outlined in Miller and Long (2008), one of the most easily recognized electrical patterns seen in the brain, the alpha wave, has a frequency band of 8 to 12 Hz in adults and 6 to 9 Hz for infants and children. Evidence suggests that the alpha wave is spontaneously occurring and has an inverse relationship

132

with brain activation, suggesting that decreased alpha wave activity relates to task-related activity. Furthermore, preliminary findings suggest that inferences of the alpha wave for infants may be opposite that of adults in that the alpha wave activity increases with brain region activation (Bell, 2002). In addition, at each frequency, a topographic EEG phase angle map can be constructed, although these are seldom reported in the published literature. We will discuss topographic EEG phase angle maps below.

Caveats

High values of EEG coherence often are interpreted as evidence for functional connectivity of the brain regions concerned. Unfortunately, this interpretation may be invalid due to the presence of three confounding factors: volume conduction, the influence of a common reference (cf. Nunez et al., 1999), and a paucity of data on developmentally normative rates (Bell & Wolfe, 2008). The first two confounding factors can give rise to spuriously high coherence values even in the absence of any cortical interaction. The best way to correct for these confounding effects is to estimate topographic EEG coherence maps based on equivalent dipole modeling, to be discussed below (Grasman, Huizenga, Waldorp, Böcker, & Molenaar, 2004). This, however, requires the use of montages containing a large number of leads (cf. Huizenga, Heslenfeld, & Molenaar, 2002).

Several approximate solutions to correct for the confounding effects of volume conduction and common reference have been proposed if only a small number of leads are available ($K < 32$). An excellent overview of these approximate solutions is presented in Schlögl and Supp (2006), using vector-valued autoregressive (VAR) time series models to estimate coherencies $C_{km}(\omega_n)$. VAR models will be discussed later. A computer program implementing several of these approximate solutions can be obtained from the present first author.

Modeling Topographic Coherency Maps

The effective functional connectivity underlying topographic coherency maps is best manifested by means of equivalent dipole modeling. Figure 7, taken from Grasman et al. (2004), presents an illustrative result obtained in a successful application of this approach to magnetoencephalography (MEG) data. If applied to model topographic EEG maps, equivalent dipole modeling serves the combined purposes of reliably estimating the underlying functional connectivity while correcting for the confounding influences due to volume conduction and common reference.

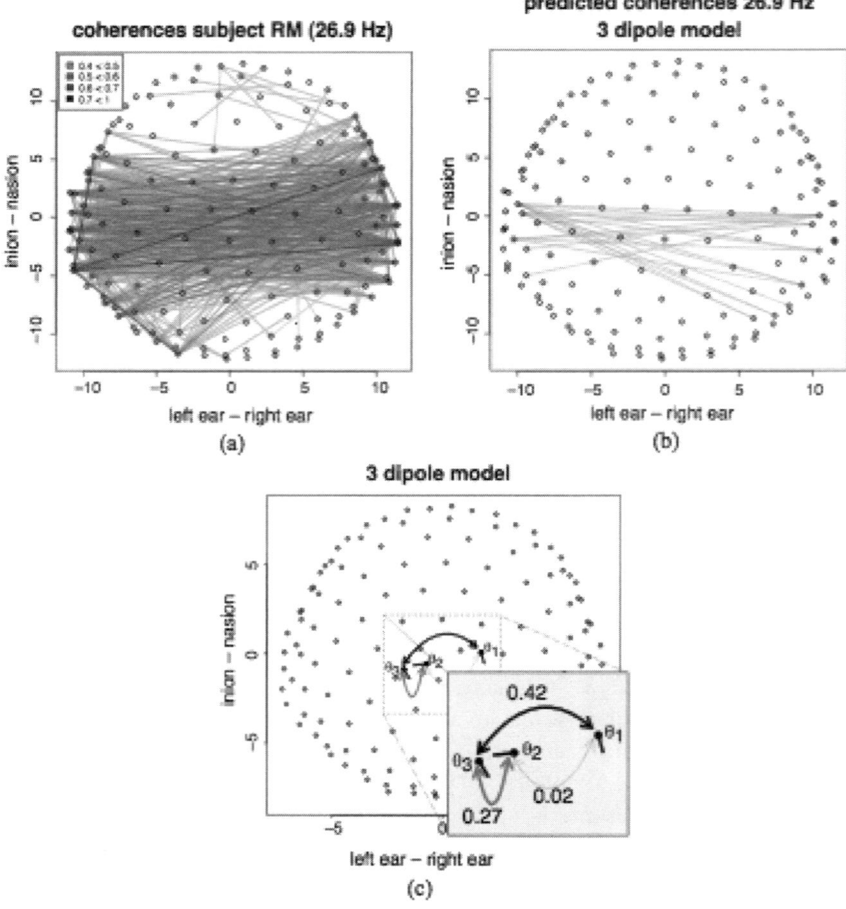

FIGURE 7.—(a) Coherence between sensors with distances greater than 9 cm. (b) Coherence between sensors predicted by the three-dipole model. (c) Three-dipole model—the arrows connecting sources indicate the coherence (averaged across frequencies) between the source activity.

If the number of leads is small ($K < 32$), Nunez's EEG wave model (Nunez & Srinivasan, 2006) constitutes an excellent alternate approach to estimate the effective functional connectivity underlying topographic EEG coherency maps. The EEG wave model can be interpreted as a complex-valued factor model in the frequency domain. Its application requires the use of a special rotation technique that is described in Molenaar (1987). The EEG wave model is simultaneously fitted to both the topographic EEG coherence maps and phase angle maps. Based on results obtained in an empirical application of the

134

EEG wave model, Molenaar (1993) concluded that the estimated functional connectivity is mainly determined by the topographic phase angle maps.

ANALYSIS OF fMRI TIME SERIES

fMRI is an increasingly popular method to investigate brain activity in response to a variety of cognitive and affective tasks. An excellent introduction for social scientists to the physical and biophysical principles underlying magnetic resonance signal generation in the brain is given in Huettel, Song, and McCarthy, (2004). Buxton (2002) and Kuperman (2000) give more technical introductions. Despite the obvious challenges to collect these data in children (e.g., movement) there has been a dramatic surge in developmental affective neuroimaging studies.

Increased amygdala activity to emotion faces relative to neutral faces has been found in studies with children (Baird et al., 1999; Thomas et al., 2001). Individual differences have been found to play a role in the associated activity of the amygdala. For instance, adults who were previously classified as behaviorally inhibited showed increased amygdala activity to negative stimuli (Schwartz, Wright, Shin, Kagan, & Rauch, 2003). In a clinical sample, anxious children showed increased activation to negative stimuli, whereas depressed children showed a diminished amygdala response (Thomas et al., 2001). Adolescents identified in toddlerhood as highly behaviorally inhibited also have been shown to exhibit greater striatal activation to reward and loss cues, compared to uninhibited adolescents (Guyer et al., 2006). Note also that asymmetry in the amygdala is also often observed (e.g., Thomas et al., 2001).

During a typical experimental fMRI run, each subject's functional activity in the brain is measured repeatedly over the course of several minutes. Since scientists seek to identify which areas of the brain increase in activity during a task, data are acquired for numerous points in the brain, ultimately yielding multivariate fMRI time series data of very large dimension. Consequently, the spatial resolution of fMRI scans can be very high—much higher that the spatial resolution of EEG/MEG. In contrast, the temporal resolution of fMRI is rather low (in seconds), about a thousand times lower than the temporal resolution of EEG/MEG (in milliseconds). Thus, emotion researchers need to ask themselves which technique would suit their questions best. For instance, someone interested in the second-by-second unfolding of the emotional process would find fMRI unsatisfactory (see Fox et al., this volume, for a discussion of timing).

Now turning to methodological considerations, fMRI time series require special preprocessing due to the way in which scans are obtained and in order to correct for head movement and other artifacts. After this preprocessing step, basically two approaches to the analysis of fMRI time series are possible:

univariate or multivariate approaches. Univariate approaches typically test for the significance of activity changes (with respect to some appropriate baseline condition) in each of the measured brain regions. Because in whole brain scans the number of measured brain regions can be very large ($>10^4$), special statistical decision procedures are required. Sarty (2007) presents an excellent discussion of preprocessing and univariate modeling and testing of fMRI time series. Lazar's (2008) monograph is highly recommended for its discussion of statistical aspects, and in general as clear introduction to analysis of fMRI time series. Friston et al. (2008) presents convenient reviews of more advanced topics.

fMRI CONNECTIVITY MAPS

In this section, we focus on the construction of connectivity maps based on fMRI time series data, which is a multivariate approach. Such connectivity maps are the fMRI analog of EEG coherency maps discussed in the previous setting. They are considered to describe the effective functional relationships among brain regions during the execution of mental tasks and have thus given insight into brain processes across the life span. For instance, developmental changes in processes relating to narrative processing have been investigated using effective connectivity maps of fMRI data (Karunanayaka et al., 2007), and greater amygdala-frontal connectivity is associated with down regulation of negative affect following cognitive reappraisal strategies (Banks, Eddy, Angstadt, Nathan, & Phan, 2007).

The standard approach to obtain connectivity maps is to fit path models to fMRI time series by means of structural equation modeling (cf. Friston et al., 2008; McIntosh & Gonzalez-Lima, 1994; Sarty, 2007). This requires that the number of brain regions under consideration be drastically reduced to a small number of so-called regions of interest (ROI). Several inductive techniques to accomplish this reduction are described in Sarty (2007), Lazar (2008), and Friston et al. (2008). Alternatively, ROIs can be selected based on a confirmatory approach using prior knowledge.

The standard approach, however, only considers contemporaneous interactions between ROIs. By neglecting the temporal auto- and cross-correlations characterizing multivariate fMRI time series, biased estimates of contemporaneous relations occur (Gates, Molenaar, Hillary, Ram, & Rovine, 2010). Therefore, Kim, Zhu, Chang, Bentler, and Ernst, (2007) proposed a combination of structural equation modeling and VAR modeling to fit path models. This approach constitutes a special case of the dynamic factor modeling approach introduced in Molenaar (1985). Kim et al. (2007) presented an empirical application of their approach, which shows that it is more powerful than the standard approach in that it recovers more significant interactions

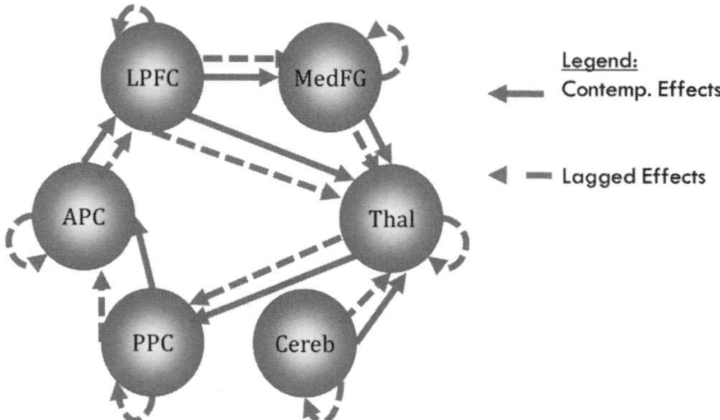

FIGURE 8.—Unified longitudinal and contemporaneous path model. Six brain regions with 13 designed longitudinal paths (dashed lines) and seven contemporaneous paths (solid lines) are described. The longitudinal connections are to one region at the current time (t) from other regions as well as itself at the past time ($t - 1$). LPDC = lateral prefrontal cortex, Brodmann area (BA) 8; MedFG = medial frontal gyrus, BA 8; APC = anterior parietal cortex, BA 7; THAL = thalamus; PPC = posterior parietal cortex, BA 40; CEREB = cerebellum.

between ROIs. Figure 8, taken from Kim et al. (2007), presents illustrative results obtained in their application.

Granger Causality Based on VAR Mapping

The key step in the approach proposed by Kim et al. (2007) is the use of VAR to model fMRI time series. The dynamic connections among ROIs recovered by means of VAR modeling may or may not be genuine causal interactions. An interaction is causal if it is directed, that is, if the cause affects the effect but the reverse is not the case. Moreover, the activity of the cause has to precede in time the resultant activity of the effect. Because VAR modeling of fMRI time series recovers dynamic interactions between ROIs, it is the perfect tool to detect such directed time-lagged interactions between ROIs causing activity in other ROIs and thus far has been used to investigate processes relating to motor activity (Abler et al., 2006), language networks in children (Wilke, Lidzba, & Krageloh-Mann, 2009), and visual spatial attention (Bressler, Tang, Sylvester, Shulman, & Corbetta, 2008).

To identify the presence of genuine causal interactions between ROIs, an approach suggested by Granger (1969) can be applied. In what follows, we will present an outline of this approach, based on Goebel, Roebroeck, Kim, and Formisano (2003). Let $\mathbf{x}(t)$ denote the fMRI time series associated with ROIs, which are expected to cause activity in other ROIs. Let $\mathbf{y}(t)$ denote the fMRI time series associated with the ROIs, the activity of which is expected to be caused by $\mathbf{x}(t)$. Moreover, let $\mathbf{q}(t)$ denote the combined time series consisting of $\mathbf{x}(t)$ and $\mathbf{y}(t)$: $\mathbf{q}(t) = [\mathbf{x}(t), \mathbf{y}(t)]$. Then, VARs are fitted to $\mathbf{x}(t)$, $\mathbf{y}(t)$, and $\mathbf{q}(t)$. For instance, the VAR fitted to $\mathbf{x}(t)$ can be represented as [similar representations pertain to $\mathbf{y}(t)$ and $\mathbf{q}(t)$]:

$$x(t) = A_1 x(t-1) + A_2 x(t-2) + \cdots + A_p x(t-p) + e_x(t).$$

The $\mathbf{A}_i$, $i = 1, 2, \ldots, p$, are square matrices of regression coefficients; $\mathbf{e}_x(t)$ denotes residual process noise.

The test for Granger causality involves comparisons between the variances of the residual process noises in the VARs for $\mathbf{x}(t)$, $\mathbf{y}(t)$, and $\mathbf{q}(t)$. Notice that in the VAR for $\mathbf{q}(t)$, the component series $\mathbf{x}(t)$ is explained by lagged instances of both $\mathbf{x}(t)$ and $\mathbf{y}(t)$. Similarly, in the VAR for $\mathbf{q}(t)$ the component series $\mathbf{y}(t)$ is explained by lagged instances of both $\mathbf{y}(t)$ and $\mathbf{x}(t)$. Now suppose that in the VAR for $\mathbf{x}(t)$ the variance of the residual process noise is larger than the variance of the residual process noise of $\mathbf{x}(t)$ in the VAR for $\mathbf{q}(t)$. Then, this implies that $\mathbf{y}(t)$ is a Granger cause for $\mathbf{x}(t)$. That is, the dynamic interaction between the ROIs associated with $\mathbf{x}(t)$ and $\mathbf{y}(t)$ is directed *from* $\mathbf{y}(t)$ (the cause) *to* $\mathbf{x}(t)$ (the effect). The reader is referred to Goebel et al. (2003) for further details concerning the tests of residual process noise variances.

CONCLUSION

As a slight departure from other chapters in this monograph, this chapter focused on state-of-the-art methods used in developmental psychophysiological research. The availability of sophisticated noninvasive brain imaging techniques enables the construction of multidimensional maps displaying the functional interconnections among the activities of brain areas during the execution of cognitive tasks. In this chapter, we focused on EEG coherency maps and fMRI connectivity maps as prime examples of these powerful tools of cognitive neuroscience, explaining important data-analytic aspects of their application and presenting some illustrations. Where traditional approaches enable researchers to assess where brain activity occurs, the newer connectivity mapping techniques allow the researcher to investigate how the brain is functioning across spatially diverse areas and time.

These maps help to understand cognitive and emotional processes across development. A few caveats must be considered when looking at different age spans. In particular, inferences from EEG coherency maps differ across developmental stages. Although a relatively young method, fMRI already offers insight into spatial integration. More research is needed regarding normative development and issues to be considered with fMRI research.

REFERENCES

Abercrombie, H. C., Schaefer, S. M., Larson, C. L., Ward, R. T., Holden, J. F., Turski, P. A., et al. (1996). Medial prefrontal and amygdala glucose metabolism in depressed and control subjects: An FDG-PET study. *Psychophysiology, 33*, S17.

Abler, B., Roebroeck, A., Goebel, R., Höse, A., Schönfeldt-Lecuona, C., Hole, G., et al. (2006). Investigating directed influences between activated brain areas in motor-response task using fMRI. *Magnetic Resonance Imaging, 24*, 181–185.

Adam, E. K. (2006). Transactions among adolescent trait and state emotion and diurnal and momentary cortisol activity in naturalistic settings. *Psychoneuroendocrinology, 31*, 664–679.

Adam, E. K., Doane, L. D., & Mendelsohn, K. (in press). Spit, sweat, and tears: Measuring biological data in naturalistic settings. In E. Hargittai (Ed.), *Research confidential: Solutions to problems that most social scientists pretend they never have.* Ann Arbor: University of Michigan Press.

Adam, E. K., Doane, L. D., Zinbarg, R. E., Mineka, S., Craske, M. G., & Griffith, J. W. (2010). Prospective prediction of major depressive disorder from cortisol awakening responses in adolescence. *Psychoneuroendocrinology, 35*, 921–931.

Adam, E. K., & Gunnar, M. R. (2001). Relationship functioning and home and work demands predict individual differences in diurnal cortisol patterns in women. *Psychoneuroendocrinology, 26*, 189–208.

Adam, E. K., Hawkley, L. C., Kudielka, B. M., & Cacioppo, J. T. (2006). Day-to-day dynamics of experience-cortisol associations in a population-based sample of older adults. *Proceedings of the National Academy of Sciences of the USA, 103*, 17058–17063.

Adam, E. K., Klimes-Dougan, B., & Gunnar, M. R. (2007). Social regulation of the adrenocortical response to stress in infants, children and adolescents: Implications for psychopathology and education. In D. Coch, G. Dawson & K. Fischer (Eds.), *Human behavior, learning, and the developing brain: Atypical development* (pp. 264–304). New York: Guilford.

Adam, E. K., & Kumari, M. (2009). Assessing salivary cortisol in large-scale, epidemiological research. *Psychoneuroendocrinology, 34*, 1423–1436.

Adam, E. K., Sutton, J. M., Doane, L. D., & Mineka, S. (2008). Incorporating hypothalamic-pituitary-adrenal axis measures into preventive interventions for adolescent depression: Are we there yet? *Development and Psychopathology, 20*, 975–1001.

Ahern, G. L., Sollers, J. J., Lane, R. D., Labiner, D. M., Herring, A. M., Weinand, M. E., et al. (2001). Heart rate and heart rate variability changes in the intracarotid sodium amobarbital test. *Epilepsia, 42*, 912–921.

Alkon, A., Goldstein, L. H., Smider, N., Essex, M. J., Kupfer, D. J., & Boyce, W. T. (2003). Developmental and contextual influences on autonomic reactivity in young children. *Developmental Psychobiology, 42*, 64–78.

Allen, J. J. B., Harmon-Jones, E., & Cavender, J. H. (2001). Manipulation of frontal EEG asymmetry through biofeedback alters self-reported emotional responses and facial EMG. *Psychophysiology, 38*, 685–693.

Alpert, J. E., Maddocks, A., Rosenbaum, J. F., & Fava, M. (1994). Childhood psychopathology retrospectively assessed among adults with early onset major depression. *Journal of Affective Disorders, 31*, 165–171.

Amaral, D. G. (2002). The primate amygdala and the neurobiology of social behavior: Implications for understanding social anxiety. *Biological Psychiatry, 51*, 11–17.

Anda, R. F., Felitti, V. J., Bremner, J. D., Walker, J. D., Whitfield, C., Perry, B. D., et al. (2006). The enduring effects of abuse and related adverse experiences in childhood: A convergence of evidence from neurobiology and epidemiology. *European Archives of Psychiatry and Clinical Neuroscience, 256*, 174–186.

Andersson, S., & Finset, A. (1998). Heart rate and skin conductance reactivity to brief psychological stress in brain-injured patients. *Journal of Psychosomatic Research, 44*, 645–656.

Ashman, S. B., Dawson, G., Panagiotides, H., Yamada, E., & Wilkinson, C. W. (2002). Stress hormone levels of children of depressed mothers. *Development and Psychopathology, 14*, 333–349.

Atzil, S., Hendler, T., & Feldman, R. (2011). Specifying the neurobiological basis of human attachment: Brain, hormones, and behavior in synchronous and intrusive mothers. *Neuropsychopharmacology, 36*, 2603–2615.

Aue, T., Lavelle, L. A., & Cacioppo, J. T. (2009). Great expectations: What can fMRI research tell us about psychological phenomena? *International Journal of Psychophysiology: Official Journal of the International Organization of Psychophysiology, 73*, 10–16.

Bachevalier, J., & Loveland, K. A. (2006). The orbitofrontal-amygdala circuit and self-regulation of social-emotional behavior in autism. *Neuroscience and Biobehavioral Reviews, 30*, 97–117.

Baird, A. A., Gruber, S. A., Fein, D. A., Maas, L. C., Steingard, R. J., Renshaw, P. F., Cohen, B. M., & Yurgelun-Todd, D. A. (1999). Functional magnetic resonance imaging of facial affect recognition in children and adolescents. *Journal of the American Academy of Child & Adolescent Psychiatry, 38*, 195–199.

Balaban, M. T. (1995). Affective influences on startle in five-month-old infants: Reactions to facial expressions of emotions. *Child Develevelopment, 66*, 28–36.

Banks, S., Eddy, K., Angstadt, M., Nathan, P. J., & Phan, K. L. (2007). Amygdala-frontal connectivity during emotion regulation. *Social Cognitive Affective Neuroscience, 2*, 303–312.

Bar-Haim, Y., Marshall, P. J., & Fox, N. A. (2000). Developmental changes in heart period and high-frequency heart period variabiligy from 4 months to 4 years of age. *Developmental Psychobiology, 37*, 44–56.

Barnett, D., Manly, J. T., & Cicchetti, D. (1993). Defining child maltreatment: The interface between policy and research. In D. Cicchetti & S. L. Toth (Eds.), *Child abuse, child development, and social policy* (pp. 7–73). Norwood, NJ: Ablex.

Bauer, A. M., Quas, J. A., & Boyce, W. T. (2002). Associations between physiological reactivity and children's behavior: Advantages of a multisystem approach. *Journal of Developmental and Behavioral Pediatrics, 23*, 102–113.

Bauer, P. M., Hanson, J. L., Pierson, R. K., Davidson, R. J., & Pollak, S. D. (2009). Cerebellar volume and cognitive functioning in children who experienced early deprivation. *Biological Psychiatry, 66*, 1100–1106.

Bazhenova, O. V., & Porges, S. W. (1997). Vagal reactivity and affective adjustment in infants: Convergent response systems. *Annals of the New York Academy of Sciences, 807*, 469–471.

Beaton, E. A., Schmidt, L. A., Schulkin, J., Antony, M. M., Swinson, R. P., & Hall, G. B. (2008). Different neural responses to stranger and personally familiar faces in shy and bold adults. *Behavioral Neuroscience*, **122**, 704–709.

Beauchaine, T. P. (2001). Vagal tone, development, and Gray's motivational theory: Toward an integrated model of autonomic nervous system functioning in psychopathology. *Development and Psychopathology*, **13**, 183–214.

Beauchaine, T. P. (2009). Physiological markers of emotional and behavioral dysregulation in externalizing psychopathology. *Monographs of the Society for Research in Child Development*, **509**, 80–88.

Beauchaine, T. P., Gatzke-Kopp, L., & Mead, H. K. (2007). Polyvagal theory and developmental psychopathology: Emotion dysregulation and conduct problems from preschool to adolescence. *Biological Psychology*, **74**, 174–184.

Beauchaine, T. P., Hinshaw, S. P., & Gatzke-Kopp, L. M. (2008). Genetic and environmental influences on behavior. In T. P. Beauchaine & S. P. Hinshaw (Eds.), *Child and adolescent psychopathology* (pp. 129–156). Hoboken, NJ: Wiley.

Beauchaine, T. P., Hinshaw, S. P., & Pang, K. (2010). Comorbidity of attention-deficit/hyperactivity disorder and early-onset conduct disorder: Biological, environmental, and developmental mechanisms. *Clinical Psychology: Science and Practice*, **17**, 327–336.

Beauchaine, T. P., Hong, J., & Marsh, P. (2008). Sex differences in autonomic correlates of conduct problems and aggression. *Journal of the American Academy of Child and Adolescent Psychiatry*, **47**, 788–796.

Beauchaine, T. P., Katkin, E. S., Strassberg, Z., & Snarr, J. (2001). Disinhibitory psychopathology in male adolescents: Discriminating conduct disorder from attention-deficit/hyperactivity disorder through concurrent assessment of multiple autonomic states. *Journal of Abnormal Psychology*, **110**, 610–624.

Beauchaine, T. P., Klein, D. N., Crowell, S. E., Derbidge, C., & Gatzke-Kopp, L. M. (2009). Multifinality in the development of personality disorders: A Biology × Sex × Environment model of antisocial and borderline traits. *Development and Psychopathology*, **21**, 735–770.

Beauchaine, T. P., & Neuhaus, E. (2008). Impulsivity and vulnerability to psychopathology. In T. P. Beauchaine & S. P. Hinshaw (Eds.), *Child and adolescent psychopathology* (pp. 129–156). Hoboken, NJ: Wiley.

Beauchaine, T. P., Neuhaus, E., Brenner, S. L., & Gatzke-Kopp, L. (2008). Ten good reasons to consider biological processes in prevention and intervention research. *Development and Psychopathology*, **20**, 745–774.

Beauchaine, T. P., Sauder, C., Gatzke-Kopp, L. M., Shannon, K. E., & Aylward, E. (in press). Neuro-anatomical correlates of heterotypic comorbidity in externalizing youth. *Journal of Clinical Child and Adolescent Psychiatry*.

Beauchaine, T. P., Webster-Stratton, C., & Reid, M. J. (2005). Mediators, moderators, and predictors of one-year outcomes among children treated for early-onset conduct problems: A latent growth curve analysis. *Journal of Consulting and Clinical Psychology*, **73**, 371–388.

Bell, K. L., & Calkins, S. D. (2000). Relationships as inputs and outputs of emotion regulation. *Psychological Inquiry*, **11**, 160–163.

Bell, M. A. (2001). Brain electrical activity associated with cognitive processing during a looking version of the A-not-B object permanence task. *Infancy*, **2**, 311–330.

Bell, M. A. (2002). Power changes in infant EEG frequency bands during a spatial working memory task. *Psychophysiology*, **39**, 450–458.

Bell, M. A. (2012). A psychobiological perspective on individual differences in working memory at 8 months. *Child Development*, **83**, 251–265.

Bell, M. A., & Deater-Deckard, K. (2007). Biological systems and the development of self-regulation: Integrating behavior, genetics, and psychophysiology. *Journal of Developmental and Behavioral Pediatrics, 28,* 409–420.

Bell, M. A., & Wolfe, C. D. (2004). Emotion and cognition: An intricately bound developmental process. *Child Development, 75,* 366–370.

Bell, M. A., & Wolfe, C. D. (2007). The cognitive neuroscience of early socioemotional development. In C. A. Brownell & C. B. Kopp (Eds.), *Socioemotional development in the toddler years* (pp. 345–369). New York: Guilford.

Bell, M. A., & Wolfe, C. D. (2008). The use of electroencephalogram in research on cognitive development. In L. A. Schmidt & S. J. Segalowitz (Eds.), *Developmental psychophysiology* (pp. 367–423). New York: Cambridge University Press.

Belsky, J., Bakermans-Kranenburg, M. J., & van IJzendoorn, M. H. (2007). For better *and* for worse: Differential susceptibility to environmental influences. *Current Directions in Psychological Science, 16,* 300–304.

Belsky, J., & Pluess, M. (2009). Beyond diathesis stress: Differential susceptibility to environmental influences. *Psychological Bulletin, 135,* 885–908.

Benarroch, E. E. (1993). The central autonomic network: Functional organization, dysfunction, and perspective. *Mayo Clinic Proceedings, 68,* 988–1001.

Bentin, S., Allison, T., Puce, A., Perez, E., & McCarthy, G. (1996). Electrophysiological studies of face perception in humans. *Journal of Cognitive Neuroscience, 8,* 551–565.

Berg, P., & Scherg, M. (1991). Dipole models of eye movements and blinks. *Electroencephalography and Clinical Neurophysiology, 79,* 36–44.

Bernardi, L., Wdowczyk-Szulc, J., Valenti, C., Castoldi, S., Passino, C., Spadacini, G., et al. (2000). Effects of controlled breathing, mental activity and mental stress with or without verbalization on heart rate variability. *Journal of American College of Cardiology, 35,* 1462–1469.

Berntson, G. G., Cacioppo, J. T., & Quigley, K. S. (1993). Cardiac psychophysiology and autonomic space in humans: Empirical perspectives and conceptual implications. *Psychological Bulletin, 114,* 296–322.

Berntson, G. G., Cacioppo, J. T., & Quigley, K. S. (1994). Autonomic cardiac control: I. Estimation and validation from pharmacological blockades. *Psychophysiology, 31,* 572–585.

Berntson, G. G., Cacioppo, J. T., & Quigley, K. S. (1995). The metrics of cardiac chronotropism: Biometric perspectives. *Psychophysiology, 32,* 162–171.

Berntson, G. G., Quigley, K. S., & Lozano, D. (2007). Cardiovascular psychophysiology. In *Handbook of psychophysiology* (3rd ed., pp. 182–210). Cambridge, UK: Cambridge University Press.

Berntson, G. G., Sarter, M., & Cacioppo, J. T. (2003). Ascending visceral regulation of cortical affective information processing. *European Journal of Neuroscience, 18,* 2103–2109.

Berridge, K. C. (2003). Comparing the emotional brain of humans and other animals. In R. J. Davidson, H. H. Goldsmith, & K. Scherer (Eds.), *Handbook of affective sciences* (pp. 25–51). New York: Oxford University Press.

Binder, E., Bradley, R., Liu, W., Epstein, M., Deveau, T., & Mercer, K. (2008). Association of FKBP5 polymorphisms and childhood abuse with risk of posttraumatic stress disorder symptoms in adults. *JAMA, 299,* 1291.

Black, J., Jones, T. A., Nelson, C. A., & Greenough, W. T. (1998). Neuronal plasticity and the developing brain. In N. E. Alessi, J. T. Coyle, S. I. Harrison, & S. Eth (Eds.), *Handbook of child and adolescent psychiatry* (pp. 31–53). New York: Wiley.

Blair, C., & Peters, R. (2003). Physiological and neurocognitive correlates of adaptive behavior in preschool among children in head start. *Developmental Neuropsychology, 24,* 479–497.

Blandon, A. Y., Calkins, S. D., Keane, S. P., & O'Brien, M. (2008). Individual differences in trajectories of emotion regulation processes: The effects of maternal depressive symptomatology and children's physiological regulation. *Developmental Psychology, 44,* 1110–1123.

Blass, E. M. (1996). Mothers and their infants: Peptide-mediated physiological, behavioral and affective changes during suckling. *Regulatory Peptides, 66,* 109–12.

Blau, V., Maurer, U., Tottenham, N., & McCandliss, B. (2007). The face-specific N170 component is modulated by emotional facial expression. *Behavioral and Brain Functions, 3,* 7–20.

Bloch, L., Moran, E. K., & Kring, A. M. (2009). On the need for conceptual and definitional clarity in emotion regulation research. In A. M. Kring & D. Sloan (Eds.), *Emotion regulation and psychopathology* (pp. 88–104). New York: Guilford Press.

Boccia, M. L., & Pedersen, C. A. (2001). Brief vs. long maternal separations in infancy: Contrasting relationships with adult maternal behavior and lactation levels of aggression and anxiety. *Psychoneuroendocrinology, 26,* 657–672.

Bornstein, M. H., & Suess, P. E. (2000). Child and mother cardiac vagal tone: Continuity, stability and concordance across the first 5 years. *Developmental Psychology, 36,* 54–65.

Bowlby, J. (1969). *Attachment and loss. Vol.1: Attachment.* New York: Basic.

Boyce, W. T. (2007). A biology of misfortune: Stress reactivity, social context, and the ontogeny of psychopathology in early life. In A. Masten (Ed.), *Multilevel dynamics in developmental psychopathology: Pathways to the future* (34th ed., pp. 45–82). Minneapolis: University of Minnesota.

Boyce, W. T., & Ellis, B. J. (2005). Biological sensitivity to context: I. An evolutionary–developmental theory of the origins and functions of stress reactivity. *Development and Psychopathology, 17,* 271–301.

Boyce, W. T., Quas, J., Alkon, A., Smider, N., Essex, M., & Kupfer, D. J. (2001). Autonomic reactivity and psychopathology in middle childhood. *British Journal of Psychiatry, 179,* 144–150.

Brenner, S. L., & Beauchaine, T. P. (2011). Cardiac pre-ejection period reactivity and psychiatric comorbidity prospectively predict substance use initiation among middle schoolers: A pilot study. *Psychophysiology, 48,* 1587–1595.

Brenner, S. L., Beauchaine, T. P., & Sylvers, P. D. (2005). A comparison of psychophysiological and self-report measures of BAS and BIS activation. *Psychophysiology, 42,* 108–115.

Bressler, S. L., Tang, W., Sylvester, C. M., Shulman, G. L., & Corbetta, M. (2008). Top-down control of human visual cortex by frontal and parietal cortex in anticipatory visual spatial attention. *Journal of Neuroscience, 28,* 10056–10061.

Brillinger, D. R. (2001). Time series: Data analysis and theory. SIAM Classics in Applied Mathematics, 36. Philadelphia: SIAM.

Bronfenbrenner, U. (1979). *The ecology of human development: Experiments by nature and design.* Cambridge, MA: Harvard University Press.

Brooker, R. J., & Buss, K. A. (2010). Dynamic measures of RSA predict distress and regulation in toddlers. *Developmental Psychobiology, 52,* 372–282.

Brown, J. D., & Cantor, J. (2000). An agenda for research on youth and the media. *Journal of Adolescent Health, 27,* 2–7.

Bubier, J., & Drabick, D. A. (2008). Affective decision-making and externalizing behaviors: The role of autonomic activity. *Journal of Abnormal Child Psychology, 36,* 941–953.

Bubier, J. L., Drabick, D. A. G., & Breiner, T. (2009). Autonomic functioning moderates the relations between contextual factors and externalizing behaviors among inner-city children. *Journal of Family Psychology, 23,* 500–510.

Buckholtz, J. W., Callicott, J. H., Kolachana, B., Hariri, A. R., Goldberg, T. E., Genderson, M., et al. (2008). Genetic variation in MAOA modulates ventromedial prefrontal circuitry mediating individual differences in human personality. *Molecular Psychiatry*, **13**, 313–324.

Bush, G., Luu, P., & Posner, M. I. (2000). Cognitive and emotional influences in anterior cingulated cortex. *Trends in Cognitive Sciences*, **4**, 215–222.

Bush, N. R., Alkon, A., Obradović, J., Stamperdahl, J., & Boyce, W. T. (2011). Differentiating challenge reactivity from psychomotor activity in studies of children's psychophysiology: Considerations for theory and measurement. *Journal of Experimental Child Psychology*, **110**, 62–79.

Buss, K. A., Davidson, R. J., Kalin, N. H., & Goldsmith, H. H. (2004). Context-specific freezing and associated physiological reactivity as a dysregulated fear response. *Developmental Psychology*, **40**, 583–594.

Buss, K. A., Goldsmith, H. H., & Davidson, R. J. (2005). Cardiac reactivity is associated with changes in negative emotion in 24-month-olds. *Developmental Psychobiology*, **46**, 118–132.

Buss, C., Lord, C., Wadiwalla, M., Hellhammer, D. H., Lupien, S. J., Meaney, M. J., et al. (2007). Maternal care modulates the relationship between prenatal risk and hippocampal volume in women but not in men. *Journal of Neuroscience*, **27**, 2592–2595.

Buss, K., Schumacher, J., Dolski, I., Goldsmith, H., Davidson, R., & Kalin, N. (2003). Right frontal brain activity, cortisol, and withdrawal behavior in 6-month-old infants. *Behavioral Neuroscience*, **117**, 11–20.

Buxton, R. B. (2002). *Introduction to functional magnetic resonance imaging: Principles and techniques.* Cambridge, UK: Cambridge University Press.

Cacioppo, J. T., & Berntson, G. G. (1999). The affect system: Architecture and operating characteristics. *Current Directions in Psychological Science*, **8**, 133–137.

Cacioppo, J. T., Berntson, G. G., Binkley, P. F., Quigley, K. S., Uchino, B. N., & Fieldstone, A. (1994). Autonomic cardiac control: II. Noninvasive indices and basal response as revealed by autonomic blockades. *Psychophysiology*, **31**, 586–598.

Cacioppo, J. T., Berntson, G. G., Larsen, J. T., Poehlmann, K. M., & Ito, T. A. (2000). The psychophysiology of emotion. In R. Lewis & J. M. Haviland-Jones (Eds.), *The handbook of emotions* (2nd ed., pp. 173–191). New York: Guilford.

Cacioppo, J. T., Berntson, G. G., Malarkey, W. B., Kiecolt-Glaser, J. K., Sheridan, J. F., Poehlmann, K. M., et al. (1998). Autonomic, neuroendocrine, and immune responses to psychological stress: The reactivity hypothesis. *Annals of the New York Academy of Sciences*, **840**, 664–673.

Cacioppo, J. T., Berntson, G. G., Sheridan, J. F., & McClintock, M. K. (2000). Multilevel integrative analyses of human behavior: Social neuroscience and the complementing nature of social and biological approaches. *Psychological Bulletin*, **126**, 829–843.

Cacioppo, J. T., Tassinary, L. G., & Berntson, G. G. (2007). *Handbook of psychophysiology.* New York: Cambridge University Press.

Calkins, S. D. (1997), Cardiac vagal tone indices of temperamental reactivity and behavioral regulation in young children. *Developmental-Psychobiology*, **31**, 125–135.

Calkins, S. D., & Bell, M. A. (2010). *Child development at the intersection of emotion and cognition.* Washington, DC: American Psychology Association Press.

Calkins, S. D., Blandon, A. Y., Williford, A. P., & Keane, S. P. (2007). Biological, behavioral, and relational levels of resilience in the context of risk for early childhood behavior problems. *Development and Psychopathology*, **19**, 675–700.

Calkins, S. D., & Dedmon, S. E. (2000). Physiological and behavioral regulation in two-year-old children with aggressive/destructive behavior problems. *Journal of Abnormal Child Psychology*, **28**, 103–118.

Calkins, S. D., Fox, N. A., & Marshall, T. R. (1996). Behavioral and physiological antecedents of inhibition in infancy. *Child Development, 67*, 523–540.

Calkins, S. D., Graziano, P. A., & Keane, S. P. (2007). Cardiac vagal regulation differentiates among children at risk for behavior problems. *Biological Psychology, 74*, 144–153.

Calkins, S. D., & Hill, A. L. (2007). Caregiver influences on emerging emotion regulation: Biological and environmental transactions in early development. In J. Gross (Ed.), *Handbook of emotion regulation* (pp. 229–248). New York: Guilford.

Calkins, S. D., & Keane, S. P. (2004). Cardiac vagal regulation across the preschool period: Stability, continuity, and implications for childhood adjustment. *Developmental Psychobiology, 45*, 101–112.

Caltagirone, C., Zoccolotti, P., Orginale, G., Daniele, A., & Mamucari, A. (1989). Autonomic reactivity and facial expression of emotion in brain-damaged patients. In G. Gainotti & C. Caltagirone (Eds.), *Emotions and the dual brain* (pp. 204–221). Berlin: Springer-Verlag.

Cameron, O. G. (2009). Visceral brain-body information transfer. *NeuroImage, 47*, 787–794.

Campbell, S. B., Shaw, D. S., & Gilliom, M. (2000). Early externalizing behavior problems: Toddlers and preschoolers at risk for later maladjustment. *Development and Psychopathology, 12*, 467–488.

Campos, J. J., Frankel, C. B., & Camras, L. (2004). On the nature of emotion regulation. *Child Development, 75*, 377–394.

Carlson, S. M., & Wang, T. S. (2007). Inhibitory control and emotion regulation in preschool children. *Cognitive Development, 22*, 489–510.

Carpenter, L. L, Carvalho, J. P., Tyrka, A. R., Wier, L. M., Mello, A. F., et al. (2007). Decreased adrenocorticotropic hormone and cortisol responses to stress in healthy adults reporting significant childhood maltreatment. *Biological Psychiatry, 62*, 1080–1087.

Carter, C. S. (1998). Neuroendocrine perspectives on social attachment and love. *Psychoneuroendocrinology, 23*, 779–818.

Caspi, A., McClay, J., Moffitt, T. E., Mill, J., Martin, J., Craig, I. W., et al. (2002). Role of genotype in the cycle of violence in maltreated children. *Science, 297*, 851–854.

Caspi, A., Sugden, K., Moffitt, T. E., Taylor, A., Craig, I. W., Harrington, H., et al. (2003). Influence of life stress on depression: Moderation by a polymorphism in the 5-HTT gene. *Science, 301*, 386–389.

Cheek, J. M., & Buss, A. H. (1981). Shyness and sociability. *Journal of Personality and Social Psychology, 41*, 330–339.

Chen, E., Matthews, K. A., Salomon, K., & Ewart, C. K. (2002). Cardiovascular reactivity during social and nonsocial stressors: Do children's personal goals and expressive skills matter? *Health Psychology, 21*, 16–24.

Chen, E., Miller, G. E., Kobor, M. S., & Cole, S. W. (2010). Maternal warmth buffers the effects of low early-life socioeconomic status on pro-inflammatory signaling in adulthood. *Molecular Psychiatry.* Available: http://www.nature.com/mp/journal/v16/n7/full/mp201053a.html.

Chida, Y., & Steptoe, A. (2006). Cortisol awakening response and psychosocial factors: A systematic review and meta-analysis. *Biological Psychiatry, 80*, 265–278

Chomsky, N. (1968). *Language and mind.* New York: Harcourt Brace Jovanovich.

Christopolous, C., Cohn, D. A., Shaw, D. S., Joyce, S., Sullivan-Hanson, J., Draft, S. P., et al.(1987). Children of abused women: Adjustment at time of shelter residence. *Journal of Marriage and the Family, 49*, 611–619.

Chung, T., Martin, C. S., & Winters, K. C. (2006). Diagnosis, course and assessment of alcohol abuse and dependence in adolescents. In M. Galanter (Ed.), *Alcohol problems in adolescents and young adults: Epidemiology, neurobiology, prevention, and treatment* (pp. 5–27). New York: Springer.

Cicchetti, D. (1990). The organization and coherence of socioemotional, cognitive, and representational development: Illustrations through a developmental psychopathology perspective on Down syndrome and child maltreatment. In R. Thompson (Ed.), *Nebraska symposium on motivation: Socioemotional development* (Vol. 36, pp. 259–366). Lincoln: University of Nebraska Press.

Cicchetti, D. (1993). Developmental psychopathology: Reactions, reflections, projections. *Developmental Review, 13*, 471–502.

Cicchetti, D. (1996). Child maltreatment: Implications for developmental theory. *Human Development, 39*, 18–39.

Cicchetti, D. (2002a). How a child builds a brain: Insights from normality and psychopathology. In W. W. Hartup & R. A. Weinberg (Eds.), *The Minnesota symposia on child psychology: Child psychology in retrospect and prospect* (Vol. 32, pp. 23–71). Mawah, NJ: Lawrence Erlbaum Associates.

Cicchetti, D. (2002b). The impact of social experience on neurobiological systems: Illustration from a constructivist view of child maltreatment. *Cognitive Development, 17*, 1407–1428.

Cicchetti, D., Ackerman, B. P., & Izard, C. E. (1995). Emotions and emotion regulation in developmental psychopathology. *Development and Psychopathology, 7*, 1–10.

Cicchetti, D., & Barnett, D. (1991). Toward the development of a scientific nosology of child maltreatment. In W. Grove & D. Cicchetti (Eds.), *Thinking clearly about psychology: Essays in honor of Paul E. Meehl: Personality and psychopathology* (Vol. 2, pp. 346–377). Minneapolis: University of Minnesota Press.

Cicchetti, D., & Curtis, W. J. (2005). An event-related potential (ERP) study of processing of affective facial expressions in young children who have experienced maltreatment during the first year of life. *Development and Psychopathology, 17*, 641–677.

Cicchetti, D., & Hesse, P. (1983). Affect and intellect: Piaget's contributions to the study of infant emotional development. In R. Plutchik & H. Kellerman (Eds.), *Emotion: Theory, research and experience* (Vol. 2, pp. 115–169). New York: Academic.

Cicchetti, D., & Lynch, M. (1995). Failures in the expectable environment and their impact on individual development: The case of child maltreatment. In D. Cicchetti & D. J. Cohen (Eds.), *Developmental psychopathology: Risk, disorder, and adaptation* (Vol. 2, pp. 32–71). New York: John Wiley & Sons.

Cicchetti, D., & Manly, J. T. (1990). A personal perspective on conducting research with maltreating families: Problems and solutions. In G. Brody & I. Sigel (Eds.), *Methods of family research: Families at risk* (Vol. 2, pp. 87–133). Hillsdale, NJ: Lawrence Erlbaum Associates.

Cicchetti, D., & Manly, J. T. (2001). Operationalizing child maltreatment: Developmental processes and outcomes. *Development and Psychopathology, 13*, 755–757.

Cicchetti, D., & Rogosch, F. A. (1996). Equifinality and multifinality in developmental psychopathology. *Development and Psychopathology, 8*, 597–600.

Cicchetti, D., & Rogosch, F. A. (1997). The role of self-organization in the promotion of resilience in maltreated children. *Development and Psychopathology, 9*, 799–817.

Cicchetti, D., & Rogosch, F. A. (2001a). Diverse patterns of neuroendocrine activity in maltreated children. *Development and Psychopathology, 13*, 677–694.

Cicchetti, D., & Rogosch, F. A. (2001b). The impact of child maltreatment and psychopathology upon neuroendocrine functioning. *Development and Psychopathology, 13*, 783–804.

Cicchetti, D., & Rogosch, F. A. (2007). Personality, adrenal steroid hormones, and resilience in maltreated children: A multi-level perspective. *Development and Psychopathology*, **19**, 787–809.

Cicchetti, D., Rogosch, F. A., Gunnar, M. R., & Toth, S. L. (2010). The differential impacts of early abuse on internalizing problems and diurnal cortisol activity in school-aged children. *Child Development*, **81**, 252–269.

Cicchetti, D., Rogosch, F. A., & Sturge-Apple, M. L. (2007). Interactions of child maltreatment and 5-HTT and monoamine oxidase A polymorphisms: Depressive symptomatology among adolescents from low-socioeconomic status backgrounds. *Development and Psychopathology*, **19**, 1161–1180.

Cicchetti, D., Rogosch, F. A., Sturge-Apple, M., & Toth, S. L. (2010). Interaction of child maltreatment and 5-HTT polymorphisms: Suicidal ideation among children from low SES backgrounds. *Journal of Pediatric Psychology*, **35**, 536–546.

Cicchetti, D., & Schneider-Rosen, K. (1984a). Theoretical and empirical considerations in the investigation of the relationship between affect and cognition in atypical populations of infants: Contributions to the formulation of an integrative theory of development. In C. Izard, J. Kagan, & R. Zajonc (Eds.), *Emotions, cognition, and behavior* (pp. 366–406). New York: Cambridge University Press.

Cicchetti, D., & Schneider-Rosen, K. (1984b). Toward a transactional model of childhood depression. *New Directions for Child Development*, **26**, 5–27.

Cicchetti, D., & Toth, S. L. (1995). A developmental psychopathology perspective on child abuse and neglect. *Journal of the American Academy of Child and Adolescent Psychiatry*, **34**, 541–565.

Cicchetti, D., & Toth, S. L. (2003). Child maltreatment: A research and policy agent for the dawn of the millennium. In R. P. Weissberg, L. H. Weiss, O. Reyes, & H. J. Walberg (Eds.), *Trends in the well-being of children and youth* (Vol. 2, pp. 181–206). Washington, DC: CWLA Press.

Cicchetti, D., & Toth, S. L. (2005). Child maltreatment. *Annual Review of Clinical Psychology*, **1**, 409–438.

Cicchetti, D., & Valentino, K. (2006). An ecological transactional perspective on child maltreatment: Failure of the average expectable environment and its influence upon child development. In D. Cicchetti & D. J. Cohen (Eds.), *Developmental psychopathology* (Vol. 3, 2nd ed., pp. 129–201). New York: Wiley.

Cicchetti, D., & Walker, E. F. (2001). Stress and development: Biological and psychological consequences. *Development and Psychopathology*, **13**, 413–418.

Cole, P. M., Martin, S. E., & Dennis, T. A. (2004). Emotion regulation as a scientific construct: Methodological challenges and directions for child development research. *Child Development*, **75**, 317–333.

Cole, P. M., Zahn-Waxler, C., Fox, N. A., Usher, B. A., & Welsh, J. D. (1996). Individual differences in emotion regulation and behavior problems in preschool children. *Journal of Abnormal Psychology*, **105**, 518–529.

Colombo, J., Mitchell, D., Coldren, J., & Freeseman, L. (1991). Individual differences in infant visual attention: Are short lookers faster processors or feature processors? *Child Development*, **62**, 1247–1257.

Colombo, J., & Saxon, T. F. (2002). Infant attention and the development of cognition: Does the environment moderate continuity? In H. E. Fitzgerald, K. H. Karraker, & T. Luster (Eds.), *Infant development: Ecological perspectives* (pp. 35–60). Washington, DC: Garland Press.

Compas, B. E., Connor-Smith, J. K., Saltzman, H., Thomsen, A. H., & Wadsworth, M. E. (2001). Coping with stress during childhood and adolescence: Problems, progress, and potential in theory and research. *Psychological Bulletin, 127*, 87–127.

Courchesne, E. (1978). Neurophysiological correlates of cognitive development: Changes in long-latency event-related potentials from childhood to adulthood. *Electroencephalography and Clinical Neurophysiology, 45*, 468–482.

Craig, A. D. (2002). How do you feel? Interoception: The sense of the physiological condition of the body. *Nature Reviews Neuroscience, 3*, 655–666.

Craig, A. D. (2005). Forebrain emotional asymmetry: A neuroanatomical basis? *Trends in Cognitive Sciences, 9*, 566–571.

Crick, N. R., & Dodge, K. A. (1994). A review and reformulation of social information processing mechanisms in children's social adjustment. *Psychological Bulletin, 115*, 74–101.

Croft, R. J., & Barry, R. J. (2000). Removal of ocular artifact from the EEG: A review. *Neurophysiologie Clinique, 30*, 5–19.

Crowell, S., Beauchaine, T. P., Gatzke-Kopp, L., Sylvers, P., Mead, H., & Chipman-Chacon, J. (2006). Autonomic correlates of attention-deficit/hyperactivity disorder and oppositional defiant disorder in preschool children. *Journal of Abnormal Psychology, 115*, 174–178.

Crowell, S. E., Beauchaine, T. P., & Lenzenwger, M. F. (2008). The development of borderline personality disorder and self-injurious behavior. In T. P. Beauchaine and S. P. Hinshaw (Eds.), *Child and adolescent psychopathology* (pp. 510–539). Hoboken, NJ: Wiley.

Crowell, S. E., Beauchaine, T. P., & Linehan, M. (2009). The development of borderline personality: Extending Linehan's theory. *Psychological Bulletin, 135*, 495–510.

Crowell, S., Beauchaine, T. P., McCauley, E., Smith, C., Stevens, A. L., & Sylvers, P. (2005). Psychological, autonomic, and serotonergic correlates of parasuicidal behavior in adolescent girls. *Development and Psychopathology, 17*, 1105–1127.

Crowell, S. E., Beauchaine, T. P., McCauley, M., Smith, C. J., Vasilev, C. A., & Stevens, A. L. (2008). Parent-child interactions, peripheral serotonin, and self-inflicted injury in adolescents. *Journal of Consulting and Clinical Psychology, 76*, 15–21.

Cullerton-Sen, C., Cassidy, A. R., Murray-Close, D., Cicchetti, D., Crick, N. R., & Rogosch, F. A. (2008). Childhood maltreatment and the development of relational and physical aggression: The importance of a gender-informed approach. *Child Development, 79*, 1736–1751.

Cummings, E. M., & Davies, P. T. (1996). Emotional security as a regulatory process in normal development and the development of psychopathology. *Development and Psychopathology, 8*, 123–139.

Cummings, M. E., El-Sheikh, M., Kouros, C. D., & Keller, P. S. (2007). Children's skin conductance reactivity as a mechanism of risk in the context of parental depressive symptoms. *Journal of Child Psychology and Psychiatry, 48*, 436–445.

Curtis, W. J., & Cicchetti, D. (2007). Emotion and resilience: A multi-level investigation of hemispheric electroencephalogram asymmetry and emotion regulation in maltreated and non-maltreated children. *Development and Psychopathology, 19*, 811–840.

Cuthbert, B. N., Bradley, M. M., & Lang, P. J. (1996). Probing picture perception: Activation and emotion. *Psychophysiology, 33*, 103–111.

Dahl, R. E. (1996). The regulation of sleep and arousal: Development and psychopathology. *Development and Psychopathology, 8*, 3–27.

Dahl, R. E. (2004). Adolescent brain development: A period of opportunities and vulnerabilities. *Annals of the New York Academy of Science, 1021*, 1–22.

Dahl, R. E., & Gunnar, M. R. (2009). Introduction to special section on heightened stress responsiveness and emotional reactivity during pubertal maturation: Implications for psychopathology. *Development and Psychopathology*, **21**, 1–6.

Dahl, R. E., & Lewin, D. S. (2002). Pathways to adolescent health sleep regulation and behavior. *Journal of Adolescent Health*, **31**, 175–184.

Dallman, M. F., Akana, S. F., Bradbury, M. J., Strack, A. M., Hanson, E. S., & Scribner, K. A. (1994). Regulation of the hypothalamo-pituitary-adrenal axis during stress: Feedback, facilitation and feeding. *Seminars in Neuroscience*, **6**, 205–213.

Dalton, K. M., Kalin, N. H., Grist, T. M., & Davidson, R. J. (2005). Neural-cardiac coupling in threat-evoked anxiety. *Journal of Cognitive Neuroscience*, **17**, 969–980.

Damasio, A. R. (1994). *Descartes' error: Emotion, reason and the human brain*. New York: Avon Books.

Damasio, A. R. (1999). *The feeling of what happens: Body and emotion in the making of consciousness*. New York: Harcourt.

Darrow, C. W. (1929). Differences in the physiological reactions to sensory and ideational stimuli. *Psychological Bulletin*, **26**, 185–201.

Davenport, M. D., Tiefenbacher, S., Lutz, C. K., Novak, M. A., & Meyer, J. S. (2006). Analysis of endogenous cortisol concentrations in the hair of rhesus macaques. *General and Comparative Endocrinology*, **147**, 255–261.

Davidson, R. J. (1993). The neuropsychology of emotion and affective style. In M. Lewis & J. M. Haviland (Eds.), *Handbook of emotions* (pp.143–154). New York: Guilford.

Davidson, R. J. (1994a). Asymmetric brain function, affective style and psychopathology: The role of early experience and plasticity. *Development and Psychopathology*, **6**, 741–758.

Davidson, R. J. (1994b). Complexities in the search for emotion-specific physiology. In P. Ekman & R. J. Davidson (Eds.), *The nature of emotion: Fundamental questions* (pp. 237–242). New York: Oxford University Press.

Davidson, R. J. (2000). Affective style, psychopathology, and resilience: Brain mechanisms and plasticity. *American Psychologist*, **55**, 1196–1214.

Davidson, R. J. (2002). Anxiety and affective style: Role of prefrontal cortex and amygdala. *Biological Psychiatry*, **51**, 68–80.

Davidson, R. J. (2003). Affective neuroscience and psychophysiology: Toward a synthesis. *Psychophysiology*, **40**, 655–665.

Davidson, R. J., Coe, C. C., Dolski, I., & Donzella, B. (1999). Individual differences in prefrontal activation asymmetry predict natural killer cell activity at rest and in response to challenge. *Brain, Behavior and Immunity*, **13**, 93–108.

Davidson, R. J., Ekman, P., Saron, C. D., Senulis, J. A., & Friesen, W. V. (1990). Approach-withdrawal and cerebral asymmetry: Emotional expression and brain physiology. *Journal of Personality and Social Psychology*, **58**, 330–341.

Davidson, R. J., & Fox, N. A. (1989). Frontal brain asymmetry predicts infants' response to maternal separation. *Journal of Abnormal Psychology*, **98**, 127–131.

Davidson, R. J., Jackson, D. C., & Kalin, N. H. (2000). Emotion, plasticity, context, and regulation: Perspectives from affective neuroscience. *Psychological Bulletin*, **126**(6), 890–909.

Davies, P. T., & Forman, E. M. (2002). Children's patterns of preserving emotional security in the interparental subsystem. *Child Development*, **73**, 1880–1903.

Davies, P. T., Sturge-Apple, M. L., Cicchetti, D., & Cummings, E. M. (2007). The role of child adrenocortical functioning in pathways between interparental conflict and child maladjustment. *Developmental Psychology*, **43**, 918–930.

Davis, M. (2006). Neural systems involved in fear and anxiety measured with fear-potentiated startle. *American Psychologist*, **61**, 741–756.

Dawson, M. E., Schell, A. M., & Filion, D. L. (2007). The electrodermal system. In *Handbook of psychophysiology* (3rd ed., pp. 159–180). Cambridge, UK: Cambridge University Press.

De Bellis, M. D. (2001). Developmental traumatology: The psychobiological development of maltreated children and its implications for research, treatment, and policy. *Development and Psychopathology, 13*, 539–564.

De Bellis, M. D. (2005). The psychobiology of neglect. *Child Maltreatment, 10*, 150–172.

De Bellis, M. D., Hallb, J., Boringb, A. M., Frustacib, K., & Moritzb, G. (2001). A pilot longitudinal study of hippocampal volumes in pediatric maltreatment-related posttraumatic stress disorder. *Biological Psychiatry, 50*, 305–309.

De Bellis, M. D., Narasimhan, A., Thatcher, D. L., Keshavan, M. S., Soloff, P., & Clark, D. B. (2005). Prefrontal cortex, thalamus, and cerebellar volumes in adolescents and young adults with adolescent-onset alcohol use disorders and comorbid mental disorders. *Alcoholism: Clinical and Experimental Research, 29*, 1590–1600.

De Geus, E. J. C. (2002). Introducing genetic psychophysiology. *Biological Psychology, 61*, 1–10.

De Haan, M., & Matheson, A. (2009). The development and neural bases of processing emotion in faces and voices. In M. de Haan & M. R. Gunnar (Eds.), *Handbook of developmental social neuroscience* (pp. 107–121). New York: Guilford Press.

De Haan, M., & Nelson, C. A. (1999). Brain activity differentiates face and object processing in 6-month-old infants. *Developmental Psychology, 35*, 1113–1121.

De Kloet, R., Vreugdenhil, E., Oitzl, M., & Joels, A. (1998). Brain corticosteroid receptor balance in health and disease. *Endocrine Reviews, 19*, 269–301.

Dedovic, K., Duchesne, A., Andrews, J., Engert, V., & Pruessner, J. C. (2009). The brain and the stress axis: The neural correlates of cortisol regulation in response to stress. *Neuroimage, 47*, 864–871.

Dedovic, K., Wadiwalla, M., Engert, V., & Pruessner, J. C. (2009). The role of sex and gender socialization in stress reactivity. *Developmental Psychology, 45*, 45–55.

DeGangi, P. A., DiPietro, J. A., Greenspan, S. I., & Porges, S. W. (1991). Psychophysiological characteristics of the regulatory disordered infant. *Infant Behavior and Development, 14*, 37–50.

Denenberg, V. H. (1981). Hemispheric laterality in animals and the effects of early experience. *Behavioral and Brain Sciences, 4*, 1–49.

Dennis, T. A. (2010). Neurophysiological markers for child emotion regulation from the perspective of emotion-cognition integration: Current directions and future challenges. *Developmental Neuropsychology, 35*, 212–230.

Dennis, T. A., & Chen, C.-C. (2007). Neurophysiological mechanisms in the emotional modulation of attention: The interplay between threat sensitivity and attentional control. *Biological Psychology, 76*, 1–10.

Dennis, T. A., Malone, M. M., & Chen, C.-C. (2009). Emotional face processing and emotion regulation in children: An ERP study. *Developmental Neuropsychology, 34*, 85–102.

DeSantis, A. S., Adam, E. K., Doane, L. D., Mineka, S., Zinbarg, R. E., & Craske, M. G. (2007). Racial/ethnic differences in cortisol diurnal rhythms in a community sample of adolescents. *Journal of Adolescent Health, 41*, 3–13.

Dettling, A. C., Gunnar, M. R., & Donzella, B. (1999). Cortisol levels of young children in full-day childcare centers: Relations with age and temperament. *Psychoneuroendocrinology, 24*, 505–518.

Diaz, A., & Bell, M. A. (2010a). *Fear reactivity and recognition memory at 10 months.* Manuscript in preparation.

Diaz, A., & Bell, M.A. (2010b, March). *Temperament-related fear reactivity in infancy: EEG and recognition memory*. Poster presented at International Conference on Infant Studies, Baltimore, MD.

Diaz, A., & Bell, M.A. (2011a). Frontal EEG asymmetry and fear reactivity in different contexts at 10 months. *Developmental Psychobiology*. doi:10.1002/dev.20612

Diaz, A., & Bell, M. A. (2011b). Information processing efficiency and regulation at five months. *Infant Behavior and Development, 34*, 239–247.

Dichter, G. S., Tomarken, A. J., & Baucom, B. R. (2002). Startle modulation before, during and after exposure to emotional stimuli. *International Journal of Psychophysiology, 43*, 191–196.

Dickerson, S. S., & Kemeny, M. E. (2004). Acute stressors and cortisol responses: A theoretical integration and synthesis of laboratory research. *Psychological Bulletin, 130*, 355–391.

Dickinson, A., & Dearing, M. F. (1979). Appetitive-aversive interactions and inhibitory processes. In A. Dickinson & R. A. Boakes (Eds.), *Mechanisms of learning and motivation* (pp. 203–231). Hillsdale, NJ: Erlbaum.

Di Luig, I. L., Guidetti, L., Baldari, C., Gallotta, M. C., Sgrò, P., Perroni, F., et al. (2006). Cortisol, dehydroepiandrosterone sulphate and dehydroepiandrosterone sulphate/cortisol ratio responses to physical stress in males are influenced by pubertal development. *Journal of Endocrinological Investigation, 29*, 796–804.

Diorio, D., Viau, V., & Meaney, M. J. (1993). The role of the medial prefrontal cortex (cingulate gyrus) in the regulation of hypothalamic-pituitary-adrenal responses to stress. *Journal of Neuroscience: The Official Journal of the Society for Neuroscience, 13*, 3839–3847.

DiPietro, J. A., Porges, S. W., & Uhly, B. (1992). Reactivity and developmental competence in preterm and full-term infants. *Developmental Psychology, 28*, 831–841.

Doane, L. D., & Adam, E. K. (2010). Loneliness and cortisol: Momentary, day-to-day, and trait associations. *Psychoneuroendocrinology, 35*, 430–441.

Dodge, K. A., Pettit, G. S., Bates, J. E., & Valente, E. (1995). Social information-processing patterns partially mediate the effect of early physical abuse on later conduct problems. *Journal of Abnormal Psychology, 104*, 632–643.

Donchin, E. (1978). Use of scalp distribution as a dependent variable in event-related potential studies: Excerpts of preconference correspondence. In D. Otto (Ed.), *Multidisciplinary perspectives in event-related brain potentials research* (pp. 501–510). Washington, DC: U.S. Government Printing Office.

Doussard-Roosevelt, J. A., Montgomery, L. A., & Porges, S. W. (2003). Short-term stability of physiological measures in kindergarten children: Respiratory sinus arrhythmia, heart period and cortisol. *Developmental Psychobiology, 43*, 231–242.

Dowlati, Y., Herrmann, N., Swardfager, W., Liu, H., Sham, L., Reim, E. K., et al. (2010). A meta-analysis of cytokines in major depression. *Biological Psychiatry, 67*, 446–457.

Dozier, M., Peloso, E., Gordon, M. K., Manni, M., & Gunnar, M. R. (2006). Foster children's diurnal production of cortisol: An exploratory study. *Child Maltreatment, 11*, 189–197.

Durston, S. (2003). A review of the biological bases of ADHD: What have we learned from imaging studies? *Mental Retardation and Developmental Disabilities Reviews, 9*, 184–195.

Eatough, E. M., Shirtcliff, E. A., Hanson, J. L., & Pollak, S. D. (2009). Hormonal reactivity to MRI scanning in adolescents. *Psychoneuroendocrinology, 34*, 1242–1246.

Edelman, G. M. (2004). *Wider than the sky: The phenomenal gift of consciousness*. New Haven, CT: Yale University Press.

Edleson, J. L. (1999). Children's witnessing of adult domestic violence. *Journal of Interpersonal Violence, 14*, 839–870.

Eidelman, M., Goldstein, A., Berger, A., & Feldman, R. (2010). *Mother's face enhances infant neural recognition of emotions*. Paper submitted for publication.

Ekman, P. (1992). Facial expressions of emotion: An old controversy and new findings. *Philosophical Transactions: Biological Sciences*, **335**, 63–69.

Ekman, P., & Davidson, R. J. (1994). *The nature of emotion: Fundamental questions*. New York: Oxford University Press.

Ekman, P., Levenson, R. W., & Friesen, W. V. (1983). Autonomic nervous system activity distinguishes among emotions. *Science*, **221**, 1208–1210.

Ekman, P., Sorenson, E. R., & Friesen, W. V. (1969). Pan-cultural elements in facial displays of emotions. *Science*, **164**, 86–88.

Ekman, P., Sorenson, E. R., & Friesen, W. V. (1984). Expression and the nature of emotion. In K. Scherer & P. Ekman (Eds.), *Approaches to emotion* (pp. 319–344). Hillsdale, NJ: Lawrence Eribaum.

Ellsworth, P. C. (1994). William James and emotion: Is a century of fame worth a century of misunderstanding? *Psychological Review*, **101**, 222–229.

El-Sheikh, M. (2005a). Stability of respiratory sinus arrhythmia in children and young adolescents: A longitudinal examination. *Developmental Psychobiology*, **46**, 66–74.

El-Sheikh, M. (2005b). Does poor vagal tone exacerbate child maladjustment in the context of parental problem drinking? A longitudinal examination. *Journal of Abnormal Psychology*, **114**, 735–741.

El-Sheikh, M., Erath, S. A., Buckhalt, J. A., Granger, D. A., & Mize, J. (2008). Cortisol and children's adjustment: The moderating role of sympathetic nervous system activity. *Journal of Abnormal Child Psychology*, **36**, 601–611.

El-Sheikh, M., Harger, J. A., & Whitson, S. M. (2001). Exposure to interparental conflict and children's adjustment and physical health: The moderating role of vagal tone. *Child Development*, **72**, 1617–1636.

El-Sheikh, M., Keller, P. S., & Erath, S. A. (2007). Marital conflict and risk for child maladjustment over time: Skin conductance level reactivity as a vulnerability factor. *Journal of Abnormal Child Psychology*, **35**, 715–727.

El-Sheikh, M., Kouros, C. D., Erath, S., Cummings, E. M., Keller, P., & Staton, L. (2009). Marital conflict and children's externalizing behavior: Interactions between parasympathetic and sympathetic nervous system activity. *Monograph of the Society for Research in Child Development*, **74**, (1, Serial No. 292), 1–79.

El-Sheikh, M., & Whitson, S. A. (2006). Longitudinal relations between marital conflict and child adjustment: Vagal regulation as a protection factor. *Journal of Family Psychology*, **20**, 30–39.

Elbert, T., Lutzenberger, W., Rockstroh, B., & Birbaumer, N. (1985). Removal of ocular artifacts from the EEG—A biophysical approach to the EOG. *Electroencephalography and Clinical Neurophysiology*, **60**, 455–463.

Elzinga, B. M., Roelofs, K., Tollenaar, M. S., Bakvis, P., van Pelt, J., & Spinhoven, P. (2008). Diminished cortisol responses to psychosocial stress associated with lifetime adverse events: A study among healthy young subjects. *Psychoneuroendocrinology*, **33**, 227–237.

Engle, R.W. (2002). Working memory capacity as executive attention. *Current Directions in Psychological Science*, **11**, 19–23.

Eppinger, H., & Hess, L. (1910). *Vagatonia*. New York: The Nervous and Mental Disease Publishing Company.

Essl, M., & Rappelsberger, P. (1998). EEG coherence and reference signals: Experimental results and mathematical explanations. *Medical and Biological Engineering and Computing*, **36**, 399–406.

152

Evans, G. W., & Kim, P. (2007). Childhood poverty and health: Cumulative risk exposure and stress dysregulation. *Psychological Science*, **18**, 953–957.

Fabes, R. A., Eisenberg, N., & Eisenbud, L. (1993). Behavioral and physiological correlates of children's reactions to others in distress. *Developmental Psychology*, **29**, 655–663.

Fantuzzo, J. W., & Mohr, W. K. (1999). Prevalence and effects of child exposure to domestic violence. *The Future of Children*, **9**, 21–32.

Feldman, R. (2003). Infant-mother and infant-father synchrony: The coregulation of positive arousal. *Infant Mental Health Journal*, **24**, 1–23.

Feldman R. (2006). From biological rhythms to social rhythms: Physiological precursors of mother-infant synchrony. *Developmental Psychology*, **42**, 175–188.

Feldman, R. (2007a). Parent-infant synchrony and the construction of shared timing: Physiological precursors, developmental outcomes, and risk conditions. *Journal of Child Psychology and Psychiatry*, **48**, 329–354.

Feldman, R. (2007b). Parent-infant synchrony: Biological foundations and developmental outcomes. *Current Directions in Psychological Science*, **16**, 340–346.

Feldman, R. (2007c). Mother-infant synchrony and the development of moral orientation in childhood and adolescence: Direct and indirect mechanisms of developmental continuity. *American Journal of Orthopsychiatry*, **77**, 582–597.

Feldman, R. (2007d). On the origins of background emotions: From affect synchrony to symbolic expression. *Emotion*, **7**, 601–611.

Feldman, R. (2009a). The development of regulatory functions from birth to five years: Insights from premature infants. *Child Development*, **80**, 544–561.

Feldman, R. (2009b). *Oxytocin and bonding: The Neurobiological Foundation of Human Affiliation*. Invited Address at the 41st European Brain and Behaviour Society Meeting. Frontiers in Behavioral Neuroscience. Rhodes, Greece. Conference Abstract. doi: 10.3389/conf.neuro.08.2009.09.024.

Feldman, R. (2010). The relational basis of adolescent adjustment: Trajectories of mother-child interactive behaviors from infancy to adolescence shape adolescents' adaptation. *Attachment and Human Development*, **12**, 173–192.

Feldman, R., & Eidelman, A. I. (2003). Direct and indirect effects of maternal milk on the neurobehavioral and cognitive development of premature infants. *Developmental Psychobiology*, **43**, 109–119.

Feldman, R., & Eidelman, A. I. (2007). Maternal postpartum behavior and the emergence of infant-mother and infant-father synchrony in preterm and full-term infants: The role of neonatal vagal tone. *Developmental Psychobiology*, **49**, 290–302.

Feldman, R., Gordon, I., Schneiderman, I., Weisman, O., & Zagoory-Sharon, O. (2010). Natural variations in maternal and paternal care are associated with systematic changes in oxytocin following parent-infant contact. *Psychoneuroendocrinology*, **35**, 1133–1141.

Feldman, R., Gordon, I., & Zagoory-Sharon, O. (2010). The cross-generation transmission of oxytocin in humans. *Hormones and Behavior*, **58**, 669–676.

Feldman, R., Granat, A., Pariente, C., Kaneti, H., Kuint, J., & Gilboa-Schechtman, E. (2009). Maternal affective disorder across the postpartum year and infant social engagement, fear regulation, and stress reactivity. *Journal of the American Academy of Child and Adolescent Psychiatry*, **48**, 919–927.

Feldman, R., Greenbaum, C. W., & Yirmiya, N. (1999). Mother-infant affect synchrony as an antecedent to the emergence of self-control. *Developmental Psychology*, **35**, 223–231.

Feldman, R., Magori-Cohen, R., Galili, G., Singer, M., & Louzoun, Y. (2011). Mother and infant coordinate heart rhythms through episodes of interaction synchrony. *Infant Behavior and Development*, **34**, 569–577.

Feldman, R., & Masalha, S. (2010). Parent-child and triadic antecedents of children's social competence: Cultural specificity, shared process. *Developmental Psychology, 46*, 455–467.

Feldman, R., Singer, M. & Zagoory, O. (2010). Touch attenuates infants' physiological reactivity to stress. *Developmental Science, 12*, 271–278.

Feldman, R., Weller, A., Zagoory-Sharon, O., & Levine, A. (2007). Evidence for a neuroendocrinological foundation of human affiliation: Plasma oxytocin levels across pregnancy and the postpartum predict mother-infant bonding. *Psychological Science, 18*, 965–970.

Fichtenholtz, H. M., Dean, H. L., Dillon, D. G., Yamasaki, H., McCarthy, G., & LaBar, K. S. (2004). Emotion-attention network interactions during visual-oddball task. *Cognitive Brain Research, 20*, 67–80.

Fisher, L., Ames, E. W., Chisholm, K., & Savoie, L. (1997). Problems reported by parents of Romanian orphans adopted to British Columbia. *International Journal of Behavioral Development, 20*, 67–82.

Fisher, P. A., Gunnar, M. R., Dozier, M., Bruce, J., & Pears, K. C. (2006). Effects of therapeutic interventions for foster children on behavioral problems, caregiver attachment, and stress regulatory neural systems. *Annals of the New York Academy of Sciences, 1094*, 215–225.

Fleming, A. S., O'Day, D. H., & Kraemer, G. W. (1999). Neurobiology of mother-infant interaction: Experience and central nervous system plasticity across development and generations. *Neuroscience and Biobehavioral Review, 23*, 673–685.

Flinn, M., & England, B. G. (1995). Childhood stress and family environment. *Current Anthropology, 36*, 854–866.

Forbes, E. E., Fox, N. A., Cohn, J. F., Galles, S. F., & Kovacs, M. (2006). Children's affect regulation during a disappointment: Psychophysiological responses and relation to parent history of depression. *Biological Psychology, 71*, 264–277.

Foster, P. S., & Harrison, D. W. (2006). Magnitude of cerebral asymmetry at rest: Covariation with baseline cardiovascular activity. *Brain and Cognition, 61*, 286–297.

Fowles, D., Kochanska, G., & Murray, K. (2000). Electrodermal activity and temperament in preschool children. *Psychophysiology, 37*, 777–787.

Fox, E. (2008). *Emotion science.* London: Palgrave Macmillan.

Fox, N. A. (1991). If it's not left, it's right: Electroencephalograph asymmetry and the development of emotion. *American Psychologist, 46*, 863–872.

Fox, N. A. (1994). Dynamic cerebral processes underlying emotion regulation. *Monographs for the Society for Research in Child Development, 59*, 152–166.

Fox, N. A., Hane, A. E., & Pine, D. S. (2007). Plasticity for affective neurocircuitry: How the environment affects gene expression. *Current Directions in Psychological Science, 16*, 1–5.

Fox, N. A., Nicols, K., Henderson, H., Rubin, K. H., Schmidt, L. A., Hamer, D., et al. (2005). Evidence for a gene-environment interaction in predicting behavioral inhibition in middle childhood. *Psychological Science, 16*, 921–926.

Fox, N. A., Rubin, K. H., Calkins, S. D., Marshall, T. R., Coplan, R. J., Porges, S. W., et al. (1995). Frontal activation asymmetry and social competence at four years of age. *Child Development, 66*, 1770–1784.

Fox, N. A., Schmidt, L. A., Calkins, S. D., Rubin, K. H., & Coplan, R. J. (1996). The role of frontal activation in the regulation and dysregulation of social behavior during the preschool years. *Development and Psychopathology, 8*, 89–102.

Fox, N. A., Schmidt, L. A., Henderson, H. A., & Marshall, P. (2006). Developmental psychophysiology: Conceptual and methodological issues. In T. Cacioppo, L. G. Tassinary, & G. G. Berntson (Eds.), *Handbook of psychophysiology* (3rd ed., pp. 453–481). New York: Cambridge University Press.

Fries, A. B., Shirtcliff, E. A., & Pollak, S. D. (2008). Neuroendocrine dysregulation following early social deprivation in children. *Developmental Psychobiology, 50,* 588–599.

Fries, A. B., Ziegler, T. E., Kurian, J. R., Jacoris, S., & Pollak, S. D. (2005). Early experience in humans is associated with changes in neuropeptides critical for regulating social behavior. *Proceedings of the National Academy of Sciences of the USA, 102,* 17237–17240.

Fries, E., Dettenborn, L., & Kirschbaum, C. (2009). The cortisol awakening response (CAR): Facts and future directions. *International Journal of Psychophysiology, 72,* 67–73.

Fries, E., Hesse, J., Hellhammer, J., & Hellhammer, D. (2005). A new view on hypocortisolism. *Psychoneuoendocrinology, 30,* 1010–1016.

Friston, K. J., Ashburner, J. T., Kiebel, S. J., Nichols, T. E., & Penny, W. D. (2008). *Statistical parametric mapping: The analysis of functional brain images.* London: Academic Press.

Gaab, J., Sonderegger, L., Scherrer, S., & Ehlert, U. (2006). Psychoneuroendocrine effects of cognitive-behavioral stress management in a naturalistic setting—A randomized controlled trial. *Psychoneuoendocrinology, 31,* 428–438.

García Coll, C., Kagan, J., & Reznick, J. S. (1984). Behavioral inhibition in young children. *Child Development, 55,* 1005–1019.

Gates, K. M., Molenaar, P. C. M., Hillary, F., Ram., N., & Rovine, M. (2010). Automatic search for fMRI connectivity mapping: An alternative to Granger causality testing using formal equivalences between SEM path modeling, VAR, and unified SEM. *NeuroImage, 50,* 1118–1125.

Gatzke-Kopp, L. M., Beauchaine, T. P., Shannon, K. E., Chipman, J., Fleming, A. P., Crowell, S. E., et al. (2009). Neurological correlates of reward responding in adolescents with and without externalizing behavior disorders. *Journal of Abnormal Psychology, 118,* 203–213.

Gatzke-Kopp, L. M., Raine, A., Loeber, R., Stouthamer-Loeber, M., & Steinhauer, S. R. (2002). Serious delinquent behavior, sensation seeking, and electrodermal arousal. *Journal of Abnormal Child Psychology, 30,* 477–486.

Geselowitz, D. B. (1998). The zero of potential. *IEEE Engineering in Medicine and Biology, 17,* 128–132.

Geva, R., & Feldman, R. (2008). A neurobiological model for the effects of brainstem functioning on the development of behavior and emotion regulation in infants: Implications for prenatal and perinatal risk. *Journal of Child Psychology and Psychiatry, 49,* 1031–1041.

Gevins, A., & Smith, M. E. (2000). Neurophysiological measures of working memory and individual differences in cognitive ability and cognitive style. *Cerebral Cortex, 10,* 829–839.

Giancola, P. R., Peterson, J. B., & Pihl, R. O. (2006). Risk for alcoholism, antisocial behavior, and response perseveration. *Journal of Clinical Psychology, 49,* 423–428.

Gibson, E. L., Checkley, S., Papadopoulos, A., Poon, L., Daley, S., & Wardle, J. (1999). Increased salivary cortisol reliably induced by a protein-rich midday meal. *Psychosomatic Medicine, 61,* 214–224.

Giedd, J. N., Schmitt, J. E., & Neale, M. C. (2007). Structural brain magnetic resonance imaging of pediatric twins. *Human Brain Mapping, 28,* 474–481.

Gilbert, R., Widom, C. S., Browne, K., Fergusson, D., Webb, E., & Janson, S. (2009). Burden and consequences of child maltreatment in high-income countries. *Lancet, 373,* 68–81.

Gilissen, R., Bakermans-Kranenburg, M. J., van IJzendoorn, M. H., & Van der Veer, R. (2008). Parent–child relationship, temperament, and physiological reactions to fear-inducing film clips: Further evidence for differential susceptibility. *Journal of Experimental Child Psychology, 99,* 182–195.

Gilissen, R., Koolstra, C. M., van IJzendoorn, M. H., Bakermans-Kranenburg, M. J., & Van der Veer, R. (2007). Physiological reactions of preschoolers to fear-inducing film clips: Effects of temperamental fearfulness and quality of the parent–child relationship. *Developmental Psychobiology, 49*, 187–195.

Gillespie, C., Phifer, J., Bradley, B., & Ressler, K. (2009). Risk and resilience: Genetic and environmental influences on development of the stress response. *Depression and Anxiety, 26*, 984–992.

Goebel, R., Roebroeck, A., Kim, D. S., & Formisano, E. (2003). Investigating directed cortical interactions in time-resolved fMRI data using vector autoregressive modeling and Granger causality mapping. *Magnetic Resonance Imaging, 21*, 1251–1261.

Goenjian, A. K., Yehuda, R., Pynoos, R. S., Steinberg, A. M., Tashjian, R. K., Yang, L. M., et al. (1996). Basal cortisol, dexamethasone suppression of cortisol, and MHPG in adolescents after the 1988 earthquake in Armenia. *American Journal of Psychiatry, 153*, 929–934.

Gogtay, N., Giedd, J. N., Lusk, L., Hayashi, K. M., Greenstein, D., Vaituzis, A. C., et al. (2004). Dynamic mapping of human cortical development during childhood through early adulthood. *Proceedings of the National Academy of Sciences of the USA, 101*, 8174–8179.

Goldsmith, H. H., & Davidson, R. J. (2004). Disambiguating the components of emotion regulation. *Child Development, 75*, 361–365.

Goldsmith, H. H., Pollak, S. D., & Davidson, R. J. (2008). Developmental neuroscience perspectives on emotion regulation. *Child Development Perspectives, 2*, 132–140.

Goldstein, A., Berger, A., & Feldman, R. (2009). *Mother's face enhances infant neural recognition of emotions.* Paper submitted for publication.

Goldstein, J. M., Jerram, M., Abbs, B., Whitfield-Gabrieli, S., & Makris, N. (2010). Sex differences in stress response circuitry activation dependent on female hormonal cycle. *Journal of Neuroscience, 30*, 431–438.

Goodyer, I. M., Park, R. J., Netherton, C. M., & Herbert, J. (2001). Possible role of cortisol and dehydroepiandrosterone in human development and psychopathology. *British Journal of Psychiatry: The Journal of Mental Science, 179*, 243–249.

Gordis, E. B., Granger, D. A., Susman, E. J., & Trickett, P. K. (2006). Asymmetry between salivary cortisol and a-amylase reactivity to stress: Relation to aggressive behavior in adolescents. *Psychoneuroendocrinology, 31*, 976–987.

Gordon, I., & Feldman, R. (2008). Synchrony in the triad: A micro-level process model of coparenting and parent-child interactions. *Family Process, 47*, 465–479.

Gordon, I., Zagoory-Sharon, O., Leckman, J. F., & Feldman, R. (2010a). Oxytocin and the development of parenting in humans. *Biological Psychiatry, 68*, 377–382.

Gordon, I., Zagoory-Sharon, O., Leckman, J. F., & Feldman, R. (2010b). Parental oxytocin and triadic family interactions. *Physiology and Behavior.* doi: 1016/j.physbeh.2010.08.008.

Gordon, I., Zagoory-Sharon, O., Leckman, J. F., & Feldman, R. (2010c). Prolactin, oxytocin, and the development of paternal behavior across the first six months of fatherhood. *Hormones and Behavior, 58*, 513–518.

Gordon, I., Zagoory-Sharon, O., Leckman, J. F., Weller, A., & Feldman, R. (2009). *Maternal and paternal bonding in the postpartum: Hormones, parenting behavior, and mental representations.* Presented at the biannual meeting of the Society for Research in Child Development, Denver, CO.

Gordon, I., Zagoory-Sharon, O., Schneiderman, I., Leckman, J. F., Weller, A., & Feldman, R. (2008). Oxytocin and cortisol in romantically unattached young adults: Associations with bonding and psychological distress. *Psychophysiology, 45*, 349–352.

Goto, M., Nagashima, M., Baba, R., Nagano, Y., Yokota, M., Nishibata, K., et al. (1997). Analysis of heart rate variability demonstrates effects of development on vagal modulation of heart rate in healthy children. *Journal of Pediatrics, 130*, 725–729.

Gottesman, I. I., & Gould, T. D. (2003). The endophenotype concept in psychiatry: Etymology and strategic intentions. *American Journal of Psychiatry*, **160**, 636–645.

Gottman, J., & Mettetal, G. (1986). Speculations about social and affective development: Friendship and acquaintanceship through adolescence. In J. Gottman & J. Parker (Eds.), *Conversations with friends: Speculations on affective development* (pp. 192–237). New York: Cambridge University Press.

Gottman, J. M., & Katz, L. F. (1989). Effects of marital discord on children's peer interaction and health. *Developmental Psychology*, **25**, 373–381.

Grace, A. A., & Rosenkranz, J. A. (2002). Regulation of conditioned responses of basolateral amygdala neurons. *Physiology and Behavior*, **77**, 489–493.

Graham Bermann, S. A., & Levendosky, A. A. (1998). Traumatic stress symptoms in children of battered women. *Journal of Interpersonal Violence*, **13**, 111–128.

Granger, C. W. J. (1969). Investigating causal relations by econometric models and cross-spectral methods. *Econometrics*, **37**, 424–438.

Grasman, R. P. P. P., Huizenga, H. M., Waldorp, L. J., Böcker, K. B., & Molenaar, P. C. M. (2004). Frequency domain simultaneous source and source coherence estimation with an application to MEG. *IEEE Transactions on Biomedical Engineering*, **51**, 45–55.

Gratton, G., Coles, M. G. H., & Donchin, E. (1983). A new method for the off-line removal of ocular artifact. *Electroencephalography and Clinical Neurophysiology*, **55**, 468–484.

Gray, J. A., & McNaughton, N. (2000). *The neuropsychology of anxiety: An enquiry into the functions of the septo-hippocampal system,* (2nd ed.). Oxford, UK: Oxford University Press.

Gray, J. R. (2001). Emotion modulation of cognitive control: Approach-withdrawal states double-dissociate spatial from verbal two-back task performance. *Journal of Experimental Psychology: General*, **130**, 436–452.

Gray, J. R. (2004). Integration of emotion and cognitive control. *Current Directions in Psychological Science*, **13**, 46–48.

Grillon, C., & Baas, J. (2003). A review of the modulation of the startle reflex by affective states and its application in psychiatry. *Clinical Neurophysiology*, **114**, 1557–1579.

Grillon, C., & Davis, M. (1997). Fear-potentiated startle conditioning in humans: Explicit and contextual cue conditioning following paired vs. unpaired training. *Psychophysiology*, **34**, 451–458.

Grillon, C., Dierker, L., & Merikangas, K. R. (1998). Fear-potentiated startle in adolescent offspring of parents with anxiety disorders. *Biological Psychiatry*, **44**, 990–997.

Groome, L. J., Loizou, P. C., Holland, S. B., Smith, L. A., & Hoff, C. (1999). High vagal tone is associated with more efficient regulation of homeostasis in low-risk human fetuses. *Developmental Psychobiology*, **35**, 25–34.

Gross, J., & Thompson, R. A. (2007). Conceptual foundations for the field. In J. Gross (Ed.), *Handbook of emotion regulation* (pp. 3–24). New York: Guilford.

Gross, J. J., & Munoz, R. E. (1995). Emotion regulation and mental health. *Clinical Psychology: Science and Practice*, **2**, 151–164.

Gunnar, M. R. (2006). Stress neurobiology and developmental psychopathology. In D. Cicchetti & D. J. Cohen, (Eds.), *Developmental psychopathology: Developmental neuroscience* (Vol. 2, 2nd ed., pp. 533–577). Hoboken, NJ: John Wiley & Sons.

Gunnar, M. R., & Donzella, B. (2002). Social regulation of the cortisol levels in early human development. *Psychoneuroendocrinology*, **27**, 199–220.

Gunnar, M. R., Hertsgaard, L., Larson, M., & Rigatuso, J. (1991). Cortisol and behavioral responses to repeated stressors in the human newborn. *Developmental Psychobiology*, **24**, 487–506.

Gunnar, M. R., & Quevedo, K. (2007). The neurobiology of stress and development. *Annual Review of Psychology, 58*, 145–173.

Gunnar, M. R., Sebanc, A. M., Tout, K., Donzella, B., & van Dulmen, M. M. H. (2003). Temperament, peer relationships, and cortisol activity in preschoolers. *Developmental Psychobiology, 43*, 346–358.

Gunnar, M. R., & Talge, N. M. (2007). Neuroendocrine measures in developmental research. In L. A. Schmidt & S. J. Segalowitz (Eds.), *Developmental psychophysiology: Theory, systems, and methods* (pp. 343–366). Cambridge, UK: Cambridge University Press.

Gunnar, M. R., Talge, N. M., & Herrera, A. (2009). Stressor paradigms in developmental studies: What does and does not work to produce mean increases in salivary cortisol. *Psychoneuroendocrinology, 34*, 953–967.

Gunnar, M. R., & Vazquez, D. (2001). Low cortisol and a flattening of the expected daytime rhythm: Potential indices of risk in human development. *Development and Psychopathology, 13*, 515–538.

Gunnar, M. R., & Vazquez, D. (2006). Stress neurobiology and developmental psychopathology. In D. Cicchetti & D. Cohen (Eds.), *Developmental psychopathology: Developmental neuroscience* (Vol. 2, 2nd ed., pp. 533–577). New York: Wiley.

Gunnar, M. R., Wewerka, S., Frenn, K., Long, J. D., & Griggs, C. (2009). Developmental changes in HPA activity over the transition to adolescence: Normative changes and associations with puberty. *Development and Psychopathology, 21*, 69–85.

Guyer, A. E., Nelson, E. E., Perez-Edgar, K., Hardin, M. G., Roberson-Nay, R., Monk, C. S., Bjork, J. M., Henderson, H. A., Pine, D. S., Fox, N. A., & Ernst, M. (2006). Striatal functional alteration in adolescents characterized by early childhood behavioral inhibition. *Journal of Neuroscience, 26*, 6399–6405.

Haas, B. W., Omura, K., Constable, R. T., & Canli, T. (2006). Interference produced by emotional conflict associated with anterior cingulate activation. *Cognitive, Affective, and Behavioral Neuroscience, 6*, 152–156.

Haas, S. M., Frei, M. G., Osorio, I., Pasik-Duncan, B., & Radel, J. (2003). EEG ocular artifact removal through ARMAX model system identification using extended least squares. *Communications in Information and Systems, 3*, 19–40.

Hagan, M. J., Luecken, L. J., Sandler, I. N., & Tein, J. Y. (2009). Prospective effects of postbereavement negative events on cortisol activity in parentally bereaved youth. *Developmental Psychobiology, 52*, 394–400.

Halit, H., de Haan, M., & Johnson, M. H. (2003). Cortical specialisation for face processing: Face-sensitive event-related potential components in 3- and 12-month-old infants. *Neuroimage, 19*, 1180–1193.

Halligan, S. L., Herbert, J., Goodyer, I. M., & Murray, L. (2004). Exposure to postnatal depression predicts elevated cortisol in adolescent offspring. *Biological Psychiatry, 55*, 376–381.

Halligan, S. L., Herbert, J., Goodyer, I., & Murray, L. (2007). Disturbances in morning cortisol excretion in association with maternal postnatal depression predict subsequent depressive symptomatology in adolescents. *Biological Psychiatry, 62*, 40–46.

Hannesdottir, D. K., Doxie, J., Bell, M. A., Ollendick, T. H., & Wolfe, C. D. (2010). A longitudinal study of emotion regulation and anxiety in middle childhood: Associations with frontal EEG asymmetry in early childhood. *Developmental Psychobiology, 52*, 197–204.

Hanson, J. L., Chung, M. K., Avants, B. B., Shirtcliff, E. A., Gee, J. C., Davidson, R. J., et al. (2010). Early stress is associated with alterations in the orbitofrontal cortex: A tensor-based morphometry investigation of brain structure and behavioral risk. *Journal of Neuroscience, 30*, 7466–7472.

Hariri, A. R., Tessitore, A., Mattay, V. S., Fera, F., & Weinberger, D. R. (2002). The amygdala response to emotional stimuli: A comparison of faces and scenes. *Neuroimage, 17*, 317–323.

Hart, J., Gunnar, M., & Cicchetti, D. (1996). Altered neuroendocrine activity in maltreated children related to depression. *Development and Psychopathology, 8*, 201–214.

Hastings, P. D., Nuselovici, J. N., Utendale, W. T., Coutya, J., McShane, K. E., & Sullivan, C. (2007). Applying the polyvagal theory to children's emotion regulation: Social context, socialization, and adjustment. *Biological Psychology, 79*, 229–306.

Hastings, P. D., Nuselovici, J. N., Utendale, W. T., Coutya, J., McShane, K. E., & Sullivan, C. (2008). Applying the polyvagal theory to children's emotion regulation: Social context, socialization, and adjustment. *Biological Psychology, 79*, 229–306.

Hauner, K. Y., Adama, E. K., Mineka, S., Doane, L. D., DeSantis, A. S., Zinbarg, R., et al. (2008). Neuroticism and introversion are associated with salivary cortisol patterns in adolescents. *Psychoneuroendocrinology, 33*, 1344–1356.

Heim, C., & Nemeroff, C. B. (2001). The role of childhood trauma in the neurobiology of mood and anxiety disorders: Preclinical and clinical studies. *Biological Psychiatry, 49*, 1023–1039.

Heim, C., Newport, D. J., Bonsall, R. W., Miller, A. H., & Nemroff, C. B. (2001). Altered pituitary-adrenal axis responses to provocative challenge tests in adult survivors of childhood abuse. *American Journal of Psychiatry, 158*, 575–581.

Heim, C., Newport, D. J., Mietzko, T., Miller, A. H., & Nemeroff, C. B. (2008). The link between childhood trauma and depression: Insights from HPA axis studies in humans. *Psychoneuroendocrinology, 33*, 693–710.

Heim, C., Owens, M. J., Plotsky, P. M., & Nemeroff, C. B. (1997). Persistent changes in corticotropin-releasing factor systems due to early life stress: Relationship to the pathophysiology of major depression and post-traumatic stress disorder. *Psychopharmacology Bulletin, 33*, 185–192.

Heim, C., Plotsky, P., & Nemeroff, C. B. (2004). The importance of studying the contributions of early adverse experiences to the neurobiological findings in depression. *Neuropsychopharmacology, 29*, 641–648.

Henderson, H. A., & Wachs, T. D. (2007). Temperament theory and the study of cognition-emotion interactions across development. *Developmental Review, 27*, 396–427.

Hennessy, J. W., & Levine, S. (1979). Stress, arousal, and the pituitary-adrenal system: A psychoendocrine hypothesis. In J. M. Sprague & A. N. Epstein (Eds.), *Progress in psychobiology and physiological psychology* (Vol. 8, pp. 133–178). New York: Academic Press.

Henry, J. P. (1993). Psychological and physiological responses to stress: The right hemisphere and the hypothalamic-pituitary-adrenal axis, an inquiry into problems of human bonding. *Integrative Physiological and Behavioral Science, 28*, 369–387.

Herman, J. P., & Cullinan, W. E. (1997). Neurocircuitry of stress: Central control of the hypothalamo-pituitary-adrenocortical axis. *Trends in Neurosciences, 20*, 78–84.

Herman, J. P., Ostrander, M. M., Mueller, N. K., & Figueiredo, H. (2005). Limbic system mechanisms of stress regulation: Hypothalamo-pituitary-adrenocortical axis. *Progress in Neuropsychopharmacology and Biological Psychiatry, 29*, 1201–1213.

Herman, J. P., Tasker, J. G., Ziegler, D. R., & Cullinan, W. E. (2002). Local circuit regulation of paraventricular nucleus stress integration glutamate-GABA connections. *Pharmacology Biochemistry and Behavior, 71*, 457–468.

Herpertz, S. C., Mueller, B., Wenning, B., Qunaibi, M., Lichterfeld, C., & Herpertz-Dahlmann, B. (2003). Autonomic responses in boys with externalizing disorders. *Journal of Neural Transmission, 110*, 1181–1195.

Hertsgaard, L., Gunnar, M. R., Larson, M., Brodersen, L., & Lehman, H. (1992). First time experiences in infancy: When they appear to be pleasant, do they activate the adrenocortical stress response? *Developmental Psychobiology, **25**, 319–334.

Hesse, P., & Cicchetti, D. (1982). Perspectives on an integrative theory of emotional development. *New Directions for Child Development,* **16**, 3–48.

Hibel, L. C., Granger, D. A., Cicchetti, D., & Rogosch, F. (2007). Salivary biomarker levels and diurnal variation: Associations with medications prescribed to control children's problem behavior. *Child Development,* **78**, 927–937.

Hilz, M. J., Dutsch, M., Perrine, K., Nelson, P. K., Rauhut, U., & Devinsky, O. (2001). Hemispheric influence on autonomic modulation and baroreflex sensitivity. *Annals of Neurology,* **49**, 575–584.

Hinnant, J. B., & El-Shiekh, M. (2009). Children's externalizing and internalizing symptoms over time: The role of individual differences in patterns of RSA responding. *Journal of Abnormal Child Psychology,* **37**, 1049–1061.

Hinrichs, H., & Machleidt, W. (1992). Basic emotions reflected in EEG-coherences. *International Journal of Psychophysiology,* **13**, 225–232.

Hofer, M. A. (1971). Cardiac rate regulated by nutritional factor in young rats. *Science,* **172**, 1039–1041.

Hofer, M. A. (1995). Hidden regulators: Implications for a new understanding of attachment, separation, and loss. In S. Golberg, R. Muir, & J. Kerr (Eds.), *Attachment theory: Social, developmental, and clinical perspectives* (pp. 203–230). Hillsdale, NJ: Analytic Press.

Hoffmann, S., & Falkenstein, M. (2008). The correction of eye blink artifacts in the EEGL: A comparison of two prominent methods. *PLoS ONE,* **3**, 1–11.

Hopkins, W. D., & Cantalupo, C. (2008). Theoretical speculations on the evolutionary origins of hemispheric specialization. *Current Directions in Psychological Science,* **17**, 233–237.

Horne, J. (1993). Human sleep, sleep loss and behaviour: Implications for the prefrontal cortex and psychiatric disorder. *British Journal of Psychiatry,* **162**, 413–419.

Hrdy, S. B. (1999). *Mother nature.* New York: Ballantine Books.

Huettel, S. A., Song, A. W., & McCarthy (2004). *Functional magnetic resonance imaging.* Sunderland, MA: Sinauer Associates.

Huffman, L. C., Bryan, Y. E., del Carmen, R., Pedersen, F. A., Doussard-Roosevelt, J. A., & Porges, S. W. (1998). Infant temperament and cardiac vagal tone: Assessments at twelve weeks of age. *Child Development,* **69**, 624–635.

Hughdahl, K. (1995). *Psychophysiology: The mind-body perspective.* Cambridge, MA: Harvard University Press.

Hughdahl, K., Franzon, M., Andersson, B., & Walldebo, G. (1983). Heart-rate responses (HRR) to lateralized visual stimuli. *Pavlovian Journal of Biological Science,* **18**, 186–198.

Huizenga, H. M., Heslenfeld, D. J., & Molenaar, P. C. M. (2002). Optimal measurement conditions for spatiotemporal EEG/MEG source analysis. *Psychometrika,* **67**, 299–313.

Human Rights Watch. (1998). *Abandoned to the state: Cruelty and neglect in Russian orphanages.* New York: Human rights watch.

Insel T. R. (1997). A neurobiological basis of social attachment. *American Journal of Psychiatry,* **154**, 726–735.

Isreal, J. B., Chesney, G. L., Wickens, C. D., & Donchin, E. (1980). P300 and tracking difficulty: Evidence for multiple resources in dual-task performance. *Psychophysiology,* **17**, 259–273.

Izard, C. (1993). Four systems for emotion activation: Cognitive and noncognitive processes. *Psychological Review,* **100**, 68–90.

Izard, C. E., & Harris, P. (1995). Emotional development and developmental psychopathology. In D. Cicchetti & D. J. Cohen (Eds.), *Developmental psychopathology: Theory and methods* (Vol. 1, pp. 467–503). New York: Wiley.

Jackson, D. C., Malmstadt, J. R., Larson, C. L., & Davidson, R. J. (2000). Suppression and enhancement of emotional response to unpleasant pictures. *Psychophysiology, 37*, 515–522.

Jackson, D. C., Mueller, C. J., Dolski, I., Dalton, K. M., Nitschke, J. B., Urry, H. L., et al. (2003). Now you feel it, now you don't: Frontal brain electrical asymmetry and individual differences in emotion regulation. *Psychological Science, 14*, 612–617.

Jaffe, F., Beebe, B., Feldstein, S., Crown, C. L., & Jasnow, M. D. (2001). Rhythms of dialogue in infancy. *Monographs of the Society for Research in Child Development, 66*, Serial No. 265.

Jaffe, P., Wolfe, D. A., Wilson, S., & Zak, L. (1986). Emotional and physical health problems of battered women. *Canadian Journal of Psychiatry, 31*, 625–629.

James, W. (1890). *The principles of psychology.* New York: Henry Holt.

Joëls, M., & Baram, T. Z. (2009). The neuro-symphony of stress. *Nature Review Neuroscience, 10*, 459–466.

Johnson, M. H., Griffin, R., Csibra, G., Halit, H., Farroni, T., de Haan, M., et al. (2005). The emergence of the social brain network: Evidence from typical and atypical development. *Development and Psychopathology, 17*, 599–619.

Johnstone, T., van Reekum, C. M., Urry, H. L., Kalin, N. H., & Davidson, R. J. (2007). Failure to regulate: Counterproductive recruitment of top-down prefrontal-subcortical circuitry in major depression. *Journal of Neuroscience, 27*, 8877–8884.

Jouriles, E. N., McDonald, R., & Skopp, N. A. (2005). Partner violence and children. In W. M. Pinsof & J. L. Lebow (Eds.), *Family psychology: The art of the science* (pp. 223–242). New York: Oxford University Press.

Jouriles, E. N., Norwood, W. D., McDonald, R. & Peters, B. (2001). Domestic violence and child adjustment. In J. H. Grych & F. D. Fincham (Eds.), *Interparental conflict and child development: Theory, research, and applications* (pp. 315–336). New York: Cambridge University Press.

Jung, T. P., Makeig, S., Humphries, C., Lee, T. W., McKeown, M. J., Iragui, V., et al. (2000). Removing electroencephalographic artifacts by blind source separation. *Psychophysiology, 37*, 163–178.

Kagan, J. (1994). *Galen's prophecy: Temperament in human nature.* New York: Basic Books.

Kagan, J. (2006). Biology's useful contribution: A comment. *Human Development, 49*, 310–314.

Kagan, J., Reznick, J. S., & Snidman, N. (1987). The physiology and psychology of behavioral inhibition in children. *Child Development, 58*, 1459–1473.

Kagan, J., Reznick, J. S., & Snidman, N. (1988). Biological bases of childhood shyness. *Science, 240*, 167–171.

Kagan, J., Snidman, N., Zentner, M., & Peterson, E. (1999). Infant temperament and anxious symptoms in school age children. *Development and Psychopathology, 11*, 209–224.

Kalin, N. H., Larson, C., Shelton, S. E., & Davidson, R. J. (1998). Asymmetric frontal brain activity, cortisol, and behavior associated with fearful temperament in rhesus monkeys. *Behavioral Neuroscience, 112*, 286–292.

Kalin, N. H., Shelton, S. E., & Davidson, R. J. (2004). The role of the central nucleus of the amygdala in mediating fear and anxiety in the primate. *Journal of Neuroscience, 24*, 5506–5515.

Kamarck, T. W., & Lovallo, W. R. (2003). Cardiovascular reactivity to psychological challenge: Conceptual and measurement considerations. *Psychosomatic Medicine, 65*, 9–21.

Karunanayaka, P., Holland, S. K., Schmithorst, V. J., Solodkin, A., Chen, E. E., Szaflarski, J. P., et al. (2007). Age-related connectivity changes in fMRI data from children listening to stories. *NeuroImage, 34*, 349–360.

Katz, L. F. (2000). Living in a hostile world: Toward an integrated model of family, peer and physiological processes in childhood aggression. In K. A. Kerns, J. Contreras & A. M. Neal-Barnett (Eds.), *Linking two social worlds: Family and peers.* Westport, CT: Praeger.

Katz, L. F. (2007). Domestic violence and vagal reactivity to peer provocation. *Biological Psychology, 74*, 154–164.

Katz, L. F., & Gottman, J. M. (1995). Vagal tone protects children from marital conflict. *Development and Psychopathology, 7*, 83–92.

Katz, L. F., & Gottman, J. M. (1997). Buffering children from marital conflict and dissolution. *Journal of Clinical Child Psychology, 26*, 157–171.

Katz, L. F., Hessler, D. H., & Annest, A. (2007). Domestic violence, child emotional competence, and child adjustment. *Social Development, 16*, 513–538.

Katz, L. F., Hunter, E., & Klowden, A. (2008). Intimate partner violence and children's reactions to peer provocation: The moderating role of emotion coaching. *Journal of Family Psychology, 22*, 614–621.

Katz, L. F., & Windecker-Nelson, B. (2006). Domestic violence, emotion coaching and child adjustment. *Journal of Family Psychology, 20*, 56–67.

Kaufman, J. (1991). Depressive disorders in maltreated children. *Journal of the American Academy of Child and Adolescent Psychiatry, 30*, 257–265.

Kaufman, J., Birmaher, B., Perel, J., Dahl, R. E., Moreci, P., Nelson, B., et al. (1997). The corticotropin-releasing hormone challenge in depressed abused, depressed nonabused, and normal control children. *Biological Psychiatry, 42*, 669–679.

Kaufman, J., & Charney, D. (2001). Effects of early stress on brain structure and function: Implications for understanding the relationship between child maltreatment and depression. *Development and Psychopathology, 13*, 451–471.

Kendrick, K. M., Keverne, E. B., Baldwin, B. A., & Sharman, D. F. (1986). Cerebrospinal fluid levels of acetylcholinesterase, monoamines and oxytocin during labour, parturition, vaginocervical stimulation, lamb separation and suckling in sheep. *Neuroendocrinology, 44*, 149–156.

Kenemans, J. L., Molenaar, P. C. M., Verbaten, M. N., & Slangen, J. L. (1991). Removal of the ocular artifacts from the EEG: A comparison of time and frequency domain methods with simulated and real data. *Psychophysiology, 28*, 115–121.

Kerr, A., & Zelazo, P. D. (2004). Development of "hot" executive function: The children's gambling task. *Brain and Cognition, 55*, 148–157.

Key, A. P., Dove, G. O., & Maguire, M. J. (2005). Linking brainwaves to the brain: An ERP primer. *Developmental Neuropsychology, 27*, 183–215.

Kibler, J. L., Prosser, V. L., & Ma, M. (2004). Cardiovascular correlates of misconduct in children and adolescents. *Journal of Psychophysiology, 18*, 184–189.

Kierkels, J. J. M., van Boxtel, G. J. M., & Vogten, L. L. M. (2006). A model-based objective evaluation of eye movement correction in EEG recordings. *IEEE Transactions on Biomedical Engineering, 53*, 246–253.

Kim, J., Cicchetti, D., Rogosch, F. A., & Manly, J. T. (2009). Child maltreatment and trajectories of personality and behavioral functioning: Implications for the development of personality disorder. *Development and Psychopathology, 21*, 889–912.

Kim, J., Zhu, W., Chang, L., Bentler, P. M., & Ernst, T. (2007). Unified structural equation modeling approach for the analysis of multisubject, multivariate functional MRI data. *Human Brain Mapping, 28*, 85–93.

Kim, P., Feldman, R., Leckman, J. F., Mayes, L. C., & Swain, J. E. (2011). Breastfeeding, mothers' brain activation to own infant stimuli, and maternal sensitivity. *Journal of Child Psychology and Psychiatry*, **52**, 907–915.

King, A. P., & Liberzon, I. (2009). Assessing the neuroendocrine stress response in the functional neuroimaging context. *Neuroimage*, **47**, 1116–1124.

King, J. A., Mandansky, D., King, S., Fletcher, K., & Brewer, J. (2001). Early sexual abuse and low cortisol. *Psychiatry and Clinical Neurosciences*, **55**, 71–74.

Kirschbaum, C., & Hellhammer, D. H. (1989). Salivary cortisol in psychobiological research: An overview. *Neuropsychobiology*, **22**, 150–169.

Kirschbaum, C., & Hellhammer, D. H. (1994). Salivary cortisol in psychoneuroendocrine research: Recent developments and applications. *Psychoneuroendocrinology*, **19**, 313–333.

Kirschbaum, C., Tietze, A., Skoluda, N., & Dettenborn, L. (2009). Hair as a retrospective calendar of cortisol production-increased cortisol incorporation into hair in the third trimester of pregnancy. *Psychoneuoendocrinology*, **34**, 32–37.

Kivlighan, K. T., Granger, D. A., Schwartz, E. B., Nelson, V., Curran, M., & Shirtcliff, E. A. (2004). Quantifying blood leakage into the oral mucosa and its effects on the measurement of cortisol, dehdroepiandrosterone, and testosterone in saliva. *Hormones and Behavior*, **46**, 39–46.

Koikegami, H., & Yoshida, K. (1953). Pupillary dilation induced by stimulation of amygdaloid nuclei. *Folia Pychiatrica Neurologica Japonica*, **7**, 109–125.

Konorski, J. (1967). *Integrative activity of the brain: An interdisciplinary approach*. Chicago: University of Chicago Press.

Kopp, C. B. (2002). The co-development of attention and emotion regulation. *Infancy*, **3**, 199–208.

Korosi, A., & Baram, T. Z. (2008). The central corticotropin releasing factor system during development and adulthood. *European Journal of Pharmacology*, **583**, 204–214.

Korpelainen, J. T., Sotaniemi, K. A., Huikuri, H. V., & Myllyla, V. V. (1996). Abnormal heart rate variability as a manifestation of autonomic dysfunction in hemispheric brain infarction. *Stroke*, **27**, 2059–2063.

Kosfeld, M., Heinrichs, M., Zak, P. J., Fischbacher, U., & Fehr, E. (2005). Oxytocin increases trust in humans. *Nature*, **435**, 673–676.

Krueger, R. F., Hicks, B., Patrick, C. J., Carlson, S. R., Iacono, W. G., & McGue, M. (2002). Etiologic connections among substance dependence, antisocial behavior, and personality: Modeling the externalizing spectrum. *Journal of Abnormal Psychology*, **111**, 411–424.

Kuperman, V. (2000). *Magnetic resonance imaging: Physical principles and applications*. San Diego, CA: Academic Press.

Kupper, N., Willemsen, G., Posthuma, D., deBoer, D., Boomsma, D. I., & DeGeus, E. J. C. (2005). A genetic analysis of ambulatory cardiorespiratory coupling. *Psychophysiology*, **42**, 202–212.

Laakso, A., Wallius, E., Kajander, J., Bergman, J., Eskola, O., Solin, O., et al. (2003). Personality traits and striatal dopamine synthesis capacity in healthy subjects. *American Journal of Psychiatry*, **160**, 904–910.

Lamm, C., & Lewis, M. D. (2010). Developmental change in the neurophysiological correlates of self-regulation in high- and low-emotion conditions. *Developmental Neuropsychology*, **35**, 156–176.

Lane, R. D., Novelly, R., Cornell, C., Zeitlin, S., & Schwartz, G. (1988). *Asymmetrical control of heart rate*. Paper presented at the Annual Meeting of the Society for Psychophysiological Research, San Francisco.

Lane, R. D., & Schwartz, G. (1987). Induction of lateralized sympathetic input to the heart by CNS during emotional arousal: A possible neurophysiologic trigger of sudden cardiac death. *Psychosomatic Medicine, 49,* 274–284.

Lang, P. J., Bradley, M. M., & Cuthbert, B. N. (1990). Emotion, attention and the startle reflex. *Psychological Review, 97,* 377–395.

Lang, P. J., Bradley, M. M., & Cuthbert, B. N. (1998). Emotion, motivation, and anxiety: Brain mechanisms and psychophysiology. *Biological Psychiatry, 44,* 1248–1263.

Larsen, J. T., Berntson, G. G., Poehlmann, K. M., Ito, T. A., & Cacioppo, J. T. (2008). The psychophysiology of emotion. In R. Lewis, J. M. Haviland-Jones, & L. F. Barrett (Eds.), *The handbook of emotions* (3rd ed., pp. 180–195). New York: Guilford.

Larson, M., White, B. P., Cochran, A., Donzella, B., & Gunnar, M. R. (1998). Dampening of the cortisol response to handling at 3-months in human infants and its relation to sleep, circadian cortisol activity, and behavioral distress. *Developmental Psychobiology, 33,* 327–337.

Larson, M. C., Gunnar, M. R., & Hertsgaard, L. (1991). The effects of morning naps, car trips, and maternal separation on adrenocortical activity in human infants. *Child Development, 62,* 362–372.

Larson, R. W., & Asmussen, L. (1991). Anger, worry, and hurt in early adolescence: An enlarging world of negative emotions. In M. E. Colten & S. Gore (Eds.), *Adolescent stress: Causes and consequences* (pp. 21–41). Hawthorne, NY: Aldine de Gruyter.

Lazar, N. A. (2008). *The statistical analysis of functional MRI data.* New York: Springer.

Lazarus, R. S. (1982). Thoughts on the relations between emotion and cognition. *American Psychologist, 37,* 1019–1024.

Leary, A., & Katz, L. F. (2004). Family-level processes, and peer outcomes: The moderating role of vagal tone. *Development and Psychopathology, 16,* 593–608.

Leckman J. F., & Herman A. E. (2002). Maternal behavior and developmental psychopathology. *Biological Psychiatry, 51,* 27–43.

LeDoux, J. (2000). Emotion circuits in the brain. *Annual Review of Neuroscience, 23,* 155–184.

Lee, H., Shackman, A. J., Jackson, D. C., & Davidson, R. J. (2009). Test-retest reliability of voluntary emotion regulation. *Psychophysiology, 46,* 874–879.

Lee, M. Y. (2001). Marital violence: Impact on children's emotional experiences, emotional regulation and behaviors in a post-divorce/separation situation. *Child and Adolescent Social Work Journal, 18,* 137–163.

Leppanen, J. M., Moulson, M. C., Vogel-Farley, V. K., & Nelson, C. A. (2007). An ERP study of emotional face processing in the adult and infant brain. *Child Development, 78,* 232–245.

Levine, S., & Wiener, S. G. (1989). Coping with uncertainty: A paradox. In D. S. Palermo (Ed.), *Coping with uncertainty: Behavioral and developmental perspectives* (pp. 1–16). Hillsdale, NJ: Erlbaum.

Lewis, M., Ramsay, D. S., & Sullivan, M. W. (2006). The relations of ANS and HPA activation to infant anger and sadness response to goal blockage. *Developmental Psychobiology, 48,* 397–405.

Lewis, M. D. (2005). Bridging emotion theory and neurobiology through dynamic systems modeling. *Behavioral and Brain Sciences, 28,* 169–245.

Lewis, M. D., Granic, I., Lamm, C., Zelazo, P. D., Stieben, J., Todd, R. M., et al. (2008). Changes in the neural bases of emotion regulation associated with clinical improvement in children with behavior problems. *Developemental Psychopathology, 20,* 913–939.

Lewis, M. D., Lamm, C., Segalowitz, S. J., Stieben, J., & Zelazo, P. D. (2006). Neurophysiological correlates of emotion regulation in children and adolescents. *Journal of Cognitive Neuroscience, 18,* 430–443.

164

Lewis, M. D., & Stieben, J. (2004). Emotion regulation in the brain: Conceptual issues and directions for developmental research. *Child Development, 75*, 371–376.

Lewis, M. D., & Todd, R. M. (2007). The self-regulating brain: Cortical-subcortical feedback and the development of intelligent action. *Cognitive Development, 22*, 406–430.

Lewis, M. D., Todd, R. M., & Honsberger, M. J. M. (2007). Event-related potential measures of emotion regulation in early childhood. *NeuroReport, 18*, 61–65.

Llineas, R. (2001). *I of the vortex: From neurons to self.* Cambridge, MA: MIT Press.

Logothetis, N. K. (2008). What we can do and what we cannot do with fMRI. *Nature, 453*, 869–878.

Lorber, M. F. (2004). Psychophysiology of aggression, psychopathy, and conduct problems: A meta-analysis. *Psychological Bulletin, 130*, 531–552.

Lorenz, K. Z. (1950). The comparative method in studying innate behavior patterns. *Society for experimental biology: Physiological mechanisms in animal behavior* (Society's Symposium IV) (pp. 221–268). Oxford, UK: Academic Press.

Lovallo, W. R., Farag, N. H., & Vincent A. S. (2010). Use of a resting control day in measuring the cortisol response to mental stress: Diurnal patterns, time of day, and gender effects. *Psychoneuroendocrinology, 35*, 1253–1258.

Lovic, V., & Fleming, A. S. (2004). Artificially-reared female rats show reduced prepulse inhibition and deficits in the attentional set shifting task–reversal of effects with maternal-like licking stimulation. *Behavioural Brain Research, 148*, 209–219.

Luck, S. J. (2005). *An introduction to the event-related potential technique.* Cambridge, MA: MIT Press.

Luecken, L. J., Kraft, A., Appelhans, B. M., & Enders, C. (2009). Emotional and cardiovascular sensitization to daily stress following childhood parental loss. *Developmental Psychology, 45*, 296–302.

Luecken, L. J., Kraft, A., & Hagan, M. J. (2009). Negative relationships in the family-of-origin predict attenuated cortisol in emerging adults. *Hormones and Behavior, 55*, 412–417.

Lupien, S. J., Ouellet-Morin, I., Hupbach, A., Tu, M. T., Buss, C., Walker, D., et al. (2006). Beyond the stress concept: Allostatic load—A developmental biological and cognitive perspective. In D. Cicchetti & D. Cohen (Eds.), *Developmental Psychopathology. Vol. 2: Developmental Neuroscience* (2nd ed., pp. 578–628). New York: Wiley.

Majewska, M. D. (1995). Neuronal actions of dehydroepinandrosterone: Possible roles in brain development, aging, memory, and affect. *Annals of the New York Academy of Sciences, 774*, 111–120.

Makino, S., Gold, P. W., & Schulkin, J. (1994a). Corticosterone effects on corticotropin-releasing hormone mRNA in the central nucleus of the amygdala and the parvocellular region of the paraventricular nucleus of the hypothalamus. *Brain Research, 640*, 105–112.

Makino, S., Gold, P. W., & Schulkin, J. (1994b). Effects of corticosterone on CRH mRNA and content in the bed nucleus of the stria terminals: Comparison with the effects in the central nucleus of the amygdala and the paraventricualar nucleus of the hypothalmus. *Brain Research, 657*, 141–149.

Manly, J. T., Kim, J. E., Rogosch, F. A., & Cicchetti, D. (2001). Dimensions of child maltreatment and children's adjustment: Contributions of developmental timing and subtype. *Development and Psychopathology, 13*, 759–782.

Margolin, G. (1998). Effects of domestic violence on children. In P. K. Trickett & C. J. Schellenbach (Eds.), *Violence against children in the family and the community* (pp. 57–101). Washington, DC: American Psychological Association.

Marshall, P. J., Bar-Haim, Y., & Fox, N. A. (2002). Development of the EEG from 5 months to 4 years of age. *Clinical Neurophysiology, 113*, 1199–1208.

Matthys, W., van Goozen, S. H. M., Snoek, H., & van Engeland, H. (2004). Response perseveration and sensitivity to reward and punishment in boys with oppositional defiant disorder. *European Child and Adolescent Psychiatry*, **13**, 362–364.

McCloskey, L. A., & Stuewig, J. (2001). The quality of peer relationships among children exposed to family violence. *Development and Psychopathology*, **13**, 83–96.

McEwen, B. S. (1998). Stress, adaptation, and disease: Allostasis and allostatic load. *Annals of the New York Academy of Sciences*, **840**, 33–44.

McEwen, B. S., & Stellar, E. (1993). Stress and the individual mechanisms leading to disease. *Archives of Internal Medicine*, **153**, 2093–2101.

McGowan, P., Sasaki, A., D'Alessio, A., Dymov, S., Labonté, B., Szyf, M., et al. (2009). Epigenetic regulation of the glucocorticoid receptor in human brain associates with childhood abuse. *Nature Neuroscience*, **12**, 342–348.

McIntosh, A. R., & Gonzalez-Lima, F. (1994). Structural equation modeling and its application to network analysis in functional brain imaging. *Human Brain Mapping*, **2**, 2–22.

McManis, M. H., Bradley, M. M., Berg, W. K., Cuthbert, B. N., & Lang, P. J. (2001). Emotional reactions in children: Verbal, physiological, and behavioral responses to affective pictures. *Psychophysiology*, **38**, 222–231.

Mead, H. K., Beauchaine, T. P., Brenner, S. L., Crowell, S., Gatzke-Kopp, L., Marsh, P. (2004). *Autonomic response patterns to reward and negative mood induction among children with conduct disorder, depression, and both psychiatric conditions.* Poster presented at the Annual Meeting of the Society for Psychophysiological Research, Santa Fe, NM.

Mead, H. K., Beauchaine, T. P., & Shannon, K. E. (2010). Neurobiological adaptations to violence across development. *Development and Psychopathology*, **22**, 1–22.

Meaney, M. J. (2001). Maternal care, gene expression, and the transmission of individual differences in stress reactivity across generations. *Annual Review of Neuroscience*, **24**, 1161–1192.

Merikangas, K. R., Avenevoli, S., Dierker, L., & Grillon, C. (1999). Vulnerability factors among children at risk for anxiety disorders. *Biological Psychiatry*, **46**, 1523–1535.

Merz, C. J., Tabbert, K., Schweckendiek, J., Klucken, T., Vaitl, D., Stark, R., et al. (2010). Investigating the impact of sex and cortisol on implicit fear conditioning with fMRI. *Psychoneuoendocrinology*, **35**, 33–46.

Mikolajczak, M., Quoidbach, J., Vanootighem, V., Lambert, F., Lahaye, M., Fillée, C., et al. (2010). Cortisol awakening response (CAR)'s flexibility leads to larger and more consistent associations with psychological factors than CAR magnitude. *Psychoneuroendocrinology*, **35**, 752–757.

Miller, A., & Long, J. (2008). Psychophysiology principles, pointers, and pitfalls. In L. A. Schmidt & S. J. Segalowitz (Eds.), *Developmental psychophysiology* (pp. 367–423). New York: Cambridge University Press.

Miller, G. E., & Chen, E. (2010). Harsh family climate in early life presages the emergence of a proinflammatory phenotype in adolescence. *Psychological Science*, **21**, 848–856.

Miller, G. E., Chen, E., Fok, A. K., Walker, H., Lim, A., Nicholls, E. F., et al. (2009). Low early-life social class leaves a biological residue manifested by decreased glucocorticoid and increased proinflammatory signaling. *Proceedings of the National Academy of Sciences USA*, **106**, 14716–14721.

Miller, G. E., Chen, E., & Zhou, E. S. (2007). If it goes up, must it come down? Chronic stress and the hypothalamic-pituitary-adrenocortical axis in humans. *Psychological Bulletin*, **133**, 25–45.

Miller, N. E. (1959). Liberalization of basic S-R concepts: Extensions to conflict behavior, motivation and social learning. In S. Koch (Ed.), *Psychology: A study of a science* (pp. 198–292). New York: McGraw-Hill.

Mirmiran, M., & Lunshof, S. (1996). Perinatal development of human circadian rhythms. *Progress in Brain Research, 111*, 217–226.

Miskovic, V., & Schmidt, L.A. (2010). Frontal brain electrical asymmetry and cardiac vagal tone predict biased attention to social threat. *International Journal of Psychophysiology, 75*, 332–338.

Miskovic, V., Schmidt, L. A., Georgiades, K., Boyle, M., & MacMillan, H. L. (2010). Adolescent females exposed to child maltreatment exhibit atypical EEG coherence and psychiatric impairment: Linking early adversity, the brain, and psychopathology. *Development and Psychopathology, 22*, 419–432.

Molenaar, P. C. M. (1985). A dynamic factor model for the analysis of multivariate time series. *Psychometrika, 50*, 181–202.

Molenaar, P. C. M. (1987). Dynamic factor analysis in the frequency domain: Causal modeling of multivariate psychophysiological time series. *Multivariate Behavioral Research, 22*, 329–353.

Molenaar, P. C. M. (1993). Dynamic factor analysis of psychophysiological signals. In J. R. Jennings, P. Ackles, & M. G. H. Coles (Eds.), *Advances in psycho-physiology* (Vol. 5, pp. 229–302). London: Jessica Kingsley Publishers.

Moore, G. A, Hill-Soderlund, A. L, Propper, C. B., Calkins, S. D., Mills-Koonce, W. R., & Cox, M. J. (2009). Mother-infant vagal regulation in the face-to-face still-face paradigm is moderated by maternal sensitivity. *Child Development, 80*, 209–23.

Morasch, K. C., & Bell, M. A. (2011). The role of inhibitory control in behavioral and physiological expressions of toddler executive function. *Journal of Experimental Child Psychology, 108*, 593–606.

Murray-Close, D., Han, G., Cicchetti, D., Crick, N. R., & Rogosch, F. A. (2008). Neuroendocrine regulation and aggression: The moderating roles of physical and relational aggression and child maltreatment. *Developmental Psychology, 44*, 1160–1176.

Nelson, C. A., & de Haan, M. (1996). Neural correlates of infants' visual responsiveness to facial expressions of emotion. *Developmental Psychobiology, 29*, 577–595.

Nelson, C. A., de Haan, M., & Thomas, K. M. (2006). *Neuroscience of cognitive development: The role of experience and the developing brain.* Hoboken, NJ: Wiley.

Nelson, E. E., & Panksepp, J. (1998). Brain substrates of infant-mother attachment: Contributions of opioids, oxytocin, and norepinephrine. *Neuroscience and Biobehavioral Reviews, 22*, 437–452.

Neveu, P. J. (1993). Brain lateralization and immunomodulation. *International Journal of Neuroscience, 70*, 135–143.

Nieuwenhuis, S., Yeung, N., van den Wildenberg, W., & Ridderinkhof, K. R. (2003). Electrophysiological correlates of anterior cingulate function in a go/no-go task: Effects of response conflict and trial type frequency. *Cognitive, Affective and Behavioral Neuroscience, 3*, 17–26.

Nolte, G., Bai, O., Wheaton, L., Mari, Z., Vorbach, S., & Hallett, M. (2004). Identifying true brain interaction from EEG data using the imaginary part of coherency. *Clinical Neurophysiology, 115*, 2292–2307.

Nunez, P. L., Silberstein, R. B., Shi, Z., Carpenter, M.R., Srinivasan, R., Tucker, D., et al. (1999). EEG coherency II: Experimental comparisons of multiple measures. *Clinical Neurophysiology, 110*, 469–486.

Nunez, P. L., & Srinivasan, R. (2006). *Electric fields of the brain: The neurophysics of EEG* (2nd ed.). Oxford, UK: Oxford University Press.

Nunez, P. L., Wingeier, B. M., & Silberstein, R. B. (2001). Spatial-temporal structures of human alpha rhythms: Theory, microcurrent sources, multiscale measurements, and global binding of local networks. *Human Brain Mapping*, **13**, 125–164.

Oas, P. (1985). The psychological assessment of impulsivity: A review. *Journal of Psychoeducational Assessment*, **3**, 141–156.

Oberlander, T., Weinberg, J., Papsdorf, M., Grunau, R., Misri, S., & Devlin, A. (2008). Prenatal exposure to maternal depression, neonatal methylation of human glucocorticoid receptor gene (NR3C1) and infant cortisol stress responses. *Epigenetics*, **3**, 97–106.

Obradović, J., & Boyce, W. T. (2009). Individual differences in behavioral, physiological, and genetic sensitivities to contexts: Implications for development and adaptation. *Developmental Neuroscience*, **31**, 300–308.

Obradović, J., & Boyce, W. T. (in press). The role of stress reactivity for child development: Indices, correlates and future directions. In L. C. Mayes & M. Lewis (Eds.), *The Cambridge Handbook of environment in human development: A handbook of theory and measurement*. New York, NY: Cambridge University Press.

Obradović, J., Bush, N. R., & Boyce, W. T. (2011). The interactive effect of marital conflict and stress reactivity on externalizing and internalizing symptoms: The role of laboratory stressors. *Development and Psychopathology*, **23**, 101–114.

Obradović, J., Bush, N. R., Stamperdahl, J., Adler, N. A., & Boyce, W. T. (2010). Biological sensitivity to context: The interactive effects of stress reactivity and family adversity on socio-emotional behavior and school readiness. *Child Development*, **81**, 270–289.

Ochsner, K. N., & Gross, J. J. (2005). The cognitive control of emotion. *TRENDS in Cognitive Sciences*, **9**, 242–249.

Ochsner, K. N., & Gross, J. J. (2008). Cognitive emotion regulation: Insights from social cognitive and affective neuroscience. *Current Directions in Psychological Science*, **17**, 153–158.

O'Connor, T. G., Marvin, R. S., Rutter, M., Olrick, J. T., Britner, P. A., & English and Romanian Adoptees Study Team. (2003). Child-parent attachment following early institutional deprivation. *Development and Psychopathology*, **15**, 19–38.

O'Connor, T. G., & Rutter, M. (2000). Attachment disorder behavior following early severe deprivation: Extension and longitudinal follow-up. English and Romanian adoptees study team. *Journal of the American Academy of Child and Adolescent Psychiatry*, **39**, 703–712.

Onyskiw, J. E. (2003). Domestic violence and children's adjustment: A review of research. *Journal of Emotional Abuse*, **3**, 11–45.

Oppenheimer, S. M., Gelb, A., Girvin, J. P., & Hachinski, V. C. (1992). Cardiovascular effects of human insular cortex stimulation. *Neurology*, **42**, 1727–1732.

Oppenheimer, S. M., Kedem, G., & Martin, W. M. (1996). Left-insular cortex lesions perturb cardiac autonomic tone in humans. *Clinical Autonomic Research*, **6**, 131–140.

Orekhova, E. V., Stroganova, T. A., & Posikera, I. N. (2001). Alpha activity as an index of cortical inhibition during sustained internally controlled attention in infants. *Clinical Neurophysiology*, **112**, 740–749.

Otten, L. J., & Rugg, M. D. (2004). Interpreting event-related brain potentials. In T. C. Handy (Ed.), *Event-related potentials: A methods handbook* (pp. 3–16). Cambridge, MA: MIT Press.

Out, D., Pieper, S., Bakermans-Kranenburg, M., & van IJzendoorn, M. (2010). Physiological reactivity to infant crying: A behavioral genetic study. *Genes, Brain and Behavior*, 1–9.

Page, R. M. (1990). Shyness and sociability: A dangerous combination for illicit substance use in adolescent males. *Adolescence, 25*, 803–806.

Papadimitriou, A., & Priftis, K. N. (2009). Regulation of the hypothalamic-pituitary-adrenal axis. *Neuroimmunomodulation, 16*, 265–271.

Patterson, G. R., DeGarmo, D. S., & Knutson, N. M. (2000). Hyperactive and antisocial behaviors: Comorbid or two points in the same process? *Development and Psychopathology, 12*, 91–107.

Pendry, P., & Adam, E. K. (2007). Associations between parents' marital functioning, maternal parenting quality, maternal emotion and child cortisol levels. *International Journal of Behavioral Development, 31*, 218–231.

Pérez-Edgar, K., Bar-Haim, Y., McDermott, J. M., Chronis-Tuscano, A., Pine, D. S., & Fox, N. A. (2010). Attention biases to threat and behavioral inhibition in early childhood shape adolescent social withdrawal. *Emotion, 10*, 349–357.

Perez-Edgar, K., & Fox, N. A. (2003). Individual differences in children's performance during an emotional Stroop task: A behavioral and electrophysiological study. *Brain and Cognition, 52*, 33–51.

Perez-Edgar, K., & Fox, N. A. (2005a). A behavioral and electrophysiological study of children's selective attention under neutral and affective conditions. *Journal of Cognition and Development, 6*, 89–118.

Perez-Edgar, K., & Fox, N. A. (2005b). Temperament and anxiety disorders. *Child and Adolescent Psychiatric Clinics of North America, 14*, 681–706.

Perez-Edgar, K., & Fox, N. A. (2007). Temperamental contributions to children's performance in an emotion-word processing task: A behavioral and electrophysiological study. *Brain and Cognition, 65*, 22–35.

Perkins, S., & Graham-Bermann, S. A. (2006, November). *Contribution of age of first exposure to intimate partner violence on child adjustment.* Presentation given at the 22nd Annual Meeting of the International Society for Traumatic Stress Studies, Hollywood, CA.

Peterson, C. K., Shackman, A. J., & Harmon-Jones, E. (2007). The role of asymmetrical frontal cortical activity in aggression. *Psychophysiology, 45*, 86–92.

Pfeffer, C. R., Altemus, M., Heo, M., & Jiang, H. (2007). Salivary cortisol and psychopathology in children bereaved by the September 11, 2001 terror attacks. *Biological Psychiatry, 61*, 957–965.

Phelps, E. A. (2006). Emotion and cognition: Insights from studies of the human amygdala. *Annual Review of Psychology, 57*, 27–53.

Pine, D. S., Cohen, P., Gurley, D., Brook, J., & Ma, Y. (1998). The risk for early-adulthood anxiety and depressive disorders in adolescents with anxiety and depressive disorders. *Archives of General Psychiatry, 55*, 56–64.

Polich, J. (2007). Updating P300: An integrative theory of P3a and P3b. *Clinical Neurophysiology, 118*, 2128–2148.

Polich, J., & Criado, J. R. (2006). Neuropsychology and neuropharmacology of P3a and P3b. *International Journal of Psychophysiology, 60*, 172–185.

Polk, D. E., Cohen, S., Doyle, W. J., Skoner, D. P., & Kirschbaum, C. (2004). State and trait affect as predictors of salivary cortisol in healthy adults. *Psychoneuoendocrinology, 30*, 261–272.

Pollak, S. D. (2005). Early adversity and mechanisms of plasticity: Integrating affective neuroscience with developmental approaches to psychopathology. *Development and Psychopathology, 17*, 735–752.

Pollak, S. D. (2008). Mechanisms linking early experience and the emergence of emotions: Illustrations from the study of maltreated children. *Current Directions in Psychological Science, 17*, 370–375.

Pollak, S. D., Cicchetti, D., Hornung, K., & Reed, A. (2000). Recognizing emotion in faces: Developmental effects of child abuse and neglect. *Developmental Psychology, 36,* 679–688.

Pollak, S. D., Cicchetti, D., & Klorman, R. (1998). Stress, memory, and emotion: Developmental considerations from the study of child maltreatment. *Development and Psychopathology, 10,* 811–828.

Pollak, S. D., Cicchetti, D., Klorman, R., & Brumaghim, J. (1997). Cognitive brain event-related potentials and emotion processing in maltreated children. *Child Development, 68,* 773–787.

Pollak, S. D., Cicchetti, D., Knutson, R., & Brumaghim, J. T. (1997). Cognitive brain event-related potentials and emotion processing in maltreated children. *Child Development, 68,* 773–787.

Pollak, S. D., Klorman, R., Thatcher, J. E., & Cicchetti, D. (2001). P3b reflects maltreated children's reactions to facial displays of emotion. *Psychophysiology, 38,* 267–274.

Pollak, S. D., & Sinha, P. (2002). Effects of early experience on children's recognition of facial displays of emotion. *Developmental Psychology, 38,* 784–791.

Pollak, S. D., & Tolley-Schell, S. A. (2003). Selective attention to facial emotion in physically abused children. *Journal of Abnormal Psychology, 112,* 323–338.

Porges, S. W. (1974). Heart rate indices of newborn attentional responsivity. *Merrill-Palmer Quarterly, 20,* 231–254.

Porges, S. W. (1995). Orienting in a defensive world: Mammalian modifications of our evolutionary heritage: A polyvagal theory. *Psychophysiology, 32,* 301–318.

Porges, S. W. (2001). The polyvagal theory: Phylogenetic substrates of a social nervous system. *International Journal of Psychophysiology, 42,* 123–146.

Porges, S. W. (2003). The polyvagal theory: Phylogenetic contributions to social behavior. *Physiology and Behavior, 79,* 503–513.

Porges, S. W. (2007). The polyvagal perspective. *Biological Psychology, 74,* 116–143.

Porges, S. W., Doussard-Roosevelt, J. A., & Maiti, A. K. (1994). Vagal tone and the physiological regulation of emotion. *Monographs of the Society for Research in Child Development, 59* (2–3, Serial No. 240).

Porges, S. W., Doussard-Roosevelt, J. A., Portales, A. L., & Greenspan, S. I. (1996). Infant regulation of the vagal "brake" predicts child behavior problems: A psychobiological model of social behavior. *Developmental Psychobiology, 29,* 697–712.

Porges, S. W., Heilman, K. J., Bazhenova, O. V., Bal, E., Doussard-Roosevelt, J. A., & Koledin, M. (2007). Does motor activity during psychophysiological paradigms confound the quantification and interpretation of heart rate and heart rate variability measures in young children? *Developmental Psychobiology, 49,* 485–494.

Porges, S. W., McCabe, P. M., & Yongue, B. G. (1982). Respiratory-heart rate interactions: Psychophysiological implications for pathophysiology and behavior. In J. T. Cacioppo & R. E. Petty (Eds.), *Perspectives in cardiovascular psychophysiology* (pp. 226–264). New York: Guilford Press.

Posner, M. I., & Rothbart, M. K. (2000). Developing mechanisms of self-regulation. *Development and Psychopathology, 12,* 427–441.

Price, D. A., Close, G. C., Fielding, B. A. (1983). Age of appearance of circadian rhythm in salivary cortisol values in infancy. *Archives of the Disabled Child, 58,* 454–456.

Pruessner, J. C., Gaab, J., Hellhammer, D. H., Lintz, D., Schommer, N., & Kirschbaum, C. (1997). Increasing correlations between personality traits and cortisol stress responses obtained by data aggregation. *Psychoneuroendocrinology, 22,* 615–625.

Pruessner, J. C., Kirschbaum, C., Meinlschmid, G., & Hellhammer, D. (2003). Two formulas for computation of the area under the curve represent measures of total hormone concentration versus time-dependant change. *Psychoneuroendocrinology, 28,* 916–931.

Pruessner, J. C., Wolf, O. T., Hellhammer, D. H., Buske-Kirschbaum, A., von Auer, K., Jobst, S., et al. (1997). Free cortisol levels after awakening: A reliable biological marker for the assessment of adrenocortical activity. *Life Sciences, 61*, 2539–2549.

Quas, J. A., Hong, M., Alkon, A., & Boyce, W. T. (2000). Dissociations between psychobiologic reactivity and emotional expression in children. *Developmental Psychobiology, 37*, 153–175.

Quevedo, K. M., Benning, S. D., Gunnar, M. R., & Dahl, R. E. (2009). The onset of puberty: Effects on the psychophysiology of defensive and appetitive motivation. *Development and Pyschopathology, 21*, 27–45.

Quigley, K. S., & Stifter, C. A. (2006). A comparative validation of sympathetic reactivity in children and adults. *Psychophysiology, 43*, 357–365.

Quirk, G. J., & Mueller, D. (2007). Neural mechanisms of extinction learning and retrieval. *Neuropsychopharmacology Reviews, 33*, 1–17.

Raine, A. (1996). Autonomic nervous system factors underlying disinhibited, antisocial, and violent behavior: Biosocial perspectives and treatment implications. *Annals of the New York Academy of Sciences, 794*, 46–59.

Raine, A. (2002). Biosocial studies of antisocial and violent behavior in children and adults: A review. *Journal of Abnormal Child Psychology, 30*, 311–326.

Ramsay, D. S., & Lewis, M. (2003). Reactivity and regulation in cortisol and behavioral responses to stress. *Child Development, 74*, 456–464.

Reeb-Sutherland, B. C., Helfinstein, S. M., Degnan, K. A., Perez-Edgar, K., Henderson, H. A., Lissek, S., et al. (2009). Startle response in behaviorally inhibited adolescents with a lifetime occurrence of anxiety disorders. *Journal of the American Academy of Child and Adolescent Psychiatry, 48*, 610–617.

Repetti, R., Taylor, S. E., & Seeman, T. (2002). Risky families: Family social environments and the mental and physical health of offspring. *Psychological Bulletin, 128*, 330–366.

Richards, J. E. (2003). Cortical sources of ERP in the prosaccade and antisaccade task using realistic source models based on individual MRIs. *Psychophysiology, 40*, 878–894.

Richards, J. M., & Gross, J. J. (2000). Emotion regulation and memory: The cognitive costs of keeping one's cool. *Journal of Personality and Social Psychology, 79*, 410–424.

Rieder, C., & Cicchetti, D. (1989). Organizational perspective on cognitive control functioning and cognitive-affective balance in maltreated children. *Developmental Psychology, 25*, 382–393.

Rigterink, T., & Katz, L. F. (2010). Domestic violence and longitudinal associations with children's physiological regulation abilities. *Journal of Interpersonal Violence, 25*, 1669–1683.

Riva, D., & Giorgi, C. (2000). The contribution of the cerebellum to mental and social functions in developmental age. *Fiziologiia Cheloveka, 26*, 27–31.

Rohleder, N., Beulen, S. E., Chen, E., Wolf, J. M., & Kirschbaum, C. (2007). Stress on the dance floor: The cortisol stress response to social-evaluative threat in competitive ballroom dancers. *Personality and Social Psychology Bulletin, 33*, 69–84.

Rolls, E. T. (1999). *The brain and emotion.* New York: Oxford University Press.

Romeo, R. D. (2010). Pubertal maturation and programming of hypothalamic-pituitary-adrenal reactivity. *Frontiers of Neuroendocrinology, 31*, 232–240.

Rose, A. J. (2002). Co-rumination in the friendships of girls and boys. *Child Development, 73*, 1830–1843.

Rosen, A. D., Gur, R. C., Sussman, N., Gur, R. E., & Hurtig, H. (1982). Hemispheric asymmetry in the control of heart rate. *Abstracts of Social Neuroscience, 8*, 917.

Rosen, J. B., & Schulkin, J. (1998). From normal fear to pathological anxiety. *Psychological Review, 105*, 325–350.

Rosenblatt, J. S. (1965). The basis of synchrony in the behavioral interaction between the mother and her offspring in the laboratory rat. In B. M. Foss (Ed.), *Determinants of infant behavior* (pp. 3–45). London: Methuen.

Rothbart, M. K. (2004). Temperament and the pursuit of an integrated developmental psychology. *Merrill-Palmer Quarterly*, **50**, 492–505.

Rothbart, M. K., Sheese, B. E., & Posner, M. I. (2007). Executive attention and effortful control: Linking temperament, brain networks, and genes. *Child Development Perspectives*, **1**, 2–7.

Rudolph, K. D., & Conley, C. S. (2005). The socioemotional costs and benefits of social-evaluative concerns: Do girls care too much? *Journal of Personality*, **73**, 115–138.

Rudolph, K. D., Troop-Gordon, W., & Granger, D. A. (2010). Individual differences in biological stress responses moderate the contribution of early peer victimization to subsequent depressive symptoms. *Psychopharmacology*. Available: http://www.ncbi.nlm.nih.gov/pubmed/20505926.

Rueda, M. R., Posner, M. I., & Rothbart, M. K. (2005). The development of executive attention: Contributions to the emergence of self-regulation. *Developmental Neuropsychology*, **28**, 573–594.

Ruff, H. A., & Rothbart, M. K. (1996). *Attention in early development: Themes and variations.* New York: Oxford.

Sabatinelli, D., Bradley, M. M., & Lang, P. J. (2001). Affective startle modulation in anticipation and perception. *Psychophysiology*, **38**, 719–722.

Sagvolden, T., Johansen, E., Aase, H., & Russell, V. (2005). A dynamic developmental theory of attention-deficit/hyperactivity disorder (ADHD) predominantly hyperactive/impulsive and combined subtypes. *Behavioural and Brain Sciences*, **28**, 397–468.

Saha, S. (2005). Role of the central nucleus of the amygdala in the control of blood pressure: Descending pathways to medullary cardiovascular nuclei. *Clinical and Experimental Pharmacology and Physiology*, **32**, 450–456.

Salomon, K., Matthews, K. A., & Allen, M. T. (2000). Patterns of sympathetic and parasympathetic reactivity in a sample of children and adolescents. *Psychophysiology*, **37**, 842–849.

Saltzman, K. M., Holden, G. W., & Holahan, C. J. (2005). The psychobiology of children exposed to marital violence. *Journal of Clinical Child and Adolescent Psychology*, **34**, 129–139.

Sanchez, M. M., Noble, P. M., Lyon, C. K., Plotsky, P. M., Davis, M., Nemeroff, C. B., et al. (2005). Alterations in diurnal cortisol rhythm and acoustic startle response in nonhuman primates with adverse rearing. *Biological Psychiatry*, **57**, 373–381.

Santesso, D. L., Reker, D. L., Schmidt, L. A., & Segalowitz, S. J. (2006). Frontal electroencephalogram activation asymmetry, emotional intelligence, and externalizing behaviors in 10-year old children. *Child Psychiatry and Human Development*, **36**, 311–328.

Santesso, D. L., Schmidt, L. A., & Fox, N. A. (2004). Are shyness and sociability still a dangerous combination for substance use? Evidence from a US and Canadian sample. *Personality and Individual Differences*, **37**, 5–17.

Santucci, A. K., Silk, J. S., Shaw, D. S., Gentzler, A., Fox, N. A., & Kovacs, M. (2008). Vagal tone and temperament as predictors of emotion regulation strategies in young children. *Developmental Psychobiology*, **50**, 205–216.

Sapolsky, R. M. (1994). Individual differences and the stress response. *Seminars in the Neurosciences*, **6**, 261–269.

Sapolsky, R. M., Romero, L. M., & Munck, A. U. (2000). How do glucocorticoids influence stress responses? Integrating permissive, suppressive, stimulatory, and preparative actions. *Endocrine Reviews*, **21**, 55–89.

Sarty, G. E. (2007). *Computing brain activity maps from fMRI time-series images.* Cambridge, UK: Cambridge University Press.

Saxbe, D. E. (2008). A field (researcher's) guide to cortisol: Tracking HPA axis functioning in everyday life. *Health Psychology Review, 2,* 163–190.

Scarpa, A., Raine, A., Venables, P. H., & Mednick, S. A. (1997). Heart rate and skin conductance in behaviorally inhibited Mauritian children. *Journal of Abnormal Psychology, 106,* 182–190.

Scherer, K. R. (2003). Introduction: Cognitive components of emotion. In R. J. Davidson, K. R. Scherer, & H. H. Goldsmith (Eds.), *Handbook of affective sciences* (pp. 563–571). New York: Oxford.

Scherg, M., & Berg, P. (1991). Use of prior knowledge in brain electromagnetic source analysis. *Brain Topography, 4,* 143–150.

Scherg, M., & Picton, T. W. (1991). Separation and identification of event-related potential components by brain electric source analysis. *Electroencephalography Clinical Neurophysiology Supplement, 42,* 24–37.

Schlögl A., & Supp, G. (2006). Analyzing event-related EEG data with multivariate autoregressive parameters. In C. Neuper & W. Klimesch (Eds.), *Event-related dynamics of brain oscillations* (pp. 135–147). Amsterdam: Elsevier.

Schmahmann, J. D., Weilburg, J. B., & Sherman, J. C. (2007). The neuropsychiatry of the cerebellum—Insights from the clinic. *Cerebellum (London, England), 6,* 254–267.

Schmidt, L. A. (1999). Frontal brain electrical activity in shyness and sociability. *Psychological Science, 10,* 316–320.

Schmidt, L. A. (2008). Patterns of second-by-second resting frontal brain (EEG) asymmetry and their relation to heart rate and temperament in 9-month-old human infants. *Personality and Individual Differences, 44,* 216–225.

Schmidt, L. A., & Fox, N. A. (1994). Patterns of cortical electrophysiology and autonomic activity in adults' shyness and sociability. *Biological Psychology, 38,* 183–198.

Schmidt, L. A., & Fox, N. A. (1998a). Electrophysiological studies: I. Quantitative electroencephalography. In C. E. Coffey & R. A. Brumback (Eds.), *Textbook of Pediatric Neuropsychiatry: Section II. Neuropsychiatric assessment of the child and adolescent* (pp. 315–329). Washington, DC: American Psychiatric Press.

Schmidt, L. A., & Fox, N. A. (1998b). Fear-potentiated startle responses in temperamentally different human infants. *Developmental Psychobiology, 32,* 113–120.

Schmidt, L. A., & Fox, N. A. (1999). Conceptual, biological, and behavioral distinctions among different categories of shy children. In L. A. Schmidt & J. Schulkin (Eds.), *Extreme fear, shyness and social phobia: Origins, biological mechanisms and clinical outcomes* (pp. 47–66). New York: Oxford University Press.

Schmidt, L. A., Fox, N. A., & Hamer, D. H. (2007). Evidence for a gene–gene interaction in predicting children's behavior problems: Association of 5-HTT short and DRD4 long genotypes with internalizing and externalizing behaviors in seven year-old children. *Development and Psychopathology, 19,* 1103–1114.

Schmidt, L. A., Fox, N. A., Perez-Edgar, K., & Hamer, D. H. (2009). Linking gene, brain, and behavior: DRD4, frontal asymmetry, and temperament. *Psychological Science, 20,* 831–837.

Schmidt, L. A., Fox, N. A., Rubin, K. H., Sternberg, E. M., Gold, P. W., & Smith, C. C. (1997). Behavioral and neuroendocrine responses in shy children. *Developmental Psychobiology, 30,* 127–140.

Schmidt, L. A., Fox, N. A., Schulkin, J., & Gold, P. W. (1999). Behavioral and psychophysiological correlates of self-presentation in temperamentally shy children. *Developmental Psychobiology, 35,* 119–135.

Schmidt, L. A., Santesso, D. L., Schulkin, J., & Segalowitz, S. J. (2007). Shyness is a necessary but not sufficient condition for high salivary cortisol in typically developing 10 year-old children. *Personality and Individual Differences, 43,* 1541–1551.

Schmidt, L. A., & Schulkin, J. (2000). Toward a computational affective neuroscience. *Brain and Cognition, 42*, 95–98.

Schmidt, L. A., & Segalowitz, S. J. (2008). *Developmental psychophysiology: Theory, systems, and methods.* New York: Cambridge University Press.

Schneiderman, I., Zagoory-Sharon, O., Leckman, J. F., & Feldman, R. (2012). Oxytocin at the first stages of romantic attachment: Relations to couples' interactive reciprocity. *Psychoneuroendocrinology,* DOI: 10.1016/j.psyneuen.2011.12.021

Schneirla, T. C. (1946). Problems in the biopsychology of social organizations. *Journal of Abnormal and Social Psychology, 41*, 385–402.

Schneirla, T. C. (1959). An evolutionary and developmental theory of biphasic processes underlying approach and withdrawal. In M. R. Jones (Ed.), *Nebraska symposium on motivation* (Vol. 7, pp.1–42). Lincoln: University of Nebraska Press.

Schore, A. N. (1996). The experience-dependent maturation of a regulatory system in the orbital prefrontal cortex and the origin of developmental psychopathology. *Development and Psychopathology, 8*, 59–87.

Schulkin, J. (1999). *The neuroendocrine regulation of behavior.* Cambridge, UK: Cambridge University Press.

Schulkin, J. (2003). *Rethinking homeostasis: Allostatic regulation in physiology and pathophysiology.* Cambridge, MA: MIT Press.

Schulkin, J., McEwen, B. S., & Gold, P. W. (1994). Allostasis, amygdala and anticipatory angst. *Neuroscience and Biobehavioral Reviews, 18*, 385–396.

Schulkin, J., Morgan, M. A., & Rosen, J. B. (2005). A neuroendocrine mechanism for sustaining fear. *Trends in Neurosciences, 28*, 629–635.

Schulkin, J., Thompson, B. L., & Rosen, J. B. (2003). Demythologizing the emotions: Adaptation, cognition, and visceral representation of emotion in the nervous system. *Brain and Cognition, 52*, 15–23.

Schwartz, C. E., Wright, C. I., Shin, L. M., Kagan, J., & Rauch, S. L. (2003). Inhibited and uninhibited infants "grown up": Adult amygdalar response to novelty. *Science, 300*, 1952–1953.

Shackman, J. E., Shackman, A. J., Jenness, J., & Pollak, S. D. (2010). Emotion expression among abusive mothers is associated with their children's emotion processing and problem behaviors. *Cognition and Emotion, 24*, 1421–1430.

Shackman, J. E., Shackman, A. J., & Pollak, S. D. (2007). Physical abuse amplifies attention to threat and increases anxiety in children. *Emotion, 7*, 838–852.

Shannon, K. E., Beauchaine, T. P., Brenner, S. L., Neuhaus, E., & Gatzke-Kopp, L. (2007). Familial and temperamental predictors of resilience in children at risk for conduct disorder and depression. *Development and Psychopathology, 19*, 701–727.

Shea, A., Walsh, C., MacMillan, H., & Steiner, M (2004). Child maltreatment and HPA axis dysregulation: Relationship to major depressive disorder and post-traumatic stress disorder in females. *Psychoneuroendocrinology, 30*, 162–178.

Sherwood, A., Allen, M. T., Obrist, P. A., & Langer, A. W. (1986). Evaluation of beta-adrenergic influences on cardiovascular and metabolic adjustments to physical and psychological stress. *Psychophysiology, 23*, 89–104.

Shipman, K. L., Schneider, R., Fitzgerald, M. M., Sims, C., Swisher, L., & Edwards, A. (2007). Maternal emotion socialization in maltreating and non-maltreating families: Implications for children's emotion regulation. *Social Development, 16*, 268–285.

Shirtcliff, E. A., & Essex, M. J. (2008). Concurrent and longitudinal associations of basal and diurnal cortisol with mental health symptoms in early adolescence. *Developmental Psychobiology, 50*, 690–703.

174

Shirtcliff, E. A., Granger, D. A., Booth, A., & Johnson, D. (2005). Low salivary cortisol levels and externalizing behavior problems in youth. *Development and Psychopathology*, **17**, 167–184.

Shooshtari, P., Mohamadi, G., Arkedani, B. M., & Shamsollahi, M. B. (2006). Removing ocular artifacts from EEG signals using adaptive filtering and ARMAX modeling. *Proceedings of World Academy of Science, Engineering and Technology*, **11**, 277–280.

Shortt, J. W., Stoolmiller, M., Smith-Shine, J. N., Eddy, J. M., & Sheeber, L. (2010). Maternal emotion coaching, adolescent anger regulation and siblings' externalizing symptoms. *Journal of Child Psychology and Psychiatry*, **51**, 799–808.

Siegle, G. J., Granholm, E., Ingram, R. E., & Matt, G. E. (2001). Pupillary and reaction time measures of sustained processing of negative information in depression. *Biological Psychiatry*, **49**, 624–636.

Siegle, G. J., Steinhauer, S. R., Carter, C. S., Ramel, W., & Thase, M. E. (2003). Do the seconds turn into hours? Relationships between sustained pupil dilation in response to emotional information and self-reported rumination. *Cognitive Therapy and Research*, **27**, 365–382.

Siegle, G. J., Steinhauer, S. R., Friedman, E., & Thase, M. E. (in press). Prediction of response to cognitive therapy for recurrent depression using pupil dilation: Utility and neural correlates. *PLOS*.

Siegle, G. J., Steinhauer, S. R., Stenger, V., Konecky, R., & Carter, C. S. (2003). Use of concurrent pupil dilation assessment to inform interpretation and analysis of fMRI data. *Neuroimage*, **20**(1), 114–124.

Silk, J. S., Dahl, R. E., Ryan, N. D., Forbes, E. E., Axelson, D. A., Birmaher, B., et al. (2007). Pupillary reactivity to emotional information in child and adolescent depression: Links to clinical and ecological measures. *American Journal of Psychiatry*, **164**, 1873–1880.

Silk, J. S., Dahl, R. E., & Siegle, G. J. (2009). *Pupil dilation to affective words as a marker of risk for early onset depression*. Paper presented at the paper presented at the 28th International Colloquium on the Pupil, Pittsburgh, PA.

Silk, J. S., Forbes, E. E., Whalen, D. J., Jakubcak, J. L., Thompson, W. K., Ryan, N. D., et al. (2011). Understanding daily emotional and social dynamics in depressed youth: A cell-phone ecological momentary assessment study. *Journal of Experimental Child Psychology*, **110**, 241-257.

Silk, J. S., Siegle, G. J., Whalen, D. J., Ostapenko, L., Ladouceur, C. D., & Dahl, R. E. (2009). Pubertal changes in emotional information processing: Pupillary, behavioral, and subjective evidence during emotional word identification. *Development and Psychopathology*, **21**, 7–16.

Silk, J. S., Steinberg, L., & Morris, A. S. (2003). Adolescents' emotion regulation in daily life: Links to depressive symptoms and problem behavior. *Child Development*, **74**, 1869–1880.

Silk, J. S., Vanderbilt-Adriance, E., Shaw, D. S., Forbes, E. E., Whalen, D. J., Ryan, N. D., et al. (2007). Resilience among children and adolescents at risk for depression: Mediation and moderation across social and neurobiological contexts. *Development and Psychopathology*, **19**, 841–865.

Smeekens, S., Riksen-Walraven, M. J., & van Bakel, H. J. (2007). Cortisol reactions in five-year-olds to parent-child interaction: The moderating role of ego-resiliency. *Journal of Child Psychology and Psychiatry*, **48**, 649–656.

Smider, N. A., Essex, M. J., Kalin, N. H., Buss, K. A., Klein, M. H., Davidson, R. J., et al. (2002). Salivary cortisol as a predictor of socioemotional adjustment during kindergarten: A prospective study. *Child Development*, **73**, 75–92.

Smith, C. L., & Bell, M. A. (2010). Stability in infant frontal asymmetry as a predictor toddlerhood internalizing and externalizing behaviors. *Developmental Psychobiology*, **52**, 158–167.

Smyth, J. M., Ockenfels, M. C., Porter, L., Kirschbaum, C., Hellhammer, D. H., & Stone, A. A. (1998). Stressors and mood measured on a momentary basis are associated with salivary cortisol secretion. *Psychoneuroendocrinology, 23*, 353–370.

Sneider, H., Boomsma, D. I., van Doornen, L. J. P., & DeGeus, E. J. C. (1997). Heritability of respiratory sinus arrhythmia: Dependency on task and respiration rate. *Psychophysiology, 34*, 317–328.

Snidman, N., & Kagan, J. (1994). The contribution of infant temperamental differences to acoustic startle response. *Psychophysiology, 31*, S92.

Snyder, J., Schrepferman, L., & St. Peter, C. (1997). Origins of antisocial behavior: Negative reinforcement and affect dysregulation of behavior as socialization mechanisms in family interaction. *Behavior Modification, 21*, 187–215.

Spence, S., Shapiro, D., & Zaidel, E. (1996). The role of the right hemisphere in the physiological and cognitive components of emotional processing. *Psychophysiology, 33*, 112–122.

Springer, U. S., Rosas, A., McGetrick, J., & Bowers, D. (2007). Differences in startle reactivity during the perception of angry and fearful faces. *Emotion, 7*, 516–525.

Sroufe, L. A. (1979). Socioemotional develoment. In J. D. Osofky (Ed.), *Handbook of infant development* (pp. 462–516). New York: Wiley.

Sroufe, L. A. (1996). *Emotional development: The organization of emotional life in the early years.* New York: Cambridge University Press.

Stack, D. M., & Muir, D. W. (1992). Adult tactile stimulation during face-to-face interactions modulates five-month-olds' affect and attention. *Child Development, 63*, 1509–1525.

Stark, R., Wolf, O. T., Tabbert, K., Kagerer, S., Zimmermann, M., Kirsch, P., et al. (2006). Influence of the stress hormone cortisol on fear conditioning in humans: Evidence for sex differences in the response of the prefrontal cortex. *Neuroimage, 32*, 1290–1298.

Sterling, P. (2003). Allostasis, homeostasis and the costs of adaptation. In J. Schulkin (Ed.), *Allostasis, homeostasis, and the costs of adaptation* (pp. 7–64). Cambridge: MIT Press.

Stern, D. N. (1985). *The interpersonal world of the infant: A view from psycho-analysis and developmental psychology.* New York: Basic Books.

Sternberg, K. H., Lamb, M. E., Greenbaum C., Cicchetti, D., Dawud, S., Coretes, R. M., et al. (1993). Effects of domestic violence on children's behavior on children's behavior problems and depression. *Developmental Psychology, 29*, 44–52.

Stieben, J., Lewis, M. D., Granic, I., Zelazo, P. D., Segalowitz, S., & Pepler, D. (2007). Neurophysiological mechanisms of emotion regulation for subtypes of externalizing children. *Developmental Psychopathology, 19*, 455–480.

Stifter, C. A., & Fox, N. A. (1990). Infant reactivity: Physiological correlates of newborn and 5-month temperament. *Developmental Psychology, 26*, 582–588.

Stocker, C. M., Richmond, M. K., Rhoades, G. K., & Kiang, L. (2007). Family emotional processes and adolescents' adjustment. *Social Development, 16*, 310–325.

Stover, J. (2004). Fathers' meta-emotion and children's social status. *Dissertation Abstracts International, 64*, 4089.

Straus, M. A., & Gelles, R. J. (1990). *Physical violence in American families: Risk factors and adaptations to violence in 8145 families.* New Brunswick, NJ: Transaction Publishers.

Straus, M. A., Gelles, R. J., & Steinmetz, S. K. (1980). *Behind closed doors. Violence in the American family.* Garden City, NY: Anchor.

Stroud, L., Foster, E., Handwerger, K., Papandonatos, G. D., Granger, D., Kivlighan, K. T., et al. (2009). Stress response and the adolescent transition: Performance versus peer rejection stress. *Development and Psychopathology, 21*, 47–68.

Stroud, L. R., Papandonatos, G. D., Williamson, D. E., & Dahl, R. E. (2004). Sex differences in the effects of pubertal development on responses to a corticotropin-releasing hormone challenge: The Pittsburgh Psychobiologic Studies. *Annals of the New York Academy of Sciences,* **1021**, 348–351.

Suess, P. A., Porges, S. W., & Plude, D. J. (1994). Cardiac vagal tone and sustained attention in school age children. *Psychophysiology,* **31**, 17–22.

Susman, E. J., Dockray, S., Schiefelbein, V. L., Herwehe, S., Heaton, J. A., & Dorn, L. D. (2007). Morningness/eveningness, morning-to-afternoon cortisol ratio, and antisocial behavior problems during puberty. *Developmental Psychology,* **43**, 811–822.

Swain, J. E., Leckman, J. F., Mayes, L. C., Feldman, R., Hoyt, E. H., Kang, H., et al. (2007). Baby cry and picture activations of parent brains vary with gender, experience, and dyadic relationship. *Biological Psychiatry,* **61**, 34S–35S.

Swain, J. E., Lorberbaum, J. P., Kose, S., & Strathearn, L. (2007). Brain basis of early parent-infant interactions: Psychology, physiology, and in vivo functional neuroimaging studies. *Journal of Child Psychology and Psychiatry,* **48**, 262–287.

Szyf, M., McGowan, P., & Meaney, M. J. (2008). The social environment and the epigenome. *Environmental and Molecular Mutagenesis,* **49**, 46–60.

Takahashi, T., Ikeda, K., Ishikawa, M., Tsukasaki, T., Nakama, D., Tanida, S., et al. (2004). Social stress-induced cortisol elevation acutely impairs social memory in humans. *Neuroscience Letters,* **363**, 125–130.

Talge, N. M., Donzella, B., & Gunnar, M. R. (2008). Fearful temperament and stress reactivity among preschool-aged children. *Infant and Child Development,* **17**, 427–445.

Tanida, M., Sakatani, K., Takano, R., & Tagai, K. (2004). Relation between asymmetry of prefrontal cortex activities and the autonomic nervous system during a mental arithmetic task: Near infrared spectroscopy study. *Neuroscience Letters,* **369**, 69–74.

Tarullo, A. R., & Gunnar, M. R. (2006). Child maltreatment and the developing HPA axis. *Hormones and Behavior,* **50**, 632–639.

Tavano, A., Grasso, R., Gagliardi, C., Triulzi, F., Bresolin, N., Fabbro, F., et al. (2007). Disorders of cognitive and affective development in cerebellar malformations. *Brain: A Journal of Neurology,* **130**, 2646–2660.

Taylor, M. J., Batty, M., & Itier, R. J. (2004). The faces of development: A review of early face processing over childhood. *Journal of Cognitive Neuroscience,* **16**, 1426–1442.

Teicher, M. H. (2002). Scars that won't heal: The neurobiology of child abuse. *Scientific American,* **286**, 68–75.

Teicher, M. H., Ito, Y., Glod, C. A., Anderson, S. L., Dumont, N., & Ackerman, E. (1997). Preliminary evidence for abnormal cortical development in physically and sexually abused children using EEG coherence and MRI. *Annals of the New York Academy of Sciences,* **821**, 160–75.

Teisl, M., & Cicchetti, D. (2008). Physical abuse, cognitive and emotional processes, and aggressive/disruptive behavior problems. *Social Development,* **17**, 1–23.

Thatcher, R. W., Biver, C., Gomez, J. F., North, D., Curtin, R., Walker, R. A., et al. (2001). Estimation of EEG power spectrum using MRI T2 relaxation time in traumatic brain injury. *Clinical Neurophysiology,* **112**, 1729–1745.

Thatcher, R. W., North, D., & Biver, C. (2005). EEG and intelligence: Relations between EEG coherence, EEG phase delay and power. *Clinical Neurophysiology,* **116**, 2129–2141.

Thayer, J. F., & Lane, R. D. (2000). A model of neurovisceral integration in emotion regulation and dysregulation. *Journal of Affective Disorders,* **61**, 201–216.

Thayer, J. F., & Lane, R. D. (2009). Claude Bernard and the heart-brain connection: Further elaboration of a model of neurovisceral integration. *Neuroscience and Biobehavioral Reviews*, **33**, 81–88.

Theall-Honey, L. A., & Schmidt, L. A. (2006). Do temperamentally shy children process emotion differently than nonshy children? Behavioral, psychophysiological, and gender differences in reticent preschoolers. *Developmental Psychobiology*, **48**, 187–196.

Thode, K., Beuten, J., Maher, G., Birmaher, B., Ryan, N., & Williamson, D. (2008). Hypothalamic-Pituitary-Adrenal axis activation in response to stress is moderated by polymorphic variants within the corticotropin-releasing hormone receptor 1. *Biological Psychiatry*, **63**(Suppl: Sixty-Third Annual Convention and Scientific Program), Abstract #255.

Thomas, K. M., Drevets, W. C., Dahl, R. E., Ryan, N. D., Birmaher, B., Eccard, C. H., Axelson, D., Whalen, P. J., & Casey, B. J. (2001). Amygdala response to fearful faces in anxious and depressed children. *Archives of General Psychology*, **58**, 1057–1063.

Thompson, R. A. (1990). Emotion and self-regulation. In R. A. Thompson (Ed.), *Socioemotional development* (Nebraska Symposium on Motivation, Vol. 36, pp. 383–483). Lincoln: University of Nebraska Press.

Thompson, R. A. (1994). Emotion regulation: A theme in search of definition. *Monographs of the Society for Research in Child Development*, **59**, 25–52.

Thompson, R. A., & Goodvin, R. (2007). Taming the tempest in the teapot: Emotion regulation in toddlers. In C. A. Brownell & C. B. Kopp (Eds.), *Transitions in early socioemotional development: The toddler years*. New York: Guilford.

Thompson, R. A., Lewis, M. D., & Calkins, S. D. (2008). Reassessing emotion regulation. *Child Development Perspectives*, **2**, 124–131.

Thompson, R. A., & Nelson, C. A. (2001). Developmental science and the media: Early brain development. *American Psychologist*, **56**, 5–15.

Timbergen, N. (1963). On aims and methods in ethology. *Zeitschrift fur Tierpsychologie*, **20**, 410–433.

Tomarken, A. J., Davidson, R. J., & Henriques, J. B. (1990). Resting frontal brain asymmetry predicts affective responses to films. *Journal of Personality and Social Psychology*, **59**, 791–801.

Tremblay, R. E. (2005). Towards an epigenetic approach to experimental criminology: The 2004 Joan McCord Prize Lecture. *Journal of Experimental Criminology*, **1**, 397–415.

Tronick, E. Z. (1989). Emotions and emotional communication in infants. *American Psychologist*, **44**, 112–126.

Tuvblad, C., Zheng, M., Raine, A., & Baker, L. (2009). A common genetic factor explains the covariation among ADHD, ODD, and CD symptoms in 9–10 year old boys and girls. *Journal of Abnormal Child Psychology*, **37**, 153–168.

Tyrka, A., Price, L., Gelernter, J., Schepker, C., Anderson, G., & Carpenter, L. (2009). Interaction of childhood maltreatment with the corticotropin-releasing hormone receptor gene: Effects on hypothalamic-pituitary-adrenal axis reactivity. *Biological Psychiatry*, **66**, 681–685.

Ulrich-Lai, Y. M., & Herman, J. P. (2009). Neural regulation of endocrine and autonomic stress responses. *Nature Review Neuroscience*, **10**, 397–409.

Urry, H. L., van Reekum, C. M., Johnstone, T., Kalin, N. H., Thurow, M. E., Schaefer, H. S., et al. (2006). Amygdala and ventromedial prefrontal cortex are inversely coupled during regulation of negative affect and predict the diurnal pattern of cortisol secretion among older adults. *Journal of Neuroscience*, **26**, 4415–4425.

Ursin, H., Baade, E., & Levine, S. (1978). *Psychobiology of stress: A study of coping men*. New York: Academic Press.

van den Buuse, M. (1998). Role of the mesolimbic dopamine system in cardiovascular homeostasis: Stimulation of the ventral tegmental area modulates the effect of vasopressin in conscious rats. *Clinical Experimental Pharmacology and Physiology, 25,* 661–668.

van Eck, M., Berkhof, H., Nicolson, N., & Sulon, J. (1996). The effects of perceived stress, traits, mood states, and stressful daily events on salivary cortisol. *Psychosomatic Medicine, 58,* 447–458.

van Goozen, S., Matthys, W., Cohen-Kettenis, P., Buitelaar, J., & van Engeland, H. (2000). Hypothalamic-pituitary-adrenal axis and autonomic nervous system activity in disruptive children and matched controls. *Journal of the American Academy of Child and Adolescent Psychiatry, 39,* 1438–1445.

van Ijzendoorn, M. H., Caspers, K., Bakermans-Kranenburg, M. J., Beach, S. R. H., & Philibert, P. (2010). Methylation matters: Interaction between methylation density and serotonin transporter genotype predicts unresolved loss or trauma. *Biological Psychiatry, 68,* 405–407.

van Ryzin, M. J., Chatham, M., Kryzer, E., Kertes, D. A., & Gunnar, M. R. (2009). Identifying atypical cortisol patterns in young children: The benefits of group-based trajectory modeling. *Psychoneuroendocrinology, 34,* 50–61.

van Stegeren, A. H. (2009). Imaging stress effects on memory: A review of neuroimaging studies. *Canadian Journal of Psychiatry, 54,* 16–27.

Verbane, A. J., & Owens, N. C. (1998). Cortical modulation of the cardiovascular system. *Progress in Neurobiology, 54,* 149–168.

Vermeer, H. J., & van Ijzendoorn, M. H. (2006). Children's elevated cortisol levels at daycare: A review and meta-analysis. *Early Childhood Research Quarterly, 21,* 309–401.

Vlajkovic, S., Nikolic, V., Nikolic, A., Milanovic, S., & Jankovic, B. D. (1994). Asymmetrical modulation of immune reactivity in left and right-biased rats after ipsilateral ablation of the prefrontal, parietal and occipital brain neocortex. *International Journal of Neuroscience, 78,* 123–134.

Waldstein, S. R., Kop, W. J., Schmidt, L. A., Haufler, A. J., Krantz, D. J., & Fox, N. A. (2000). Frontal electrocortical and cardiovascular reactivity during happiness and anger. *Biological Psychology, 55,* 3–23.

Walker, B. B., & Sandman, C. A. (1979). Human visual evoked responses are related to heart rate. *Journal of Comparative and Physiological Psychology, 93,* 717–729.

Wallstrom, G. L., Kass, R. E., Miller, A., Cohn, J., & Fox, N. A. (2004). Automatic correction of ocular artifacts in the EEG: A comparison of regression-based and component-based methods. *International Journal of Psychophysiology, 53,* 105–119.

Wang, X., Ding, X., Su, S., Li, Z., Riese, H., Thayer, J. F., et al. (2009). Genetic influences on heart rate variability at rest and during stress. *Psychophysiology, 46,* 458–465.

Watamura, S. E., Coe, C. L., Laudenslager, M. L., & Robertson, S. S. (2010). Child care setting affects salivary cortisol and antibody secretion in young children. *Psychoneuroendocrinology, 35,* 1156–1166.

Watamura, S. E., Donzella, B., Alwin, J., & Gunnar, M. (2003). Morning to afternoon increases in cortisol concentrations for infants and toddlers at child care: Age differences and behavioral correlates. *Child Development, 74,* 1006–1020.

Waters, A. M., Neumann, D. L., Henry, J., Craske, M. G., & Ornitz, E. M. (2008). Baseline and affective startle modulation by angry and neutral faces in 4–8-year-old anxious and non-anxious children. *Biological Psychology, 78,* 10–19.

Weaver, I. C., Cervoni, N., Champagne, F. A., D'Alessio, A. C., Sharma, S., Seckl, J. R., et al. (2004). Epigenetic programming by maternal behavior. *Nature Neuroscience, 7,* 847–854.

Weems, C. F., Zakem, A. H., Costa, N. M., Cannon, M. F., & Watts, S. E. (2005). Physiological response and childhood anxiety: Association with symptoms of anxiety disorders and cognitive bias. *Journal of Clinical Child and Adolescent Psychology*, **34**, 712–723.

Weitzman, E. D., Fukushima, D., Nogeire, C., Roffwarg, H., Gallagher, T. F., & Hellman, L. (1971). Twenty-four hour pattern of the episodic secretion of cortisol in normal subjects. *Journal of Clinical Endocrinology and Metabolism*, **33**, 14–22.

Wheeler, W. M. (1928). *The social insects*. New York: Harcourt.

Whitelaw, N. C., & Whitelaw, E. (2006). How lifetimes shape epigenotype within and across generations. *Human Molecular Genetics*, **15**, R131–R137.

Wilke, M., Lidzba, K., & Krägeloh-Mann, I. (2009). Combined functional and causal connectivity analyses of language networks in children: A feasibility study. *Brain and Language*, **108**, 22–29.

Wilkinson, M. L., & Howse, R. B. (2003, April). *Continuity and stability of vagal regulation across infancy*. Paper presented at the biennial meeting of the Society for Research in Child Development. Tampa, FL.

Witt, D. M., Carter, C. S., & Walton, D. M. (1990). Central and peripheral effects of oxytocin administration in prairie voles (microtus ochrogaster). *Pharmacology, Biochemistry, and Behavior*, **37**, 63–69.

Wittling, W. (1990). Psychophysiological correlates of human brain asymmetry: Blood pressure changes during lateralized presentation of an emotionally laden film. *Neuropsychologia*, **28**, 457–470.

Wittling, W. (1995). Brain asymmetry in the control of autonomic-physiologic activity. In R. J. Davidson & K. Hugdahl (Eds.), *Brain asymmetry* (pp. 305–357). Cambridge, MA: MIT Press.

Wittling, W. (1997). Brain asymmetry and autonomic control of the heart. *European Psychologist*, **2**, 313–327.

Wittling, W., Block, A., Genzel, S., & Schweiger, E. (1997). Hemisphere asymmetry in parasympathetic control of the heart. *Neuropsychologia*, **36**, 461–468.

Wittling, W., Block, A., Schweiger, E., & Genzel, S. (1998). Hemisphere asymmetry in sympathetic control of the human myocardium. *Brain and Cognition*, **38**, 17–35.

Wittling, W., & Genzel, S. (1995). Brain asymmetries in cerebral regulation of cortisol secretion. *Homeostasis*, **36**, 1–5.

Wittling, W., & Pfluger, M. (1990). Neuroendocrine hemisphere asymmetries: Salivary cortisol secretion during lateralized viewing of emotion-related and neutral films. *Brain and Cognition*, **14**, 243–265.

Wolfe, C. D., & Bell, M. A. (2004). Working memory and inhibitory control in early childhood: Contributions from electrophysiology, temperament, and language. *Developmental Psychobiology*, **44**, 68–83.

Wolfe, C. D., & Bell, M. A. (2007). Sources of variability in working memory in early childhood: A consideration of age, temperament, language, and brain electrical activity. *Cognitive Development*, **22**, 431–455.

Wolfe, D. A., & Korsch, B. (1994). Witnessing domestic violence during childhood and adolescence. *Pediatrics*, **94**, 594–599.

Woltering, S., & Lewis, M. D. (2009). Developmental pathways of emotion regulation in childhood: A neuropsychological perspective. *Mind, Brain, and Education*, **3**, 160–169.

Wu, T., Snieder, H., & de Geus, E. (2010). Genetic influences on cardiovascular stress reactivity. *Neuroscience & Biobehavioral Reviews*, **35**, 58–68.

180

Wüst, S., Federenko, I., Hellhammer, D. H., & Kirschbaum, C. (2000). Genetic factors, perceived chronic stress, and the free cortisol response to awakening. *Psychoneuroendocrinology*, **25**, 707–720.

Wüst, S., Federenko, I., Van Rossum, E., Koper, J. W., Kumsta, R., Entringer, S., et al. (2004). A psychobiological perspective on genetic determinants of hypothalamic-pituitary-adrenal axis activity. *Annals of the New York Academy of Science*, **1032**, 52–62.

Wynne-Edwards, K. E. (2001). Hormonal changes in mammalian fathers. *Hormones and Behavior*, **40**, 139–45.

Yamada, J., Stevens, B., de Silva, N., Gibbins, S., Beyene, J., Taddio, A., et al. (2007). Hair cortisol as a potential biologic marker of chronic stress in hospitalized neonates. *Neonatology*, **92**, 42–49.

Yang, T. T., Simmons, A. N., Matthews, S. C., Tapert, S. F., Bischoff-Grethe, A., Frank, G. K. W., et al. (2007). Increased amygdala activation is related to heart rate during emotion processing in adolescent subjects. *Neuroscience Letters*, **428**, 109–114.

Yao, D. (2001). A method to standardize a reference of scalp EEG recordings to a point at infinity. *Physiological Measurement*, **22**, 693–711.

Yao, D., Wang, L., Oostenveld, R., Dremstrup Nielsen, K., Arendt-Nielsen, L., & Chen, A. C. N. (2005). A comparative study of different references for EEG spectral mapping: The issue of the neutral reference and the use of the infinity reference. *Physiological Measurement*, **26**, 173–184.

Yehuda, R. (2000). Biology of posttraumatic stress disorder. *Journal of Clinical Psychiatry*, **61**, 15–21.

Yehuda, R. (2002). Current status of cortisol findings in post-traumatic stress disorder. *Psychiatric Clinics of North American*, **25**, 341–368.

Yoon, B. W., Morillo, C. A., Cechetto, D. F., & Hachinski, V. (1997). Cerebral hemispheric lateralization in cardiac autonomic control. *Archives of Neurology*, **54**, 741–744.

Young, E. A., Haskett, R. F., Murphy-Weinberg, V., Watson, S. J., & Akil, H. (1991). Loss of glucocorticoid fast feedback in depression. *Archives of General Psychiatry*, **48**, 693–699.

Zajonc, R. B. (1980). Feeling and thinking: Preferences need no inferences. *American Psychologist*, **35**, 151–175.

Zamrini, E. Y., Meador, K. J., Loring, D. W., Nichols, F. T., Lee, G. P., Figueroa, R. E., et al. (1990). Unilateral cerebral inactivation produces differential left/right heart rate responses. *Neurology*, **40**, 1408–1411.

Zelazo, P. D., & Cunningham, W. A. (2007). Executive function: Mechanisms underlying emotion regulation. In J. J. Gross (Ed.), *Handbook of emotion regulation* (pp. 135–158). New York: Guilford.

Zillman, D. (1988). Mood management: Using entertainment to full advantage. In L. Donohew, H. E. Sypher, & E. T. Higgins (Eds.), *Communication, social cognition, and affect* (pp. 147–171). Hillsdale, NJ: Erlbaum.

CONTRIBUTORS

Emma K. Adam is Associate Professor of Human Development and Social Policy at the School of Education and Social Policy, and a Faculty Fellow at the Cells to Society Center of the Institute for Policy Research, Northwestern University. Her research examines social influences on hypothalamic pituitary adrenal (HPA) axis activity in children and adolescents, measured in naturalistic settings, and the implications of individual differences in HPA axis activity for emotional health, physical health, and academic performance.

Theodore Beauchaine is Professor of Psychology at the University of Washington. His research examines the central and peripheral nervous system substrates of psychopathology, including both internalizing and externalizing disorders, in children and adolescents.

Martha Ann Bell is Professor of Psychology at Virginia Polytechnic Institute and State University. Her research focuses on individual differences in the early development of executive functions and on the integration of cognition and emotion across infancy and early childhood.

W. Thomas Boyce is a pediatrician-epidemiologist who holds the BC Leadership Chair in Child Development at the University of British Columbia. His work addresses how neurogenomic and psychosocial processes work together to lead to the socioeconomic partitioning of child health and development.

Kristin A. Buss is Associate Professor of Psychology at The Pennsylvania State University. Her current work examines the role of fearful temperament, emotion regulation, context, and physiological reactivity for the development of anxiety-related adjustment problems.

Dante Cicchetti is the McKnight Presidential Chair and Professor of Child Psychology and Psychiatry at the University of Minnesota Institute of Child Development and Department of Psychiatry. His major research interests lie in the formulation of an integrative, multilevel developmental theory that can account for both normality and psychopathology and serve as a foundation for prevention and intervention.

Ronald E. Dahl is Professor of Public Health and Director of the Institute of Human Development at the University of California-Berkeley. A major focus of his research aims at understanding early adolescence and pubertal maturation as a developmental period with unique opportunities for early intervention in relation to a wide range of behavioral and emotional health problems.

Tracy A. Dennis is Associate Professor in the Department of Psychology and the Biopsychology and Behavioral Neuroscience doctoral program at Hunter College of the City University of New York. Her research focuses on neurobiological processes underlying the development of emotion regulation, emotional competence, and affective psychopathology in childhood and across the adult life span. In addition, her current work examines attentional biases and patterns of emotion–cognition integration that influence adjustment.

Anjolii Diaz is a graduate student in the Developmental and Biological Psychology program at Virginia Polytechnic Institute and State University. Her research is focused on associations between temperament and cognition in early development.

Lynn Fainsilber Katz is Research Professor of Child Clinical Psychology and Developmental Psychology at the University of Washington. One major focus of her research is on how marital conflict and violence relate to children's emotion regulation abilities and socioemotional adjustment.

Ruth Feldman is Professor of Psychology and Neuroscience at Bar-Ilan University, Israel with a joint appointment at Yale University, Child Study Center, and director of a community-based infant mental health clinic. Her research focuses on the biological basis of bonding, parent-infant relationship, biobehavioral processes of emotion regulation, the development of infants and young children at high risk stemming from prematurity, biological, maternal, and contextual risk conditions, and Israeli and Palestinian children exposed to war, terror, and violence.

Nathan A. Fox is Distinguished University Professor at the University of Maryland, College Park. His research focuses on the biology of infant temperament and the development of social competence in young children. He is also involved in research on the effects of early adverse experiences on the brain and behavior in young children.

Kathleen M. Gates is a postdoctoral fellow in the Human Development and Family Studies program at The Pennsylvania State University. Her research interests concern the development of novel techniques for analysing brain imaging and psychophysiological data.

Megan R. Gunnar is a Regents Professor of Child Development at the Institute of Child Development, University of Minnesota. Her work highlights the effects of early deprivation and neglect on the development of stress and emotion regulation.

Jamie L. Hanson is a graduate student at the University of Wisconsin-Madison. His research focuses on brain development and early experience, with a specific interest in how brain plasticity and environmental experience give rise to both the commonality and individual differences in a behavioral repertoire.

Paul D. Hastings is Professor of Psychology at the Center for Mind and Brain at the University of California Davis. His research is focused on the transactional and bidirectional contributions of children's regulatory systems and socialization experiences to trajectories of social and emotional development, with particular emphasis on empathy and prosocial behavior, inhibition and anxiety, and aggression and disruptive behavior.

Michael Kirwan is the Project Coordinator at the Center on the Developing Child, Harvard University. His research focuses on how anxiety influences the orientation and disengagement of attention.

Vladimir Miskovic received his doctorate from McMaster University and is currently a postdoctoral fellow at the University of Florida. His research focuses on understanding affective function in health as well as psychiatric disease and its treatment, using measures of brain electrophysiology and behavior.

Peter C. M. Molenaar is Distinguished Professor of Human Development and Psychology at The Pennsylvania State University. His research focuses on statistical methods for brain imaging, biobehavioral health, and developmental processes.

Jelena Obradović is Assistant Professor at Stanford University in the Developmental and Psychological Sciences program in the School of Education. Her current work focuses on how contextual risk and adversity interact with children's physiological reactivity and regulatory abilities to influence adaptation across multiple domains of functioning.

Seth D. Pollak is the Letters and Science Distinguished Professor of Psychology and Professor of Pediatrics, Anthropology, Psychiatry, and Public Affairs at the University of Wisconsin–Madison, where he is also an investigator at the Waisman Center for Human Development. His research focuses on children's brain and behavioral development, with particular focus on emotions and social behavior.

Bethany Reeb-Sutherland is Research Assistant Professor in the Child Development Laboratory at the University of Maryland. Her research focuses on neurobiological predictors of aberrant social and emotional behavior.

Fred A. Rogosch is Director of Research at Mt. Hope Family Center, University of Rochester, and Associate Professor in the Department of Clinical and Social Sciences in Psychology. His major research interests involve understanding diversity in developmental process and outcome among children experiencing early life adversity.

Louis A. Schmidt is Professor in the Department of Psychology, Neuroscience and Behaviour at McMaster University. His research interests include understanding the origins and outcomes of individual differences in temperament and the impact of early life events on human brain and affective development in clinical and nonclinical populations, using behavioral, molecular genetic, fMRI, and psychophysiological methods.

Greg J. Siegle is Associate Professor of Psychiatry and Psychology at the University of Pittsburgh. His research examines cognitive, physiological, and brain mechanisms of mood and anxiety disorders through the life span with a particular focus on using this information to advance treatment personalization and development.

Jennifer S. Silk is Assistant Professor in the Departments of Psychiatry and Psychology at the University of Pittsburgh. Her research focuses on the role of emotion regulation in trajectories of depression and anxiety in children and adolescents, with a focus on the integration of social and biological influences on emotion regulation and development.

Nicole M. Strang is a doctoral student in psychology at the University of Wisconsin-Madison. She is interested in developmental changes in the relationship between emotion and cognition, and the impact of early experience.

STATEMENT OF EDITORIAL POLICY

The SRCD *Monographs* series aims to publish major reports of developmental research that generates authoritative new findings and that foster a fresh perspective and/or integration of data/research on conceptually significant issues. Submissions may consist of individually or group-authored reports of findings from some single large-scale investigation or from a series of experiments centering on a particular question. Multiauthored sets of independent studies concerning the same underlying question also may be appropriate. A critical requirement in such instances is that the individual authors address common issues and that the contribution arising from the set as a whole be unique, substantial, and well integrated. Manuscripts reporting interdisciplinary or multidisciplinary research on significant developmental questions and those including evidence from diverse cultural, racial, and ethnic groups are of particular interest. Also of special interest are manuscripts that bridge basic and applied developmental science, and that reflect the international perspective of the Society. Because the aim of the *Monographs* series is to enhance cross-fertilization among disciplines or subfields as well as advance knowledge on specialized topics, the links between the specific issues under study and larger questions relating to developmental processes should emerge clearly and be apparent for both general readers and specialists on the topic. In short, irrespective of how it may be framed, work that contributes significant data and/or extends a developmental perspective will be considered.

Potential authors who may be unsure whether the manuscript they are planning would make an appropriate submission to the SRCD *Monographs* are invited to draft an outline or prospectus of what they propose and send it to the incoming editor for review and comment.

Potential authors are not required to be members of the Society for Research in Child Development nor affiliated with the academic discipline of psychology to submit a manuscript for consideration by the *Monographs*. The significance of the work in extending developmental theory and in contributing new empirical information is the crucial consideration.

Submissions should contain a minimum of 80 manuscript pages (including tables and references). The upper boundary of 150–175 pages is more flexible, but authors should try to keep within this limit. If color artwork is submitted, and the authors believe color art is necessary to the presentation of their work, the submissions letter should indicate that one or more authors or their institutions are prepared to pay the substantial costs associated with color art reproduction. Please submit manuscripts electronically to the SRCD Monographs Online Submissions and Review Site (Scholar One) at http://mc.manuscriptcentral.com/mono. Please contact the Monographs office with any questions at monographs@srcd.org.

The corresponding author for any manuscript must, in the submission letter, warrant that all coauthors are in agreement with the content of the manuscript. The corresponding author also is responsible for informing all coauthors, in a timely manner, of manuscript submission, editorial decisions, reviews received, and any revisions recommended. Before publication, the corresponding author must warrant in the submissions letter that the study has been conducted according to the ethical guidelines of the Society for Research in Child Development.

A more detailed description of all editorial policies, evaluation processes, and format requirements, is given in the "Guidelines for the Preparation of Publication Submissions," which can be found at the SRCD website by clicking on *Monographs,* or by contacting the editor.

Monographs Editorial Office
e-mail: monographs@srcd.org

Incoming Editor, Patricia J. Bauer
Department of Psychology, Emory University
36 Eagle Row
Atlanta, GA 30322
e-mail: pjbauer@emory.edu

Note to NIH Grantees

Pursuant to NIH mandate, Society through Wiley-Blackwell will post the accepted version of Contributions authored by NIH grantholders to PubMed Central upon acceptance. This accepted version will be made publicly available 12 months after publication. For further information, see http://www.wiley.com/go/nihmandate.

    individual differences in, 55, 57
    PNS stress response and, 121
    reactivity, 4–85, 124, 127
    suppression, 54, 55, 57
    withdrawal, 122
rewards
    aberrant responses, 80–81
    brain states, 72–73
    PEP and, 123
romantic partners, biological synchrony between, 49
RSA (*See* respiratory sinus arrhythmia)

sad facial expressions, 11, 12
sadness, 122
school-age children, 35, 92
SCL (skin conductance level), 121, 123, 127
selective attention, 62–63
self-injury, 85
self-regulation, 14–15, 113
self-soothing, 54
serotonin, 85
sexually-abused children, 90–92, 94
shyness
    maternal-related, 12
    temperamental, 7, 34–35
sickness behavior, 118
skin conductance level (SCL), 121, 123, 127
skin temperature, 103
skin-to-skin contact, 46–47
sleep, adolescent emotion regulation and, 74
sMRI (structural magnetic resonance imaging), 64–65
SNS (*See* sympathetic nervous system)
social behavior, hormones and, 48–49
social contingencies, 44
social environment
    context, cortisol changes and, 19
    early deprivation, 64
    interaction with biological vulnerabilities, 73–74
social information processing models, 55
social rejection, 110
social self, threats to, 110
social support, 113
socialization, emotional, 39, 40
    cortisol reactivity and, 22, 23
    parent-child relationship and, 57
socio-emotional functioning, 40

vagal tone, infant, 46–48, 99
vagus nerve, 55, 82, 83
vector-valued autoregressive time series models (VAR models), 133, 137–138
ventral striatum, underactivation, 81
ventromedial prefrontal cortex (VMPFC), 82, 85
violence-exposed children, 58–59
VMPFC (ventromedial prefrontal cortex), 82, 85

CURRENT

Physiological Measures of Emotion From a Developmental Perspective: State of the Science—*Tracy A. Dennis, Kristin A. Buss, and Paul D. Hastings* (SERIAL NO. 303, 2012)

How Socialization Happens on the Ground: Narrative Practices as Alternate Socializing Pathways in Taiwanese and European-American Families—*Peggy J. Miller, Heidi Fung, Shumin Lin, Eva Chian-Hui Chen, and Benjamin R. Boldt* (SERIAL NO. 302, 2012)

Children Without Permanent Parents: Research, Practice, and Policy—*Robert B. McCall, Marinus H. van IJzendoorn, Femmie Juffer, Christina J. Groark, and Victor K. Groza* (SERIAL NO. 301, 2011)

I Remember Me: Mnemonic Self-Reference Effects in Preschool Children—*Josephine Ross, James R. Anderson, and Robin N. Campbell* (SERIAL NO. 300, 2011)

Early Social Cognition in Three Cultural Contexts—*Tara Callaghan, Henrike Moll, Hannes Rakoczy, Felix Warneken, Ulf Liszkowski, Tanya Behne, and Michael Tomasello* (SERIAL NO. 299, 2011)

The Development of Ambiguous Figure Perception—*Marina C. Wimmer and Martin J. Doherty* (SERIAL NO. 298, 2011)

The Better Beinnings, Better Futures Project: Findings From Grade 3 to Grade 9—*Ray DeV. Peters, Alison J. Bradshaw, Kelly Petrunka, Geoffrey Nelson, Yves Herry, Wendy M. Craig, Robert Arnold, Kevin C. H. Parker, Shahriar R. Khan, Jeffrey S. Hoch, S. Mark Pancer, Colleen Loomis, Jean-Marc Bélanger, Susan Evers, Claire Maltais, Katherine Thompson, and Melissa D. Rossiter* (SERIAL NO. 297, 2010)

First-Year Maternal Employment and Child Development in the First 7 Years—*Jeanne Brooks-Gunn, Wen-Jui Han, and Jane Waldfogel* (SERIAL NO. 296, 2010)

Deprivation-Specific Psychological Patterns: Effects of Institutional Deprivation—*Michael Rutter, Edmund J. Sonuga-Barke, Celia Beckett, Jennifer Castle, Jana Kreppner, Robert Kumsta, Wolff Schlotz, Suzanne Stevens, and Christopher A. Bell* (SERIAL NO. 295, 2010)

A Dynamic Cascade Model of the Development of Substance-Use Onset—*Kenneth A. Dodge, Patrick S. Malone, Jennifer E. Lansford, Shari Miller, Gregory S. Pettit, and John E. Bates* (SERIAL NO. 294, 2009)

Flexibility in Early Verb Use: Evidence From a Multiple-*N* Diary Study—*Letitia R. Naigles, Erika Hoff, and Donna Vear* (SERIAL NO. 293, 2009)

Marital Conflict and Children's Externalizing Behavior: Interactions Between Parasympathetic and Sympathetic Nervous System Activity—*Mona El-Sheikh, Chrystyna D. Kouros, Stephen Erath, E. Mark Cummings, Peggy Keller, and Lori Staton* (SERIAL NO. 292, 2009)

The Effects of Early Social-Emotional and Relationship Experience on the Development of Young Orphanage Children—*The St. Petersburg–USA Orphanage Research Team* (SERIAL NO. 291, 2008)

Understanding Mother-Adolescent Conflict Discussions: Concurrent and Across-Time Prediction From Youths' Dispositions and Parenting—*Nancy Eisenberg, Claire Hofer, Tracy L. Spinrad, Elizabeth T. Gershoff, Carlos Valiente, Sandra Losoya, Qing Zhou, Amanda Cumberland, Jeffrey Liew, Mark Reiser, and Elizabeth Maxon* (SERIAL NO. 290, 2008)

Developing Object Concepts in Infancy: An Associative Learning Perspective—*David H. Rakison and Gary Lupyan* (SERIAL NO. 289, 2008)

The Genetic and Environmental Origins of Learning Abilities and Disabilities in the Early School Years—*Yulia Kovas, Claire M. A. Haworth, Philip S. Dale, and Robert Plomin* (SERIAL NO. 288, 2007)

The Preservation of Two Infant Temperaments Into Adolescence—*Jerome Kagan, Nancy Snidman, Vali Kahn, and Sara Towsley* (SERIAL NO. 287, 2007)

Children's Questions: A Mechanism for Cognitive Development—*Michelle M. Chouinard* (SERIAL NO. 286, 2007)

Best Practices in Quantitative Methods for Developmentalists—*Kathleen McCartney, Margaret R. Burchinal, and Kristen L. Bub* (SERIAL NO. 285, 2006)